# Real Reading 3

## Creating an Authentic Reading Experience
### Lynn Bonesteel

**Lynn Bonesteel**
*Series Editor*

**Paul Nation**
*Series Consultant*

PEARSON
Longman

# Real Reading 3: Creating an Authentic Reading Experience

Pearson Education, 10 Bank Street, White Plains, NY 10606

Staff credits: The people who made up the **Real Reading 3** team, representing editorial,
production, design, and manufacturing, are Nancy Flaggman, Ann France, Shelley Gazes,
Dana Klinek, Amy McCormick, Martha McGaughey, Robert Ruvo, Debbie Sistino, and
Jennifer Stem.

Cover art: Shutterstock.com
Text composition: TSI Graphics
Text font: Helvetica Neue
Illustrations: TSI Graphics—pages 134, 158; Gary Torrisi—pages 37, 68, 107, 108, 151
References: see page xviii

**Library of Congress Cataloging-in-Publication Data**

Bonesteel, Lynn.
  Real reading : creating an authentic reading experience / Lynn Bonesteel.
      p. cm.
  Includes index.
  ISBN-10: 0-13-606654-2 (Level 1)
  ISBN-10: 0-13-814627-6 (Level 2)
  ISBN-10: 0-13-714443-1 (Level 3)
  ISBN-10: 0-13-502771-3 (Level 4)
  [etc.]
  1.  English language--Textbooks for foreign speakers. 2.  Reading comprehension.
  3.  Vocabulary.  I. Title.
  PE1128.B6243 2010
  428.6'4--dc22

                                                                    2010017172

**PEARSON LONGMAN ON THE WEB**

**Pearsonlongman.com** offers online
resources for teachers. Access our Companion
Websites, our online catalog, and our local
offices around the world.

Visit us at **pearsonlongman.com**.

ISBN 10: 0-13-714443-1
ISBN 13: 978-0-13-714443-3

Printed in the United States of America
12   17

# CONTENTS

# Acknowledgments

I would like to express my appreciation to all of those at Pearson who made this project possible. Special thanks to Dana Klinek for her hard work and efforts to keep all of the pieces moving in the right direction; to Pietro Alongi for believing in the project in the first place; to Debbie Sistino for always being there when support was needed; to editors Martha McGaughey and Joan Poole for their hard work and careful attention to detail; and to Production Editor Shelley Gazes, Associate Managing Editor Robert Ruvo, Senior Art Director Ann France, and Photo Research Manager Aerin Csigay.

I was also fortunate to have the opportunity to work with two wonderful writers, Alice Savage and David Wiese. Their hard work, creativity, flexibility, and good humor made the collaboration a pleasure.

Finally, I would like to thank Paul Nation, whose contributions from the inception of the project to its completion were invaluable. His explanation of the authentic reading experience during an online TESOL seminar served as the spark that led to the creation of the *Real Reading* series. His ongoing feedback was instrumental in the design and content of many of the exercises in the four books of the series. Our goal was to create a reading series informed by solid research on second language acquisition. Where we have succeeded, much of the credit belongs to Paul Nation and other researchers who make their work accessible to teachers and materials writers. By doing so, they perform an invaluable service to language learners.

*Lynn Bonesteel*

# Reviewers

**William Brazda**, Long Beach City College, Long Beach, CA; **Abigail Brown**, University of Hawaii, Honolulu, HI; **David Dahnke**, North Harris Community College, Houston, TX; **Scott Fisher**, Sungshin Women's University, Seoul, Korea; **Roberta Hodges**, Sonoma State American Language Institute, Sonoma, CA; **Kate Johnson**, Union County College Institute For Intensive English, Elizabeth, NJ; **Thomas Justice**, North Shore Community College, Danvers, MA; **Michael McCollister**, Feng Chia University, Taiching, Taiwan; **Myra Medina**, Miami-Dade Community College, Miami, FL; **Lesley Morgan**, West Virginia University, Morgantown, WV; **Angela Parrino**, Hunter College, New York, NY; **Christine Sharpe**, Howard Community College, Columbia, MD; **Christine Tierney**, Houston Community College, Houston, TX; **Kerry Vrabel**, GateWay Community College, Phoenix, AZ.

# INTRODUCTION

*Real Reading 3* is the third book in a four-level (beginning, low intermediate, intermediate, and high intermediate) intensive reading series for learners of English. The books in the series feature high-interest readings that have been carefully written or adapted from authentic sources to allow effective comprehension by learners at each level. The aim is for learners to be able to engage with the content in a meaningful and authentic way, as readers do in their native language. For example, learners who use *Real Reading* will be able to read to learn or feel something new, to evaluate information and ideas, to experience or share an emotion, to see something from a new perspective, or simply to get pleasure from reading in English. High-interest topics include superstitions, shyness, neuroscience, sports, magic, and technology, among others.

##  THE *REAL READING* APPROACH

To allow for effective comprehension, the vocabulary in the readings in the *Real Reading* series has been controlled so that 95–98 percent of the words are likely to be known by a typical learner at each level. The vocabulary choices were based on analyses of the General Service Word List (GSL) (Michael West, 1953), the Academic Word List (AWL) (Averil Coxhead, 2000), and the Billuroğlu-Neufeld List (BNL) (Ali Billuroğlu and Steve Neufeld, 2007).

Research has shown that as they read a text, good readers employ a variety of skills.[1] Thus, essential reading skills, such as predicting, skimming, making inferences, and understanding text references, are presented, practiced, and recycled in each level of *Real Reading*, with level-appropriate explanations and practice. The goal is for learners to become autonomous readers in English; the reading skills are the tools that will help learners achieve this goal.

Vocabulary development skills and strategies are prominently featured in every chapter in *Real Reading*. The importance of vocabulary size to reading comprehension and fluency has been well documented in the research on both first and second language acquisition.[2] Thus, in the *Real Reading* series, learners are given extensive practice in applying level-appropriate skills and strategies to their acquisition of the target words in each chapter. This practice serves two purposes: First, because the target words have been selected from among the most frequent words in general and academic English, learners who use the books are exposed to the words that they will encounter most frequently in English texts. Second, through repeated practice with vocabulary skills and learning strategies, learners will acquire the tools they need to continue expanding their vocabulary long after completing the books in the series.

---

[1] Nation, I.S.P. *Learning Vocabulary in Another Language.* Cambridge, England: Cambridge University Press. 2001.

[2] Nation, I.S.P. *Teaching Vocabulary: Strategies and Techniques.* Boston, MA: Heinle, Cengage Learning. 2008

# VOCABULARY: FROM RESEARCH TO PRACTICE
## *By Paul Nation*

*Real Reading* puts several well-established vocabulary-based principles into practice.

1. There is the idea that meaning-focused input should contain a small amount of unknown vocabulary but that this amount should be limited so that the learners can read for understanding without being overburdened by a large number of unknown words. Research suggests that somewhere around two percent of the running words in a text may be initially unknown and still allow a reasonable level of comprehension. If the number of unknown words is too large, then the learners cannot participate in an authentic reading experience. That is, they cannot read the text and react in the same way as a native speaker would. The texts in *Real Reading* have been developed so that learners are likely to gain a high level of comprehension while encountering some new words that they can begin to learn.

2. The activities in *Real Reading*, along with the texts, provide learners with the opportunity to thoughtfully process the unknown vocabulary that they encounter. In most of the exercises, the contexts for the target words are different from the contexts provided in the texts. This helps stretch the meaning of the new words and makes them more memorable. The various exercises also require the target words to be used in ways that will help learning.

3. *Real Reading* includes a systematic approach to the development of important vocabulary learning strategies. The ultimate goal of instructed vocabulary learning should be to help learners become autonomous language learners. An important step in this process is gaining control of effective vocabulary learning strategies, such as using word cards, using word parts, and using a dictionary. *Real Reading* includes vocabulary strategies in every unit. The strategies are broken down into their components, practiced and recycled in the vocabulary practice pages at the back of the books.

4. The sequencing of the vocabulary in *Real Reading* has been carefully designed so that the new items will not interfere with each other. That is, presenting the target words together with new vocabulary that belongs to the same lexical set or consists of opposites or synonyms greatly increases the difficulty of vocabulary learning. It is much more helpful if the unknown vocabulary fits together in ways that are similar to the ways the words occur in the texts.

5. Finally, a well-balanced language course provides four major kinds of opportunities for vocabulary learning. A unique feature of *Real Reading* is its use of these research-based principles. First, there is the opportunity to learn through *meaning-focused input*, where the learners' attention is focused on the message of what they are reading or listening to. Second, there is an opportunity to learn through *meaning-focused output*, where the learners are intent on conveying messages. Third, there is the opportunity to learn through *language-focused learning*, where learners give deliberate attention to language features. Fourth, there is the opportunity to *develop fluency* with what is already known. In a variety of ways, the *Real Reading* textbooks provide these opportunities. Their main focus is on deliberate learning through conscious attention to vocabulary, and through the use of specially designed exercises.

# THE *REAL READING* UNIT

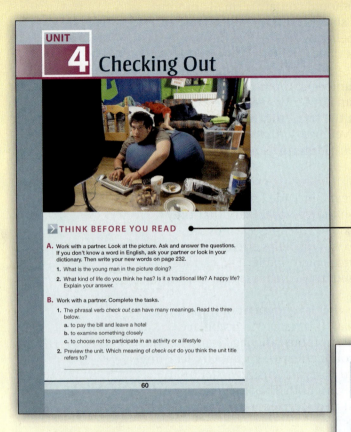

THINK BEFORE YOU READ

## THINK BEFORE YOU READ

Each unit begins with a captivating opener that introduces students to the unit theme, elicits vocabulary relevant to the theme, and includes discussion questions to activate students' prior knowledge and stimulate interest.

## PREPARE TO READ

This section previews words and phrases that students will encounter in the reading. Students reflect on what they already know and then answer questions about the topic.

**READING SKILLS** Every unit has one or two reading skills, which include previewing and predicting; understanding topics, main ideas, and details; and understanding cause and effect, among others.

**READ** The readings feature a wide variety of high-interest, contemporary topics, including business, science and nature, music and the visual arts, culture and society, sports and exercise, and health and nutrition, as well as a variety of genres, including newspaper and magazine articles, blogs, Web sites, newsletters, travel logs, personal essays, poetry, and short stories. Vocabulary is tightly controlled at each level, and target words are recycled from one chapter to the next within a unit, from unit to unit, and from one level to the next.

**Reading Skill: Recognizing Point of View**

It is important to be able to recognize a writer's opinion or attitude. We call this the writer's *point of view*. Sometimes a writer will state his or her point of view directly, but often the reader must infer it. To discover a writer's point of view, look at the way he or she uses language. Do the writer's words help you form a positive or negative idea about the topic? Or does the writer use neutral words? Is the writer using words ironically? That is, does the writer say one thing but really mean the opposite?

**C.** Skim the excerpt from the book *Welcome to Leisureville*. Then read the questions and circle the answers.

1. What is the main topic?
   a. retirement communities in the United States
   b. senior citizens in the United States
   c. how people spend their leisure time in the United States

2. What is the writer's point of view?
   a. positive
   b. negative
   c. neutral

**READ**

Read the excerpt from *Welcome to Leisureville*. As you read, circle any words or expressions that are positive. Underline any words or expressions that are negative.

### Welcome to Leisureville

In this **excerpt** from the book *Leisureville: Adventures in America's Retirement Utopias*[1], author Andrew D. Blechman describes visiting two friends and former neighbors at their new home in a retirement community called The Villages.

The Villages is located roughly in the center of Florida, about an hour north of Orlando International Airport. On the sides of the road there are billboards advertising retirement communities. Photos of seniors playing golf and relaxing in pools are covered with **slogans** such as "Life is lovelier," "On top of the world," and "Live the life you've been waiting your whole life for!"

I turn on the radio and tune into WVLG AM640, The Villages's own radio station. "It's a beautiful day in The Villages," the DJ[2]

*(continued on next page)*

[1] **utopia:** an imaginary, perfect world where everyone is happy
[2] **DJ:** a disc jockey; someone who plays records on the radio or at a party

announces. "Aren't we lucky to live here? OK folks, here is a favorite I know you're going to love. 'The Candy Man Can.' C'mon, let's sing it together."

I listen to Sammy Davis, Jr.,[3] feeling slightly claustrophobic and uneasy about living in a gated retirement community for the next month.

A few miles later, I drive by a hospital, an assisted care[4] **facility** and a large Catholic church. Then I pass some faux[5]-Spanish fort ruins[6] and suddenly I'm in the "town" of Spanish Springs. I spot Betsy outside a Starbucks, standing beside her shiny red sports car, dressed attractively in pale pink slacks[7] and a white sweater. She greets me with a relaxed smile and a friendly hug, and insists on buying me a much-welcomed cup of iced coffee.

"Isn't it nice?" she asks. "People call it 'Disney for adults,' and I'm beginning to understand why. I just can't believe I'm here. I've met people that have been here for five years, and they're still **pinching** themselves. It's like being on a **permanent** vacation."

Betsy and I take our coffee to the central square, and sit on a bench beside the Fountain of Youth, which is peppered with lucky coins. We **catch up on** neighborhood **gossip**, the miserable New England weather, and the uncertain fate of our neighborhood park. Betsy is left **pondering** her incredible luck. "If we were still living up north, those problems would be our problems." Although it isn't meant to, her comment **stings**. But she's got a point; her life down here promises to be a lot more carefree than it was back home.

We walk around the square and then enter the western-motif saloon, Katie Belle's, which is for residents and their guests only. Inside the saloon the walls are covered in dark wood, and heavy drapes hang from several large windows. There are two dozen line dancers **keeping time** to a country and western[8] tune. I look at my watch. It's just past two in the afternoon.

"Line dancing is very popular here because you can do it without a partner," Betsy explains. "They say the only problem with being a **widow** in The Villages is that you're so busy you forget you are one."

"They call it 'Florida's Friendliest Hometown'—and that's just what it is," Betsy says as she gets into her shiny red sports car. "Everyone's so friendly because everyone is so happy. So make yourself comfortable at our house and enjoy your stay."

[3] **Sammy Davis, Jr.:** American singer and entertainer (1925–1990)
[4] **assisted care:** residence for people who cannot live independently
[5] **faux:** (French) imitation; not real
[6] **ruins:** the part of a building that is left after the rest has been destroyed or fallen down
[7] **slacks:** pants or trousers
[8] **country and western:** a popular style of music from the southern and western United States

**Vocabulary Check**

Complete the sentences with the boldfaced words from *Welcome to Leisureville*. Use the correct form of the word.

1. If you haven't seen someone for a long time, it is common to take some time to _____ each other's lives.

2. You might want to read a short _____ from the book before you decide whether or not to buy it.

**VOCABULARY CHECK** This section gives students an opportunity to focus on the meaning of the target vocabulary before completing the comprehension activities.

# THE *REAL READING* UNIT (continued)

## READING GOAL
The reading goal gives students a purpose for rereading the text before completing the comprehension activities. Reading goals include completing a graphic organizer, giving an oral or written summary of a text, retelling a story, identifying the writer's point of view, and giving an opinion on the content of a text, among others.

## COMPREHENSION CHECK
Engaging and varied exercises help students achieve the reading goal. Target vocabulary is recycled, giving students additional exposure to the high frequency words and expressions.

---

**B.** Read the statements about the reading. Write *T* (true) or *F* (false). Then correct the false statements to make them true. The boldfaced words are the target words.

_____ 1. A hurricane is an example of a **violent** storm.

_____ 2. Your house is built by the side of a river. You do not have to worry about **floods**.

_____ 3. Tornadoes and snowstorms are **man-made** events.

_____ 4. If someone tells you to "**Tuck in**," they want you to start eating.

_____ 5. Businesspeople with **foresight** are usually not surprised by changes in market trends.

### ▶ READ AGAIN

Read the "Trends in Tourism" Web page again and complete the comprehension exercises. As you work, keep the reading goal in mind.

📖 READING GOAL: To understand some unusual trends in tourism

### Comprehension Check

**A.** Without looking back at the Web site article, complete as many of the sentences as you can. Some sentences need more than one word. If you can't remember, leave that sentence blank.

1. Tourism is a highly _____ industry.

2. Trips to places where both natural and man-made disasters have occurred are examples of _____ tourism.

3. According to the information on the Web site, "dark tourists" enjoy being engulfed in _____

4. There are a lot of opportunities for storm-chasing tours in _____

5. Although it is possible to make a lot of money in _____ and _____ tourism, tour operators need to be cautious. There are serious risks associated with both of these types of tourism.

*(continued on next page)*

CHAPTER 13 ■ Trends in Tourism **121**

---

**B.** On a separate sheet of paper, use the information to write a one-paragraph summary of the reading. Do not look back at the text. Include only the main idea, the main points, and one or two details that support each main point.

**C.** Reread "Being a Genius Is Hard Work." Make sure your summary accurately expresses the main idea and the main points. If any of your sentences are too close to the original sentences, use the paraphrasing techniques in the skill box on page 211 to rewrite them.

### ▶ DISCUSS

Read the statements and rate them according to your opinion. Then talk in small groups. Explain your opinions.

| strongly agree | agree | disagree | strongly disagree |
|:---:|:---:|:---:|:---:|
| 1 | 2 | 3 | 4 |

_____ 1. Parents should help their children to identify their natural talents and abilities as early as possible so that they can develop those abilities at an early age.

_____ 2. Parents should let their children discover their interests and abilities on their own.

_____ 3. Parents have a responsibility to provide their children with access to as many different types of experiences as possible, such as music lessons, sports, art classes, etc.

_____ 4. All children should have their intelligence tested at school.

_____ 5. Children who exhibit signs of genius should be taught with other children who are similarly gifted.

CHAPTER 23 ■ Being a Genius Is Hard Work **215**

---

## DISCUSS
A variety of activities for small group or pair work encourages students to use vocabulary from the current unit as well as previous units.

# VOCABULARY SKILL BUILDING

This section offers presentation and practice with skills such as identifying parts of speech, learning and using derived forms of target words, learning common affixes and roots, and recognizing common collocations, among others.

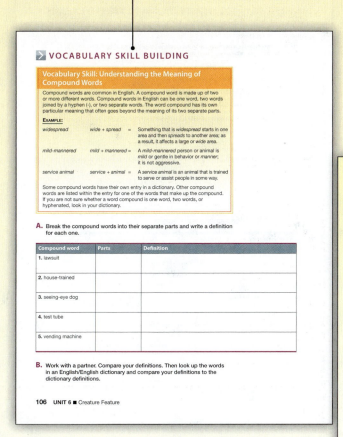

> **VOCABULARY SKILL BUILDING**

**Vocabulary Skill: Understanding the Meaning of Compound Words**

Compound words are common in English. A compound word is made up of two or more different words. Compound words in English can be one word, two words joined by a hyphen (-), or two separate words. The word compound has its own particular meaning that often goes beyond the meaning of its two separate parts.

**EXAMPLE:**

| | | | |
|---|---|---|---|
| *widespread* | *wide + spread* | = | Something that is *widespread* starts in one area and then *spreads* to another area; as a result, it affects a large or wide area. |
| *mild-mannered* | *mild + mannered* | = | A *mild-mannered* person or animal is *mild* or gentle in behavior or *manner*; it is not aggressive. |
| *service animal* | *service + animal* | = | A *service* animal is an animal that is trained to *serve* or assist people in some way. |

Some compound words have their own entry in a dictionary. Other compound words are listed within the entry for one of the words that make up the compound. If you are not sure whether a word compound is one word, two words, or hyphenated, look in your dictionary.

**A.** Break the compound words into their separate parts and write a definition for each one.

| Compound word | Parts | Definition |
|---|---|---|
| 1. lawsuit | | |
| 2. house-trained | | |
| 3. seeing-eye dog | | |
| 4. test tube | | |
| 5. vending machine | | |

**B.** Work with a partner. Compare your definitions. Then look up the words in an English/English dictionary and compare your definitions to the dictionary definitions.

106  UNIT 6 ■ Creature Feature

# LEARN THE VOCABULARY

This final section of each unit challenges students to practice strategies and techniques outlined by Paul Nation that will help them to acquire not only the target vocabulary but also vocabulary beyond the text. Activities include learning from word cards, guessing meaning from context, discovering core meaning, using a dictionary, and learning word parts, among others.

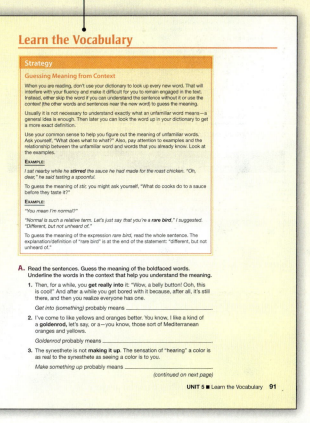

## Learn the Vocabulary

**Strategy**

**Guessing Meaning from Context**

When you are reading, don't use your dictionary to look up every new word. That will interfere with your fluency and make it difficult for you to remain engaged in the text. Instead, either skip the word if you can understand the sentence without it or use the *context* (the other words and sentences near the new word) to guess the meaning.

Usually it is not necessary to understand exactly what an unfamiliar word means—a general idea is enough. Then later you can look the word up in your dictionary to get a more exact definition.

Use your common sense to help you figure out the meaning of unfamiliar words. Ask yourself, "What does what to what?" Also, pay attention to examples and the relationship between the unfamiliar word and words that you already know. Look at the examples.

**EXAMPLE:**

*I sat nearby while he **stirred** the sauce he had made for the roast chicken. "Oh, dear," he said tasting a spoonful.*

To guess the meaning of *stir*, you might ask yourself, "What do cooks do to a sauce before they taste it?"

**EXAMPLE:**

*"You mean I'm normal?"*

*"Normal is such a relative term. Let's just say that you're a **rare bird**," I suggested. "Different, but not unheard of."*

To guess the meaning of the expression *rare bird*, read the whole sentence. The explanation/definition of "rare bird" is at the end of the statement: "different, but not unheard of."

**A.** Read the sentences. Guess the meaning of the boldfaced words. Underline the words in the context that help you understand the meaning.

1. Then, for a while, you **get really into** it: "Wow, a belly button! Ooh, this is cool!" And after a while you get bored with it because, after all, it's still there, and then you realize everyone has one.

   *Get into (something)* probably means _____

2. I've come to like yellows and oranges better. You know, I like a kind of a **goldenrod**, let's say, or a—you know, those sort of Mediterranean oranges and yellows.

   *Goldenrod* probably means _____

3. The synesthete is not **making it up**. The sensation of "hearing" a color is as real to the synesthete as seeing a color is to you.

   *Make something up* probably means _____

   *(continued on next page)*

UNIT 5 ■ Learn the Vocabulary  91

## FLUENCY PRACTICE

Four fluency practice sections address learners' extensive reading needs. Learners practice fluency strategies, read passages, check comprehension, and calculate their reading times. Fluency progress charts are provided at the back of the book for students to record their reading times and Comprehension Check scores.

## VOCABULARY PRACTICE

These pages appear at the back of the book and reinforce understanding of the target vocabulary, vocabulary skills, and vocabulary learning strategies.

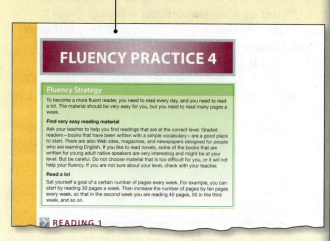

### FLUENCY PRACTICE 4

**Fluency Strategy**

To become a more fluent reader, you need to read every day, and you need to read a lot. The material should be very easy for you, but you need to read many pages a week.

**Find very easy reading material**

Ask your teacher to help you find readings that are at the correct level. Graded readers—books that have been written with a simple vocabulary—are a good place to start. There are also Web sites, magazines, and newspapers designed for people who are learning English. If you like to read novels, some of the books that are written for young adult native speakers are very interesting and might be at your level. But be careful. Do not choose material that is too difficult for you, or it will not help your fluency. If you are not sure about your level, check with your teacher.

**Read a lot**

Set yourself a goal of a certain number of pages every week. For example, you can start by reading 30 pages a week. Then increase the number of pages by ten pages every week, so that in the second week you are reading 40 pages, 50 in the third week, and so on.

▶ **READING 1**

### FLUENCY PRACTICE 4

| | Words per Minute | |
|---|---|---|
| | **First Try** | **Second Try** |
| Reading 1 | | |
| Reading 2 | | |
| Comprehension Check Score _____ % | | |

### VOCABULARY PRACTICE 9

**THINK ABOUT MEANING**

Read the statements and pay attention to the boldfaced target words. Write *T* (true), or *F* (false). Correct the false statements to make them true.

_____ 1. It is difficult to **chip** a **fragile** plate.

_____ 2. The loser of a race **trails behind** the winner.

_____ 3. If you put too much water in a glass, it will **overflow**.

_____ 4. In a flood, water from a river or ocean **overflows** and covers the land.

_____ 5. When you accommodate someone, you **insult** that person.

_____ 6. When you **get used to** something, it feels strange to you.

**PRACTICE A SKILL: Understanding idioms**

**A.** Look up the meanings of the idioms online and write the definitions. The boldfaced words are the target words.

1. **drag** one's feet: _____

2. have a **chip** on one's shoulder: _____

3. What a **drag**!: _____

4. to add **insult** to injury: _____

**B.** Complete the sentences with the idioms from Exercise A. You may need to change the form of some of the words in the idiom.

1. "I can't go to the party because I have to work."

   "_____ Can't you ask for a day off?"

2. He _____ because he didn't get invited to the party.

3. Stop _____ and get to work!

4. He lost his job. Then, _____, his wife left him.

**PRACTICE A STRATEGY: Adding visual images to word cards**

**A.** Make word cards for the four new idioms in Exercises A and B of *Practice a Skill* (above). Add visual images to those cards.

**B.** Show your cards to a classmate. See if your classmate can guess the idiom.

**242** Vocabulary Practice 9

## REAL READING COMPONENTS

- **MP3 Audio CD-ROM:** Each level has a bound-in MP3 Audio CD-ROM with recordings of all target vocabulary and readings.

- **Teacher's Manual:** The online Teacher's Manual provides a model lesson plan and includes the Student Book Answer Key. The Teacher's Manual is available at www.pearsonlongman.com/realreading.

- **Tests:** The Online Tests consist of a reading passage followed by comprehension, vocabulary, and vocabulary skill questions for each unit. An answer key is included. The Tests are available at www.pearsonlongman.com/realreading.

### HOW TO USE THE LESSON PLAN

#### Overview of Unit Format

Each unit of Real Reading 1 consists of two thematically related chapters. Compelling readings in a variety of genres have been carefully written or adapted from authentic sources and feature a principled approach to vocabulary development.

- Chapters consist of pre-reading and post-reading activities, including a reading skill, a reading goal, comprehension questions, and discussion activities.
- Reading and vocabulary skill building and vocabulary learning strategies based on Paul Nation's research help students become more confident and successful in preparation for academic reading and reading on standardized tests.

#### Suggested Methods of Instruction

This lesson plan can serve as a generic guide for any chapter in the student book.

- Suggested methods for delivering instruction for each section or activity in a chapter are presented.
- Alternative ways to handle each activity are provided under the heading *Variations*. These options allow instructors to vary the way they treat the same activity from chapter to chapter and in so doing to identify the methods that work best for a specific class or individual students.

#### Think Before You Read

The activities in this section are designed to prepare students for the topics, themes, and key vocabulary in the readings.

##### A. and B. *(approximately 10 minutes)*

1. Give students a few minutes to read the discussion questions. Answer any questions.
2. Have students form pairs to discuss their answers. Tell them they will report at least one of their answers to the class.

After 10 minutes, ask several students to share their answers.

##### Variations

- After students have discussed the questions, ask them to write for 1–3 minutes in answer to the questions. Have students exchange their writing with a partner or group member and compare their ideas.
- Ask students to answer the discussion questions in writing at home. Have them read their partner's or group members' answers in class and discuss their answers.
- Assign one discussion question per pair or small group. Have each pair or group discuss the question and report their ideas to the class.
- Choose one discussion question and have each student do a one-minute freewrite to expand ideas generated from the discussion. The students' writing can be passed around the class or reviewed in small groups to encourage further feedback and discussion. The activity may also serve as a closure to the discussion.

*Real Reading Teacher's Guide* **1**

---

NAME: _____  DATE: _____  SCORE _____ /40

#### UNIT 1
### TEST

##### Synchronized Swimming

It's part swimming, part gymnastics, and part dance. It's synchronized swimming, one of the more unusual sports in the Olympic Games. Many people love to watch it. The swimmers move their bodies in and out, forward and back, on the surface and under water. They move in perfect time with each other and the music.

Synchronized swimming was first called "water ballet." It's easy to see why. It's like ballet. And like ballet, it seems easy, but it isn't. The swimmers seem natural and relaxed, but they have to train for a long time. Many exercises are done under water, so they have to hold their breath for as long as two minutes. It takes a lot of strength, power, and energy.

Synchronized swimming first began in Europe in the 1890s. At that time, swimmers often trained outside, in rivers or in lakes. The first synchronized swimmers were men. But by the middle of the 20th century, most synchronized swimmers were women. Swimmers sometimes performed in the theater, where they swam in large water tanks on the stage! Later, some Hollywood musicals used synchronized swimmers. The actress Esther Williams starred in movies such as *Bathing Beauty* in 1944 and *Million Dollar Mermaid* in 1952.

Synchronized swimming became an Olympic sport in 1984. In the Olympic Games, swimmers work in teams of nine athletes, or in pairs. They show their skills by doing special movements above and below the water. They do not touch the bottom of the pool. Instead, they move their hands like flippers and kick their feet. This helps them stay up in the water. Like all Olympic athletes, they work very hard. Their dream is the same: to win a medal for their country in the Olympic Games.

#### Part 1

##### Comprehension

Circle the letter of the correct answer to complete each sentence.

1. In the Olympics, synchronized swimming is done _____.
   a. on land    b. to music    c. by one person

2. According to the article, synchronized swimming looks _____.
   a. easy    b. difficult    c. dangerous

3. Swimmers have to hold their breath because they need to _____.
   a. be underwater  b. train outside    c. swim on the surface

4. Synchronized swimming was first done by _____.
   a. children    b. men    c. women

5. In the early part of the twentieth century, people watched synchronized swimming _____.
   a. in the Olympics    b. in the theater    c. at the beach

6. In the Olympics, the swimmers cannot _____.
   a. kick their feet  b. move their hands    c. touch the bottom

   *Total:* _____ / 6

**2** *Real Reading Tests*

# SCOPE AND SEQUENCE

| Vocabulary Skill | Vocabulary Strategy |
|---|---|
| Parts of Speech: Review | Making Word Cards |
| The Prefix *cross-* | Using Word Cards: Different Types of Cards for Different Types of Learning |
| Collocations | Finding the Core Meaning of Words: Example Sentences |
| The Suffix *-free* | Finding the Core Meaning of Words: Using a Dictionary |
| Adverb Placement: Adverbs that Modify Verbs | Guessing Meaning from Context |
| Understanding the Meaning of Compound Words | Using the Keyword Technique |

# SCOPE AND SEQUENCE

| Unit | Chapter | Reading Skill |
|------|---------|---------------|
| **7**<br>**Getting Away From It All** | **13** Trends in Tourism | Identifying Purpose |
| | **14** Just Back: High Tide in La Serenissima | Understanding Descriptive Language |
| **8**<br>**Civilized Dining** | **15** A Blossom Lunch | Making Inferences |
| | **16** The First Home-Cooked Meal | Understanding the Relationship Between Ideas—Cause and Effect |
| **9**<br>**Family Matters** | **17** Widows | Reading Poetry |
| | **18** Lost and Found | |
| **Fluency Practice 3** | **Reading 1** The Haiku Master | |
| | **Reading 2** So You Want to Write Haiku? | |
| **10**<br>**Business** | **19** Branding and Product Placement | Skimming |
| | **20** Case Study: 3M's Entrance into the Russian Market | Recognizing Text References |
| **11**<br>**Biology: The Science of Life** | **21** Symbiosis | Understanding Definitions |
| | **22** Mixing It Up | Skimming |
| **12**<br>**Born Special** | **23** Being a Genius is Hard Work | Paraphrasing |
| | **24** Through the Eyes of Love | |
| **Fluency Practice 4** | **Reading 1** Tulip Fever | |
| | **Reading 2** Who Am I Today? | |

| Vocabulary Skill | Vocabulary Strategy |
|---|---|
| Core Meanings | Using a Dictionary to Find the Core Meaning of Related Words |
| Understanding Words that Signal Cause and Effect | Using Word Cards: Changing Order, Grouping, and Spaced Learning |
| Understanding Idioms | Using Word Cards: Adding Visual Images |
| Collocations | Using a Dictionary to Find Collocations |
| The Adjective Suffix: -ing and -ed | Choosing Words to Learn: Field-specific Terminology |
| The Prefix: extra-, hyper-, mini-, micro-, uni-, mono- | Avoiding Interference When Learning New Words |

# References

10 extraordinary child prodigies. *YouSayToo.com*. Retrieved from http://www.yousaytoo.com/10-extraordinary-child-prodigies/65567

Are Pheromones a Secret Weapon for Dating? (2005). *ABC News*. Retrieved February 20th 2009 from http://abcnews.go.com/2020/Health/story?id=1386825

Baker, B. (2008, Sept. 15). He cooked up a new theory on evolution. *The Boston Globe*. Retrieved from http://www.boston.com/news/science/articles/2008/09/15/he_cooked_up_a_new_theory_on_evolution/

Benson, E. *A Pheromone by Any Other Name*. American Psychological Association. (2002). Washington DC:

Bradt, S. (2009, June 1). Invention of cooking drove evolution of the human species, new book argues: We are what we eat, and what we cook. *Faculty of Arts and Sciences, Harvard University Press Releases*. Retrieved from http://www.fas.harvard.edu/home/news-and-notices/news/press-releases/wrangham-06012009.shtml

Brazil, Russia, India And China – BRIC. *Investopedia: A Forbes Digital Company*. Retrieved from http://www.investopedia.com/terms/b/bric.asp

Callaway, E. (2009, Feb. 5). Parasitic Butterflies Dupe Host with Ant Music. *New Scientist*. Retrieved from http://www.newscientist.com/article/dn16543-parasitic-butterflies-dupe-hosts-with-ant-music.html

Cromie, W. J. (2002, June 13). Cooking up quite a story: Ape, human theory causes evolutionary indigestion. *Harvard University Gazette*. Retrieved from http://www.news.harvard.edu/gazette/2002/06.13/01-cooking.html

Crowe, S. (2002, July 28). Sponge Commensals. *Ocean Explorer*. Retrieved from http://oceanexplorer.noaa.gov/explorations/02sab/logs/jul28/jul28.html

Custom-made worlds: Virtual Reality in Science and Business. *Science Clarified*. Retrieved from http://www.scienceclarified.com/scitech/Virtual-Reality/Custom-Made-Worlds-Virtual-Reality-in-Science-and-Business.html

TNS media intelligence reports U.S. advertising expenditures declined 14.7 percent in first nine months of 2009. *TNS Media Intelligence*. (2009, Dec. 8). Retrieved from http://www.tns-mi.com/news/2009-Ad-Spending-Q3.htm

Davis, J. Tendai Marathon Monks – The Run of a Lifetime. *How to Be Fit*. Retrieved from http://www.howtobefit.com/tendai-marathon-monks.htm

Fab 40: Brazilian Street Artists. (2009, Oct. 19). *Wallpaper*. Retrieved from http://www.wallpaper.com/art/fab-40-street-artists/3864

Flower Bulb History *International Flower Bulb Center*. Retrieved from http://www.bulb.com/

Frankel, M. (2000, April 24). When the Tulip Bubble Burst. *BusinessWeek*. Retrieved from http://www.businessweek.com/2000/00_17/b3678084.htm

Full, R. (2009). Learning from the gecko's tail. *TED Talks*. Retrieved from http://www.ted.com/talks/joshua_klein_on_the_intelligence_of_crows.html

Galouchko, K. (2009, Dec. 23). Alena Akhmadullina - the fashion designer who sets the beat in Russia. *Rossiyskaya Gazeta*, Dec. 23, 2009. Retrieved from http://www.telegraph.co.uk/sponsored/russianow/culture/6874519/Alena-Akhmadullina-the-fashion-designer-who-sets-the-beat-in-Russia.html

Garthwaite, G. R. *Khans and Shahs: A Documentary Analysis of the Bakhtiyari in Iran*. New York and Cambridge, U.K.: Cambridge University Press. 1983.

# References

Gay, G. M. (2009, July 30). Warren Faidley is America's Top Storm Chaser. *Arizona Daily Star*. Retrieved from http://www.azstarnet.com

Gladwell, M. *Outliers: The story of success*. New York: Little Brown and Company. 2008.

Gratchev, M. (2001, October 1) Making the Most of Cultural Differences. *Harvard Business Review*. Retrieved from http://hbr.org/2001/10/making-the-most-of-cultural-differences/ar/1

Gratchev, M.V., Rogovksy, N.G., & Bobina, M. (2006). 3M: Role model for emerging markets. *Thunderbird International Business Review, 48* (6), pp. 803–821.

Igne-Bianchi, B. (2008, Dec. 29). Brazilian Street Art: More Art, Less Street? *BlackBook Magazine*. Retrieved from http://www.blackbookmag.com/article/brazilian-street-art-more-art-less-street/5674

Intrigue, thievery and heart break . . . it's all in the history of the Tulip. *Tesselaar: Gardening at its best*. Retrieved from http://www.tesselaar.net.au/flowerandgarden/thetulip.asp

Koda, K. *Insights into Second Language Reading: A Cross-Linguistic Approach*. New York, NY: Cambridge University Press, 2004.

Judson, O. (2008, April 8). A Mutual Affair. *Opinionater—Exclusive Online Commentary from The Times*. Retrieved from http://opinionator.blogs.nytimes.com/2008/04/08/a-mutual-affair/

Jungwei, M. (2009, June 9). Examples of Commensalism in the Ocean: Descriptions of Marine Commensal Relationship. *Suite 101.com*. Retrieved from http://marinelife.suite101.com/article.cfm/examples_of_commensalism_in_the_ocean

Kang, C. (2008, June 27). Product Placement on TV Targeted. *The Washington Post*. Retrieved from http://www.washingtonpost.com/wp-dyn/content/article/2008/06/26/AR2008062603632.html

Ebert, Ronald & Griffin, Ricky *Business Essentials*, Sixth Edition Upper Saddle River: Pearson Education, 2007

Hass, R. (Ed.) *The Essential Haiku: Versions of Basho, Buson, & Issa*. New York: Harper Collins, 1996

Klein, J. (2008). Joshua Klein on the intelligence of crows. *TED Talks*. Retrieved from http://www.ted.com/talks/lang/eng/joshua_klein_on_the_intelligence_of_crows.html

Kurosawa, S. (2009, Aug. 29). The jewel in the crown. *Weekend Australian*, Review, p. 4.

Lightbrown, P., & Spada, N. *How Languages Are Learned*. Oxford, England: Oxford University Press, 2006.

Marietta College (2008, April 4). Symbiosis. Retrieved from http://www.marietta.edu/~biol/biomes/symbiosis.htm

Monturo, R. Brazil, Russia, India, and China—Already Cooler Than You. *Bric Pop*. Retrieved from http://www.bricpop.com/

Moore, B., Tschorn A., & Magsaysay, M. (2010, January 3). The 2010 forecast: a climate of familiar forces with a flurry of new trends. *Los Angeles Times*, p. P1.

Nation, I.S.P. *Learning Vocabulary in Another Language*. Cambridge, England: Cambridge University Press. 2001.

Nation, I.S.P. *Teaching Vocabulary: Strategies and Techniques*. Boston, MA: Heinle, Cengage Learning. 2008.

# References

Nygaard, L. (2004, April 15). Bakhtiari - travelling in Iran 1998. *Jozan Magazine*. Retrieved from http://www.jozan.net/2004/TheBactiaries.htm

O'Neill, J. (2001). Building Better Global Economic BRICs, Paper No. 66. *GS Global Economics Website*. Retrieved from http://www2.goldmansachs.com/ideas/brics/building-better-doc.pdf

Owen, J. (2004, Dec. 9). Crows as clever as great apes, study says. *National Geographic News*. Retrieved from http://news.nationalgeographic.com/news/2004/12/1209_041209_crows_apes.html

Roach, J. (2006, June 6). Crows have human-like intelligence, author says. *National Geographic News*. Retrieved from http://news.nationalgeographic.com/news/2006/06/060606-crows.html

Rudman, W.B. (2004, July 24). Symbiosis, commensalism, mutualism and parasitism. *[In] Sea Slug Forum*. Australian Museum, Sydney. Retrieved from http://www.seaslugforum.net/factsheet/symbio

Russian fashion week launches its 20th season in Moscow. *Russian Fashion Week*. Retrieved from http://www.russianfashionweek.com

Shift in world economic power means a decade of seismic change. (Jan. 22, 2010). *PriceWaterhouseCoopers Russia*. Retrieved from http://www.pwc.com/RU/en/press-releases/2010/Shift-in-World-Economic-Power.jhtml

Shore, R. (2006, Oct. 30) Virtual World, Real Cash. *The Vancouver Sun*. pp. B1, B2.

Steves, R. Taking your taste buds on a European tour. *Rick Steve's Travel News and Events*. Retrieved from http://www.ricksteves.com

Storm Chasing Adventure Tours. *Storm Chasing Tours in Tornado Alley: Frequently asked questions*. Retrieved from http://www.stormchasing.com/faq/html

Straubhaar, J. Brazil. *The Museum of Broadcast Communications*. Retrieved from http://www.museum.tv/eotvsection.php?entrycode=brazil

Street Art. (2008). *Online Tate*. Retrieved from http://www.tate.org.uk/modern/exhibitions/streetart/artists-nunca.shtm

Symbiotic Relationship. *101science.com*. Retrieved from http://101science.com/Symbiosis.htm

Tricky Caterpillars Impersonate Queen Ants to Get Worker Ant Protection. (2009, Feb. 2). *Discover Magazine Blogs/80 Beats*. Retrieved from http://blogs.discovermagazine.com/80beats/2009/02/05/tricky-caterpillars-impersonate-queen-ants-to-get-worker-ant-protection/

Tulipomania: Like beaniebabies and DrKoop, tulips used to be all the rage. *History House: An Irreverent History Magazine*. Retrieved from http://www.historyhouse.com/in_history/tulip/

Wright, T. The spirit of the running People: Three cultures you should know. *Vagabondish: The travelzine for today's vagabond*. Retrieved from http://www.vagabondish.com/running-cultures/

Zielenziger, M. *Shutting Out the Sun: How Japan Created Its Own Lost Generation*. New York: Random House. 2007.

# Pop Culture

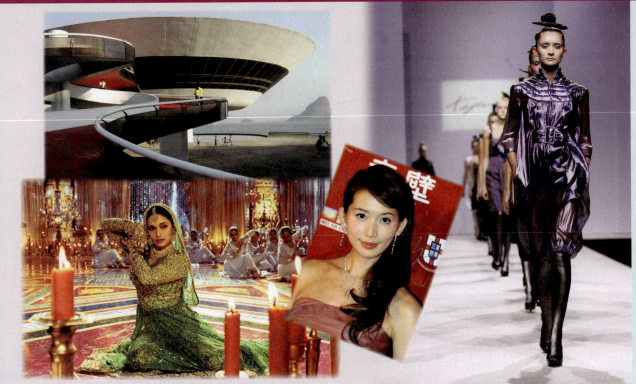

## > THINK BEFORE YOU READ

**A.** Work with a partner. Look at the pictures. Ask and answer the questions. If you don't know a word in English, ask your partner or look in your dictionary. Then write your new words on page 232.

   **1.** Can you identify which countries these pictures come from? (Each picture comes from a different country.)

   **2.** Are you familiar with anything in these pictures? Tell your partner what you know.

**B.** Work with a partner. Ask and answer the questions.

   **1.** How would you define pop culture? What kinds of music, art, fashion, writing, or film would you include in a definition of pop culture?

   **2.** In your opinion, where does the most interesting pop culture come from these days? Explain your answer with specific examples.

# Move Over, Hollywood!

 **PREPARE TO READ**

**A.** Look at the words and phrases in the list. Write the number(s) next to each word to show what you know. You may be able to write more than one number next to some of the words. You will study all of these words in this chapter.

1. I can use the word in a sentence.

2. I know <u>one meaning</u> of the word.

3. I know <u>more than one meaning</u> of the word.

4. I know how to pronounce the word.

**B.** Work with a partner. Look at the picture. Ask and answer the questions. If you don't know a word in English, ask your partner or look in your dictionary. Then write your new words on page 232.

1. Do you recognize the man in the picture? What is his name? What country is he from?

2. Why do you think he is famous?

3. Who are some famous performers (musicians, actors, etc.) in your home country today? Ask your partner if he or she has heard of them.

_____ appeal

_____ catch up with

_____ celebrity

_____ distraction

_____ implication

_____ influence

_____ inspire

_____ legend

_____ miss the boat

_____ promote

_____ role

_____ sell out

_____ slim

_____ undeniable

_____ unique

## Reading Skill: Previewing/Predicting/Skimming

You should *preview* a text before reading it. Previewing can help you . . .

- identify the general topic of the text

- activate any knowledge you already have about the topic

- *predict* (guess) what information might be in the reading

To preview, always start by reading the title and any headings and looking at any pictures. At the same time, think about what you already know about the topic and what might be new to you. Next, you can either . . .

1. read the **last sentence of the first paragraph** and the **first sentence of the other paragraphs**; or

2. *skim* the text. When you skim a text, you run your eyes over it very quickly. Do not read every word or sentence. Remember your purpose: to get a general idea about the topic.

After previewing, try to predict what the reading will be about. Then as you read, check your predictions.

**C.** Choose one of the previewing methods in the Reading Skill box and preview the blog entry "Move Over, Hollywood!" Then read the questions and check (✓) the answers. Do not spend more than two minutes previewing.

1. Which previewing method did you use?

　　＿＿＿＿＿ **a.** the first one (reading specific sentences in the text)

　　＿＿＿＿＿ **b.** the second one (skimming the text)

2. Make predictions. Which of the questions do you think the reading will answer?

　　＿＿＿＿＿ **a.** Who are these two blog entries about?

　　＿＿＿＿＿ **b.** Why is this person famous?

　　＿＿＿＿＿ **c.** Why are Hollywood movies the best in the world?

　　＿＿＿＿＿ **d.** Is Hollywood losing its influence?

　　＿＿＿＿＿ **e.** Who is Jay Chou dating?

　　＿＿＿＿＿ **f.** What is Chou's most recent movie about?

# READ

Read "Move Over, Hollywood!" Were your answers from Exercise C, question 2, correct? Underline the answers to the questions you checked (✓).

http://www.jaychoufans.com/

## MOVE OVER, HOLLYWOOD!

1  He is a **legend** all over Asia, where he is called the "King" of Chinese music. He has won almost every award in the Asian music industry, and several Western awards as well. He is a classically trained[1] pianist, writer, songwriter, pop singer, movie director, and international movie star. He sells millions of albums a year. His concerts **sell out**
5  all over the world.

This legendary singer and songwriter has a **unique** sound. His music is a combination of Chinese and Western musical styles. He specializes in R&B (rhythm and blues) and rap, with **influences** from rock and country and western music as well. His songs **inspire** listeners with lyrics[2] that touch on serious issues such as the environment,
10  domestic violence[3], and war.

If you are from Asia, you probably know who I am talking about: Taiwanese superstar Jay Chou. However, you might be surprised to hear that Chou is completely unknown to many in the West. This is about to change, as Chou is appearing in the Hollywood blockbuster[4] *The Green Hornet*.

15  What are the **implications** of Hollywood's decision to cast[5] Chou? Is Hollywood finally realizing that the future of the entertainment industry is moving from West to East? And does the pre-Hollywood success of superstar **celebrities** like Jay Chou mean that Hollywood has already **missed the boat**?

As always, I'd love to know what you think.

20  And for all of you Chou fans, check out this interview from the Shanghai Daily blog.

**Daily Blog**
Wednesday, 06 January 2010 09:01
Written by Emma Chi

Taiwanese singer-songwriter Jay Chou has been compared to Justin Timberlake, but
25  now a new comparison is being made—this time with Bruce Lee[6]. Chou recently

---

[1] **classically trained:** trained in the tradition of classical European music

[2] **lyrics:** the words of a song

[3] **domestic violence:** violence in the home, usually between a husband and a wife

[4] **blockbuster:** a very successful movie that makes a lot of money

[5] **cast:** to give someone a part in a movie or play

[6] **Bruce Lee:** Bruce Lee (1940–1973) was an actor, martial artist, film director, producer, and screenwriter. Born in the United States of Chinese parents but raised in Hong Kong, Lee is considered one of the most influential martial artists of the 20th century.

reprised[7] Lee's **role** of Kato in *The Green Hornet*, starring opposite Cameron Diaz. He told Channel New Asia, "I had to do it. It's a role that Bruce Lee once played, plus it's a positive Asian role, which is rare in Hollywood."

30 Chou's **appeal** to mainland Chinese is **undeniable**. The U.K.'s Royal Institute of International Affairs listed the performer alongside Chinese President Hu Jintao and Premier Wen Jiabao as one of the top fifty people with influence over China in the Institute's 2007 "China Power List." We **caught up with** the influential Chou, who was in town **promoting** his latest Chinese film, *The Treasure Hunter* . . .

***How was shooting** The Green Hornet in Hollywood?*

35 Oh, my English is poor, so it was really hard to recite[8] my lines, to drill them into my head. For the first month, I totally relied on a translator. I had to use body language if I wanted a drink of water! Kids, please don't learn from me, you must study English hard!

***How was acting opposite Cameron Diaz compared to Lin Zhilin in***
40 ***The Treasure Hunter?***

Well, it's quite different. Zhilin is very gentle, while Cameron is lively. When I talked with Cameron, I hated myself because I needed to use body language to get my meaning across, and it took a few minutes, but then she knew what I meant. But it's easier with Zhilin; we have a sort of common bond as people, and the language is
45 there, of course.

***You once said "I live for music." Is film more important to you now?***

No, I still live for music. I ventured[9] into movies because I felt the need for a new challenge. Movies are a source of inspiration, not **distraction**, for me. In the United States, I had lots of time to write songs after film shooting. And, you know, the
50 chances of shooting a film are **slim**, so when those good production teams invited me to join, I just jumped at the chance. As a result, though, my new album will be delayed until next year, probably January or February. But I guarantee that I'll release a new album every year.

***The Treasure Hunter** has had a pretty mediocre[10] box office reception[11].*
55 ***Did that hurt?***

We are now trying our best to promote it. There have been so many films this year; it's just like food, people have their own personal tastes. Audiences can go to as many films as they like, they're not forced to have only one choice.

***How do you think you compare to other heartthrobs/matinee idols[12]?***
60 Well, I just try my best. I can't control people making comparisons, and what they think. Every star has their own fans. For me, I won't say to my song lovers, "If you like me, you can't support others."

---

[7] **reprise:** to repeat a performance or role done at an earlier time

[8] **recite:** to say something from memory, in front of an audience

[9] **venture:** to risk going somewhere when it could be dangerous to do so

[10] **mediocre:** not very good

[11] **box office reception:** the way that the public reacts to a movie, concert, etc.

[12] **matinee idol:** popular film star

# Vocabulary Check

**A.** Read the definitions. Write the boldfaced word from the reading next to the correct definition.

1. _____ = a famous person, usually in the entertainment business

2. _____ = someone who is famous and admired for being extremely good at doing something for a long time

3. _____ = qualities that make you like someone, be interested in him or her, or want to be with him or her

4. _____ = to encourage people by making them feel confident and eager to achieve something great or to do something good

5. _____ = definitely true or certain

6. _____ = to fail to take an opportunity that will give you an advantage

7. _____ = the character played by an actor in a movie or play

8. _____ = a possible result or effect of a plan, action, etc.

**B.** Read the statements about the reading. Write *T* (true) or *F* (false). Then correct the false statements to make them true. The boldfaced words are the target words.

              *impossible*

_____ **1.** When something is **unique**, it is ~~easy~~ to find another one that is

the same.

_____ **2.** If your chances of winning are **slim**, you will probably win.

_____ **3.** When you **promote** a movie, you want people to see it.

_____ **4.** When you **catch up with** someone, you find an opportunity to

talk to him or her.

_____ **5.** A child's early **influences** include his or her parents, teachers,

and friends.

_____ **6.** When the tickets to a show **sell out**, you can buy them right

before the performance.

_____ **7.** If you are trying to study and people are talking, it can be a

**distraction**. That's why libraries are very quiet.

## ▶ READ AGAIN

Read "Move Over, Hollywood!" again and complete the comprehension exercises. As you work, keep the reading goal in mind.

> 📖 **READING GOAL:** To understand the blog writer's opinions

## Comprehension Check

**A.** Read about the celebrities mentioned in the blog. Check (✓) the true statements.

**Jay Chou**

_____ **1.** He is from mainland China.

_____ **2.** He doesn't speak any English.

_____ **3.** He likes singing more than acting.

_____ **4.** He doesn't like Cameron Diaz.

_____ **5.** He speaks Chinese.

_____ **6.** His musical style is unique.

_____ **7.** He acts in Chinese movies.

_____ **8.** He feels tired when he makes movies.

_____ **9.** He doesn't want his fans to listen to other musicians.

**Zhilin**

_____ **1.** She is a Chinese actor.

_____ **2.** She and Jay Chou made a movie in English.

_____ **3.** She is Jay Chou's girlfriend.

_____ **4.** She speaks Chinese.

**Cameron Diaz**

_____ **1.** She doesn't speak Chinese.

_____ **2.** She is Jay Chou's girlfriend.

_____ **3.** She was in the movie *The Treasure Hunter*.

_____ **4.** She did not want to be in a movie with Jay Chou.

**B.** Answer the questions about the reading.

1. Why is Jay Chou famous? What has he done to become a celebrity?

_____

_____

_____

2. What words does the writer use to describe Jay Chou?

_____

_____

_____

3. What words does the writer use to describe Hollywood?

_____

**C.** Which of the following statements does the blog writer probably agree with? Check (✓) them.

_____ **1.** Jay Chou is very talented, but he will never be successful in the United States.

_____ **2.** Jay Chou is a celebrity only among speakers of Chinese.

_____ **3.** Jay Chou's unique style will influence future musicians.

_____ **4.** Jay Chou won't become a movie star because he is more interested in music than acting or directing.

_____ **5.** Jay Chou's career will be long and successful even if he never makes another Hollywood movie.

_____ **6.** Hollywood needs Jay Chou more than Jay Chou needs Hollywood.

_____ **7.** Years from now people all over the world will remember Jay Chou as a legendary performer.

_____ **8.** Hollywood will remain the most influential force in entertainment worldwide.

## ▶ DISCUSS

Work with a partner. Compare your answers from Exercise C. Refer to specific sentences in the blog to explain your answers.

1. Do you agree with the blog writer's opinions? Which one(s)? Why or why not?

2. Have you ever seen Jay Chou in a movie or listened to his music? If so, what is your opinion of his talent? Do you think his talent matches his celebrity? Explain.

# CHAPTER 2

# MARKETING THE FUTURE: Pop Culture Trends in the BRICs

## > PREPARE TO READ

**A.** Look at the words in the list. Write the number(s) next to each word to show what you know. You may be able to write more than one number next to some of the words. You will study all of these words in this chapter.

1. I can use the word in a sentence.

2. I know <u>one meaning</u> of the word.

3. I know <u>more than one meaning</u> of the word.

4. I know how to pronounce the word.

**B.** Work with a partner. Look at the picture. Ask and answer the questions. If you don't know a word in English, ask your partner or look in your dictionary. Then write your new words on page 232.

1. What is this a picture of? Where was the picture taken?

2. Do you like it? Why or why not?

3. Is this kind of street art common in your country?

4. Who creates this kind of art? Are the artists paid?

_____ contemporary

_____ currently

_____ explosion

_____ luxury

_____ marketing

_____ motivate

_____ movement

_____ resources

_____ significant

_____ trend

_____ vivid

**C.** Scan the newsletter "MARKETING THE FUTURE: Pop Culture Trends in the BRICs." Then answer the questions.

**1.** Which countries does BRIC include? _____

**2.** What are two examples of pop culture mentioned in the article?

_____ , _____

**3.** When will the BRICs become top players in the world economy? _____

**4.** What is one area of pop culture that Brazil is known for? _____

Russia? _____

India? _____

China? _____

**D.** What is the topic of the article? Check (✓) it.

_____ **1.** the BRICs' position in the world economy

_____ **2.** the role the BRICs play in pop culture

_____ **3.** art and film in the BRICs

Read "MARKETING THE FUTURE: Pop Culture Trends in the BRICs."
Were your answers from Exercises C and D correct?

# MARKETING THE FUTURE

**POP CULTURE TRENDS IN THE BRICS**                      **VOLUME I  ISSUE 3**

### What are the BRICs?

BRIC is a term first used by global investment company[1] Goldman Sachs in 2001. It refers to Brazil, Russia, India, and China. In an influential article, Goldman Sachs claimed that the BRICs would have four of the six largest economies in the world by the year 2050.

### The BRICs and Pop Culture

Economists are watching the BRICs very closely. However, people who are interested in pop culture should also pay attention. Why? It is possible that the BRICs will soon replace the United States, Western Europe, and Japan as global pop culture trendsetters[2]. In fact, just look around you. It's happening already!

In this newsletter, we use our experience in global **marketing** to identify the most **significant** trends in the BRICs today. We predict that these **trends** will continue to influence popular culture for many years.

## BRAZIL

There has been an **explosion** of creativity in Brazil in recent years. That creativity, together with a very young population, are making Brazil a global leader in pop culture.

### Street art

Street art is a **movement** that is getting a lot of attention in the art world. Brazilian street art began as graffiti[3] on buildings in Brazil's largest city, São Paulo. Today, Brazilian street artists are producing some of the most exciting **contemporary** art in the world. Influential museums such as the Tate Modern in London have started showing their work. World-famous companies such as Adidas and Nike are using Brazilian street art to promote their products. International celebrities are buying it.

*Prediction*? The Street Art Movement is here to stay, and Brazilian artists will lead the way.

### Television

Very few countries produce their own television programs, and even fewer export programs to other countries. Instead, they import programs. Until very recently, most programs came from the United States. Brazil, however, is now one of the largest producers and exporters of television programs in the world. Brazilian television network TV Globo is the fourth largest commercial network worldwide. **Currently**, Brazil exports its programs to more than one hundred countries.

*(continued on next page)*

---

[1] **investment company:** a company that advises people and businesses on how to make money, and also invests other people's money

[2] **trendsetter:** someone who starts a trend

[3] **graffiti:** writing and pictures that are drawn illegally on the walls of buildings, trains, etc.

55 *Prediction*? Brazilian cultural exports will soon catch up to U.S. exports.

# RUSSIA

If current trends continue, Americans might soon be looking to Moscow rather than Hollywood and New York for the latest in film 60 and fashion.

### Film

Russia is becoming a leader in high-quality, low-budget film production. Russian films such as *Nightwatch* and *Daywatch* are two 65 examples. *Nightwatch* cost only $5 million to make, but it has excellent special effects[4] and was a big success at the box office. These new Russian films are popular outside of Russia as well. Their appeal is global, and young people 70 everywhere are starting to pay attention.

*Prediction*? Watch out Hollywood—here comes Russia!

### Fashion designers

Some of the hottest new fashion designers 75 are not working in Paris, but in Moscow. Alena Akhmadullina is one of these new Russian designers. In 2005, her unique designs were the talk of Paris Fashion Week.

*Prediction*? Russian Fashion Week will 80 become THE place to be seen in the fashion world.

# INDIA

India has one of the fastest growing economies in the world. With a population of 85 more than a billion people, many under the age of 25, and a rapidly growing middle class, India's influence on pop culture gets stronger every day.

### Design, Music, and Dance

Films produced in Bollywood—India's 90 answer to Hollywood—have been popular in Asia for a long time. Bollywood's influence on global pop culture, however, is just getting started. You can see it in home designs inspired by the **vivid** colors so popular in India. You can 95 hear it in pop music that is clearly influenced by Indian classical music. You can watch it at your local dance club, in dance moves inspired by Bollywood dance numbers.

*Prediction*? India's star has just begun 100 to rise.

# CHINA

### Video games

The Chinese love video games. However, most Chinese cannot afford the **luxury** of 105 expensive game consoles[5] such as PlayStation and Wii. This has **motivated** creative Chinese gamers to develop games that you can play without a console. For about 25 cents an hour at Internet cafés all over China, gamers play 110 MMORPGs—massively[6] multi-player online role-playing games. But MMORPGs are not just for people without the **resources** to buy console-based games. They appeal to gamers from all countries and backgrounds.

115 *Prediction*? Say goodbye to those expensive game consoles.

---

[4] **special effects:** images or sounds that have been produced artificially to be used in a television program, movie, or video game

[5] **game console:** a flat board or machine that contains the controls needed to play a video game

[6] **massive:** very big in number or size

# Vocabulary Check

**A.** Read the definitions. Write the boldfaced word from the reading next to the correct definition.

1. _____ = at the present time

2. _____ = the activity of deciding how to advertise a product, what price to charge for it, etc.

3. _____ = a sudden, large increase

4. _____ = a way of doing something or a way of thinking that is becoming fashionable

**B.** Complete the sentences with the boldfaced words from the reading. Use the correct form of the word.

1. My grandparents don't like _____ music. They prefer the music that they listened to fifty years ago.

2. Good teachers know how to make their students want to study. They know how to _____ them.

3. Poor people do not have a lot of economic _____. When poor people lose their jobs, they might not have the money to buy food or pay the rent.

4. We don't have the money to buy _____ items such as expensive cars, fur coats, and diamond jewelry.

5. Pablo Picasso was a legend even before he died. He was one of the most influential painters of the early twentieth century art _____ called Cubism.

6. Young children often like _____ colors such as bright blue, red, and yellow.

7. He will probably win the race. He's far ahead of everyone else. He has a _____ lead. It will be almost impossible for any other runner to catch up.

## > READ AGAIN

Read "Marketing the Future: Pop Culture Trends in the BRICs" again and complete the comprehension exercises on the next page. As you work, keep the reading goal in mind.

> **READING GOAL:** To understand the purpose of the article

# Comprehension Check

**A.** Read the details from the newsletter. Write *B* (Brazil), *R* (Russia), *I* (India), or *C* (China) next to the correct detail. More than one country is possible.

1. _____: four of the six largest economies in the world by 2050

2. _____: creativity

3. _____: influential television programs

4. _____: good movies that don't cost a lot to make

5. _____: Bollywood influences

6. _____: exciting contemporary art

7. _____: hot new fashion

8. _____: original design ideas

9. _____: new dances

10. _____: a completely new kind of computer gaming

**B.** Which of the statements would the author of the article probably agree with? Check (✓) them.

_____ **1.** Pop culture is a lot of fun, but it is not very significant to a country's economy.

_____ **2.** In the future the United States and Japan will probably not be the leading producers of pop culture.

_____ **3.** Business people all over the world should pay attention to what is happening in the BRICs.

_____ **4.** Young people in the BRICs are smart and interesting.

_____ **5.** In 2050, the United States will not have the world's largest economy.

**C.** Which group of readers is the writer of the article <u>most</u> interested in reaching? Check (✓) it.

_____ **1.** artists and musicians

_____ **2.** business people

_____ **3.** people living in the BRICs

**D.** Work with a partner. Talk about how the information from the newsletter could be useful to each of the following groups of people.

1. Hollywood movie executives

2. music and television producers

3. people who work in marketing

4. museum directors

5. young fashion designers

6. companies that make computer games

**E.** Choose two of your answers from Exercise D and share them with the class.

## > DISCUSS

Work in groups. Ask and answer the questions.

1. Are you familiar with any of the pop culture trends mentioned in the article? For example, have you played an online game created in China? Watched an Indian movie? Seen Russian fashions? Watched a Brazilian TV show?

2. Why do you think there has been an explosion of creativity in the BRIC countries recently?

3. Do you agree with the predictions in the article? Explain.

## > VOCABULARY SKILL BUILDING

### Vocabulary Skill: Parts of Speech

To use a word correctly, you need to know its part of speech: noun, verb, adjective, or adverb. Knowing a word's part of speech will help you understand how to use it. Study the chart.

| Part of speech | Purpose | Grammar and clause placement |
|---|---|---|
| noun | to name people, places, things, and ideas | *as the subject or complement of a verb*<br>subject<br>Example: The explosion of creativity was not a<br>complement<br>surprise.<br><br>*as the object of a verb*<br>object of verb<br>Example: I don't understand marketing.<br><br>*as the object of a preposition*<br>object of preposition<br>Example: I enjoy learning about new trends. |
| | to describe another noun | *in front of another noun, to describe that noun*<br>describes noun<br>Example: Street artists are becoming celebrities. |

*(continued on next page)*

| Part of speech | Purpose | Grammar and clause placement |
|---|---|---|
| verb | to describe actions, experiences, states, or conditions | *after the subject*<br>Example: You <u>inspire</u> me.<br><br>*at the beginning of the clause in a command*<br>Example: You can do it! <u>Inspire</u> them! |
| | to express purpose or how to do something (infinitive form only) | *at the beginning of the clause, followed by a comma* OR *at the end of the clause (no comma)*<br>Example: <u>To inspire</u> teenagers, you first need to get their attention.<br>OR<br>You need to get teenagers' attention <u>to inspire</u> them. |
| adjective | to describe or modify nouns | *in front of nouns*<br>Example: That is a <u>significant</u> problem.<br><br>*after a linking verb such as* be, feel, seem, appear<br>Example: That problem is <u>significant</u>. |
| adverb | to modify verbs, adjectives, or an entire sentence. Many adverbs are formed by adding -*ly* to the adjective form of the word. For example: *significant* (adjective)/*significantly* (adverb) | Clause placement varies, depending on what the adverb modifies<br><br>*To modify a verb: before or after the verb*<br>Examples: His paintings <u>vividly</u> show the effects of war.<br><br>The BRICs' influence has grown <u>significantly</u>.<br><br>*to modify an adjective: immediately before the adjective*<br>Example: His music is <u>significantly</u> different from mine.<br><br>*to modify an entire sentence: at the beginning of the sentence, followed by a comma*<br>Example: <u>Undeniably</u>, Picasso was one of the most significant painters of the twentieth century. |

**A.** Read the sentences. Identify the part of speech of the underlined words. Write *N* for nouns, *V* for verbs, *A* for adjectives, and *ADV* for adverbs.

_____ **1.** It has major <u>implications</u> for the entertainment and media industries in Europe.

_____ **2.** <u>Celebrity</u> and money do not always go together.

_____ **3.** Come to Brazil and live <u>luxuriously</u>!

_____ **4.** The shopping opportunities in India come from small <u>luxury</u> boutiques.

_____ **5.** What trends <u>influence</u> you?

_____ **6.** His talent is <u>legendary</u>.

_____ **7.** That CD is <u>currently</u> unavailable.

_____ **8.** Chou was in town to <u>promote</u> his new film.

_____ **9.** Movies are a source of <u>distraction</u> for me.

_____ **10.** To <u>motivate</u> your workers, you need to pay them well.

**B.** Read the sentences. Are the underlined words from Exercise A used correctly in the sentences? If the word is used correctly, put a check (✓) in the space. If the word is used incorrectly, write an *X*.

_____ **1.** <u>Promote</u> movies is an important part of his job.

_____ **2.** <u>Currently</u>, that film is very popular.

_____ **3.** Everyone enjoys <u>luxury</u>.

_____ **4.** I can't afford to buy a <u>luxuriously</u> car.

_____ **5.** I'm bored. <u>Distraction</u> me.

_____ **6.** <u>Motivate</u> your students, or they won't learn.

_____ **7.** You can't <u>influence</u> me.

_____ **8.** <u>Celebrity</u> performers are difficult to work with.

_____ **9.** Music <u>legendary</u> Jay Chou is also a movie star.

_____ **10.** The <u>implications</u> of the government's policy are not well understood, even by economists.

# Learn the Vocabulary

---

*influence (n., v.)*

*My father has a big influence on my life.*

*My father influences many of my decisions.*

---

*(n.) an effect*

*(v.) to have an effect on someone or something*

---

A. Make cards for the words from Chapters 1 and 2 that were new to you when you started the unit. Include target words and words that you wrote on page 232. Make sure you spell the new words correctly!

B. Work with a partner. Take one of your partner's cards and show him or her the back side of it (the side with the translation, drawing, or definition on it). You look at the front side of the card. Your partner will say and spell the word in English. If your partner makes a mistake, correct him or her. Then your partner will do the same with one of your cards. Continue until you review all of the cards.

C. Go back to the vocabulary list at the beginning of each chapter. What did you learn about the target words? Add numbers to the lists.

---

**Vocabulary Practice 1,** see page 234

# UNIT 2

# Personal Best

*[Handwritten notes in margin: 3rd times to read a novel every Thursday. Vocabulary Card every Wednesday total 50 card]*

## > THINK BEFORE YOU READ

**A.** Work with a partner. Look at the picture. Ask and answer the questions. If you don't know a word in English, ask your partner or look in your dictionary. Then write your new words on page 232.

1. What is happening in the picture? What is this kind of event called?

2. What are the participants in the event called?

3. Do you enjoy participating in or watching events like the one in the picture? Why or why not?

**B.** Work with a partner. Ask and answer the questions.

1. Is running a popular sport in your home country? Explain your answer.

2. Do you like to run? What is the longest distance that you have ever run?

3. Why do you think people enjoy running?

# Running around the World

## ▶ PREPARE TO READ

**A.** Look at the words and phrases in the list. Write the number(s) next to each word to show what you know. You may be able to write more than one number next to some of the words. You will study all of these words in this chapter.

**1.** I can use the word in a sentence.

**2.** I know <u>one meaning</u> of the word.

**3.** I know <u>more than one meaning</u> of the word.

**4.** I know how to pronounce the word.

**B.** Work with a partner. Look at the pictures. Ask and answer the questions. If you don't know a word in English, ask your partner or look in your dictionary. Then write your new words on page 232.

**1.** Where are the pictures from? Why is each person running?

2:5:29 **2.** Are there any famous runners from your home country? Who are they?
↓            Yes, there are. Naoko Takahashi and Yuki Kawauch are famous.
2:4:15 **3.** Do you know if there is a famous marathon in your home country or city
every year? When is it?
February 2nd    Syguru Asako    renewed Japanese man marathon record

2004 Athens Olympics Mizuki Noguchi got a gold medal.
My city has a marathon    2000 Sydney Olympics Naoko Takahashi got a gold medal
every year

_____ appreciation (n)

_____ capacity

_____ cycle

_____ dramatic (⊖)

_____ elite  best

_____ enormous  huge

_____ give someone
            an edge  Advantage

_____ intense  strong
                    激しい

_____ lung  肺

_____ play a role

_____ reward

_____ rigorous 厳しい(物)

_____ sweat

## Reading Skill: Understanding Basic Text Organization

Many texts in English are organized in a predictable way. If you understand this basic organization, you will be able to find the most important information quickly in many different kinds of texts.

- **The Hook**
  Many texts begin with a hook. A hook catches your attention and makes you want to keep reading. The hook could be one or two sentences or a whole paragraph.

- **The Main Idea**
  After the hook, the writer introduces the general topic of the reading. This introduction is usually in the first or second paragraph of the reading, depending on how long the hook is. At the end of the introduction, the writer often gives the main idea of the text. Sometimes the main idea is more than one sentence.

- **The Main Points that Support the Main Idea**
  The main points are developed in the *body* of the text—that is, the paragraphs between the introduction and the conclusion. Some main points are developed in one paragraph. Other main points are more complex and require two or more paragraphs.

- **Supporting Examples and Details**
  Examples and details illustrate and support the main points. The examples and details are in the main point paragraphs.

- **The Conclusion**
  The conclusion brings together all of the information and ends the text smoothly. The conclusion is usually one or two paragraphs. The main idea is often restated in the conclusion.

**C.** Read the first two paragraphs of the magazine article "Running around the World" on the next page and preview the rest of it. Then answer the questions.

1. Is there a hook? If so, is it in its own paragraph?

2. What is the main idea? Underline it.

3. How many points does the writer make about the main idea?

4. How many paragraphs are there in the conclusion?

5. Is the main idea restated in the conclusion? If so, underline it.

Read "Running around the World." Check your answers from Exercise C.

# Running around the World

1 [1] If a cheetah[1], a wolf, and a well-trained human all entered a marathon, who would win? The cheetah would definitely take an early lead. The wolf would probably pass the cheetah after

5 a few miles. But at the end of the 26 miles, the human would be the first to cross the finish line.
[2] Humans have only two legs but an incredible **capacity** for running. Our powerful **lungs** give us the stamina[2] needed to run great distances.

10 And because we can **sweat**, we can control our body temperature while we run. Why are we so good at running? Running was necessary for early human survival. Of course, we don't often need to run for survival these days. All the

15 same, running continues to **play an** important **role** in human cultures all over the world.
[3] Marathon running is perhaps the best-known example of human running culture. That is because it is big business. Millions of people

20 worldwide watch as **elite** runners compete for millions of dollars on television. And, of course, businesses promote products such as athletic shoes during the competition.
[4] How does someone become an elite

25 marathoner? The legendary runners of Kenya seem to have found the answer. Iten is a small farming town in Kenya's western highlands. It is also home to seven of the world's top ten marathon winners. Most of them are

30 members of the Kalenjin tribe. The Kalenjini tend to have ideal bodies for running. Their slim bodies, long legs, and short waists[3] concentrate power where a runner needs it most—the legs. And because Iten is 8,000

35 feet above sea level, the Kalenjini develop an **enormous** lung capacity. They need it to get oxygen out of the thin air. This **gives** the Kalenjini **an** important **edge** when they compete in races at lower altitudes[4].

40 [5] Thousands of miles away from Iten, in the mountains in western Mexico, live the Tarahumara. They call themselves the running people. The Tarahumara do not have much contact with the outside world. However, their

45 amazing capacity for long-distance running has caught the attention of researchers. Unlike elite marathon runners, the Tarahumara do not compete for prize money. Instead, they run when playing traditional games and when

50 competing in two- to three-day-long races over mountains. There is no million-dollar prize waiting for them. For the Tarahumara, running seems to be its own **reward**.
[6] Some monks[5] high in the mountains near

55 Kyoto, Japan, run for a different reason. They run to reach enlightenment[6]. The 1,000-day challenge of the monks of Hiei involves **intense** periods of running, as well as a period of extreme physical deprivation[7]. The challenge

60 takes seven years to complete. Only forty-six

---

[1] **cheetah:** a member of the cat family that can run fast

[2] **stamina:** physical or mental strength that lets you do something for a long time

[3] **waist:** the part in the middle of your body just above the hips

[4] **altitude:** the height of a place above the surface of the ocean

[5] **monk:** a man who is a member of a group of religious men who live together

[6] **enlightenment:** the state in the Buddhist and Hindu religions of not having any more human desires

[7] **deprivation:** a lack of something you need or want

monks have finished it since 1885, and only six men have attempted the race since World War II. Undeniably, the motivation to succeed is high: Any monk who fails must take his own life[8].

65  A monk begins the challenge by running about 25 miles (40 kilometers) every day for 100 days. The distance is similar to that of a marathon. The monk completes three of these 100-day **cycles**. There are periods of rest
70  between the cycles. Next, the monk must run about 25 miles a day for 200 days without a single day of rest. Then comes a different type of challenge. For nine days, the monk cannot eat, drink, or sleep. At the end of the nine
75  days, he is often near death.

If the monk survives, he will go on to complete the final year of the challenge. There are two 100-day cycles in the final year. During each cycle, the monk runs about 57 miles
80  (84 kilometers) every day. He must complete

the run within eighteen hours. Then he must repeat it again the next day. That means that in each 100-day cycle, he is running two marathons a day.

85  The few monks who have completed the **rigorous** 1,000-day challenge say that they now see the world in a new way. They report that they experience things more **intensely**. They notice a **dramatic** improvement in all of their
90  senses; they can see, hear, taste, and smell much better than before. They also say that they have a much greater **appreciation** for life.

It is undeniable that the running cultures of the Kalenjini, the Tarahumara, and the monks
95  of Hiei are very different. However, they all remind us that running has always played a significant role in human life and culture. The tradition continues today as people all over the world continue to run for money, sport,
100  exercise, enlightenment, or just plain fun.

---

[8] **take (his) own life:** to kill oneself

*Conculusion*

# Vocabulary Check

**A.** Complete the sentences with the words from the list. Be careful. There are two extra answers. The boldfaced words are the target words.

| | | | | |
|---|---|---|---|---|
| advantage | easy | fail | respect | succeed |
| difficult | exactly | remember | significant | |

1. If you have an **appreciation** for something, you ___respect___ it.

2. The training for that event is **rigorous**. It is not ___easy___.

3. If you have an **intense** experience, you will probably ___remember___ it.

4. If you ___succeed___, you will get a **reward**.

5. If something **gives** you **an edge**, you have a(n) ___advantage___.

6. To complete three **cycles**, you will need to repeat ___exactly___ the same process three times.

7. If there is a **dramatic** change in something, the change is very ___significant___.

**B.** Write the letter of the correct definition next to the target word. Be careful. There are two extra definitions.

_f_ **1.** play a role

_a_ **2.** capacity

_e_ **3.** elite

_g_ **4.** enormous

_b_ **5.** lungs

_c_ **6.** sweat

**a.** the ability to do or produce something

**b.** the two organs in your body that you use for breathing

**c.** to have liquid coming out through your skin, especially when you are hot or nervous

**d.** unpopular

**e.** the best and most skilled

**f.** to have an effect or influence on something

**g.** extremely large in size or amount

**h.** insignificant

## > READ AGAIN

Read "Running around the World" again and complete the comprehension exercises. As you work, keep the reading goal in mind.

> **READING GOAL:** To demonstrate your understanding of the text by completing a graphic organizer

## Comprehension Check

**A.** Read the sentences from the text. Write *MI* for main idea, *MP* for main point, *SD* for supporting detail, or *H* for hook.

_MP_ **1.** Marathon running is perhaps the best-known example of running culture today. That's because running is big business.

_MP_ **2.** They run to reach enlightenment.

_SD_ **3.** For the Tarahumara, running seems to be its own reward. *(MP)*

_H_ **4.** The cheetah would take an early lead, and the wolf might pass the cheetah after a few miles.

_SD_ **5.** For nine days, the monk cannot eat, drink, or sleep.

_SD_ **6.** There is no million-dollar prize waiting for them.

_MP_ **7.** The Kalenjini tend to have ideal bodies for running. *(SD)*

_MI_ **8.** They all remind us that running has always played a significant role in human life and culture.

**B.** Where can you find the different parts of the reading? Write the paragraph number(s).

_2_ **1.** the main idea          _5 6_ **3.** the second main point

3 _4_ **2.** the first main point    _6_ **4.** the third main point

**C.** Complete the graphic organizer with information from the reading.

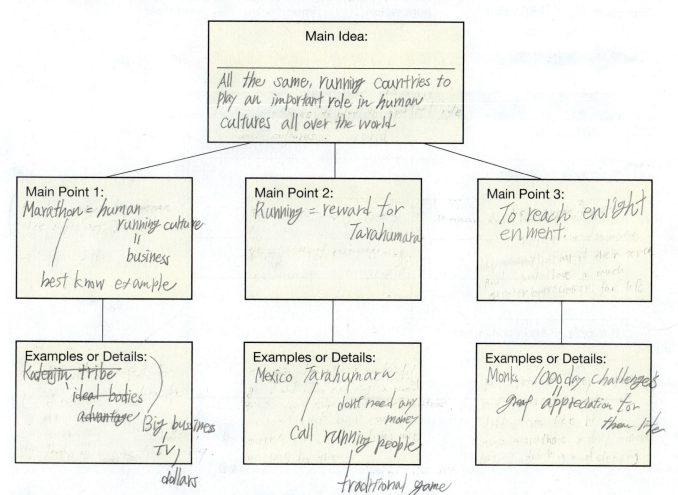

**Main Idea:**

All the same, running countries to play an important role in human cultures all over the world.

**Main Point 1:**
Marathon = human running culture
" business
best know example

**Main Point 2:**
Running = reward for Tarahumara

**Main Point 3:**
To reach enlighten ment.

**Examples or Details:**
Kalenjin tribe
ideal bodies
advantage Big bussiness
TV,
dollars

**Examples or Details:**
Mexico Tarahumara
dont need any money
Call running people
traditional game

**Examples or Details:**
Monks 1000 day challenges
" great appreciation for them life

**D.** Work with a partner. Compare your graphic organizers.

## ▶ DISCUSS

How important do you think the features in the chart are to an athlete's success? Rate them using the numbers on the scale. Then talk in small groups. Explain your opinions.

| least important 1 | not very important 3 | important 5 | very important 7 | most important 9 |
|---|---|---|---|---|

| Feature | Rating |
|---|---|
| 1. lung capacity | |
| 2. personal motivation | |
| 3. rigorous training | |
| 4. natural ability | |
| 5. a good coach | |
| 6. support of family and friends | |
| 7. intelligence | |

**CHAPTER 4**

# Bigger Is Better, Except When It's Not

## PREPARE TO READ

**A.** Look at the words and phrases in the list. Write the number(s) next to each word to show what you know. You may be able to write more than one number next to some of the words. You will study all of these words in this chapter.

**1.** I can use the word in a sentence.

**2.** I know <u>one meaning</u> of the word.

**3.** I know <u>more than one meaning</u> of the word.

**4.** I know how to pronounce the word.

**B.** Work with a partner. Look at the pictures. Ask and answer the questions. If you don't know a word in English, ask your partner or look in your dictionary. Then write your new words on page 232.

**1.** How are the athletes in the two photographs similar? How are they different? Compare their height, weight, body shape, and size.

**2.** In which sport do you think each of the athletes competes? Explain your answer.

| _____ | accurate |
| _____ | at first glance |
| _____ | beneficial |
| _____ | championship |
| _____ | cross-section |
| _____ | exception |
| _____ | horizontal |
| _____ | initially |
| _____ | load |
| _____ | muscle |
| _____ | rank |
| _____ | reasoning |
| _____ | store |
| _____ | stride |

## Reading Skill: Understanding Text Organization

As you saw in the previous chapter, most texts in English have this basic organizational structure:
- introductory paragraph(s) with a hook and the main idea
- body paragraph(s) that develop the main points and support the main idea
- a concluding paragraph that often contains a restatement of the main idea

Although this basic organizational structure is usually the same, there are many different ways to present and organize the main points. For example, in "Running around the World," the writer used three examples of different running cultures to illustrate and develop the main idea. That pattern of organization is called *exemplification*. Other common patterns of organization are compare/contrast, cause/effect, and problem/solution. Writers often use a combination of patterns.

**C.** Preview the newspaper article "Bigger Is Better, Except When It's Not." Which two types of organization does the writer use to develop the main points? Check (✓) the two types.

_____ **a.** exemplification and problem/solution

_____ **b.** compare/contrast and problem/solution

_____ **c.** cause/effect and compare/contrast

## > READ

Read "Bigger Is Better, Except When It's Not." Check your answer from Exercise C.

# *Bigger Is Better, Except When It's Not*

1  LOOKING back, Dr. Michael Joyner thinks he chose the wrong sport when he became a distance runner. He should have been a swimmer or a rower. Dr. Joyner, an
5  anesthesiologist[1] and exercise researcher, was fast—he ran a marathon in 2 hours 25 minutes. But, at 6 foot 5, and 175 pounds at his lightest, he was simply too big to be great.

The rules of physics can explain why the
10  best distance runners look so different from the best swimmers or rowers. Physics can also explain why being big is **beneficial** for some sports and not others. However, parents should not push their children into
15  a sport based on their body type, exercise physiologists[2] say. Most people who do sports do it because they love the sport; they are not aiming for the Olympic Games. Many also choose a sport because they discover they are
20  good at it.

For example, Dr. Niels H. Secher, an anesthesiologist, exercise researcher, and rower at the University of Copenhagen, started rowing when he was fourteen. He always was big—he
25  weighs 205 pounds—and he immediately loved to row and went with it. "If it works well, you think you are great and you follow up on your success," he said.

---
[1] **anesthesiologist:** a doctor who gives anesthetic to patients to make them fall asleep before an operation
[2] **physiologist:** a scientist who studies how the bodies of living things work

But understanding why body size matters in certain sports can open your eyes to other possibilities, exercise researchers say. "I've told people: 'You're tall. Why not try swimming?'" Dr. Joyner said.

The rules of physics say that distance cycling and distance running are for small people. Rowing and swimming are for people who are big. The physics is very exact. When Dr. Secher tried to predict how fast competitive rowers could go, based only on their sizes and the weights of their boats, he was **accurate** to within 1 percent.

**At first glance**, a big rower (and elite male rowers can weigh as much as 250 pounds) may seem to be at a disadvantage. But because water holds the boat up, weight becomes less important compared with the enormous benefits of having strong **muscles**. Their bigger muscles allow bigger people to use more oxygen. That gives them more power. It's like having a bigger motor, Dr. Secher said. Bigger muscles, with their larger **cross-section**, also are stronger. And bigger muscles can **store** more glycogen[3], their fuel for short intense spurts[4].

The same **reasoning** explains why elite swimmers are big. Great male swimmers often are 6 foot 4 inches tall, and muscular. And because of the advantage that large muscles give for sprints[5] over short distances, the shorter the distance an athlete must swim, the greater the advantage it is to be big.

Tall swimmers also have another advantage. Because swimmers are **horizontal** in the water, their long bodies give them an automatic edge. "It's the difference between long canoes[6] and short canoes," Dr. Joyner said.

Distance running is different. Tall people naturally have longer **strides**, but stride length does not determine speed. Running requires that you lift your body off the ground with each step, propelling[7] yourself forward. The more you weigh, the harder you have to work to lift your body and the slower you will be. The best runners are small and light, with slim legs. "If you have large legs, you have to move a big **load**," Dr. Secher said.

Of course, there are **exceptions** to the rules. Tom Fleming won the New York City Marathon in 1973 and 1975. He is 6 foot 1 and weighed 159 pounds when he ran his fastest marathon at 2 hours 12 minutes. And he ran the Boston Marathon in 2 hours 14 minutes when he weighed 179 pounds. "I tell people that's the fat-man record of Boston," he said.

The tallest elite marathoner today, Robert Cheruiyot, is 6 foot 2, but he weighs only 143 pounds. Most elite male marathoners, Dr. Joyner notes, are between 5 foot 7 and 5 foot 11 and weigh between 120 and 140 pounds.

The decision for high school coaches, said Hayden Smith, a cross-country[8] coach, is whether to say anything when a young teenager seems set on the wrong sport. The best high school athlete Mr. Smith ever coached **initially** wanted to play football. The football coach refused to let him join the team. "He told the kid, 'You'll be a great runner,'" Mr. Smith recalled. The coach was right. The boy started running and ended up one of the top ten in the nation.

No one ever told Dr. Joyner not to run. Injuries, though, finally forced him to look for another sport. He chose swimming, knowing that his size would be to his advantage. Dr. Joyner got a coach, worked hard, and recently **ranked** fifteenth swimming a mile in a U.S. Masters Swimming **championship** race (for people over age twenty-five). He started too late, he said, to know what he might have been as a swimmer.

*(continued on next page)*

---

[3] **glycogen:** a molecule that stores energy in the muscles

[4] **spurt:** a short sudden increase of activity or speed

[5] **sprint:** the act of moving very fast for a short time

[6] **canoe:** a long narrow boat, pointed at both ends

[7] **propel:** to move, drive, or push something forward

[8] **cross-country:** a sport in which you run across fields, not around a track

But that is OK, Dr. Joyner said. He loved
110 running. And there is more to performance than
simply having the right sort of body for the
sport. There is hard work and rigorous training,
and, of course, there is motivation.

"I always remember something Bill
115 Bowerman[9] said," he added, referring to the
legendary distance running coach. "Sometimes
what matters is not what dog is in the fight but
how much fight is in the dog."

---

[9] **Bill Bowerman (1911–1999):** an American track and field coach and the cofounder of Nike, Inc., the sports
clothing and equipment company

## Vocabulary Check

Read the statements about the reading. Write *T* (true) or *F* (false). Then
correct the false statements to make them true. The boldfaced words are
the target words.

    *completely*
  **F** 1. When numbers are **accurate**, they are ~~almost~~ correct.

    2. If you look at the **cross-section** of a **muscle** under a

        microscope, you will see pieces of muscle tissue going in two

        different directions.

    3. When we stand up, our bodies are **horizontal**.

        *legs*
    4. We **stride** with our ~~arms~~.

    5. **At first glance** means the first time you look at something

        quickly.

    6. When people explain their **reasoning**, they explain ~~how they do~~

        ~~something.~~

        *later*
    7. When you **store** energy, you use it ~~right away~~.

    8. The team won the **championship**, so it is **ranked** number one.

        *bigger*
    9. If you lift heavy **loads** every day, your **muscles** will get ~~smaller~~.

    10. Most great swimmers are tall. Tom is an **exception**; he is only 5

        foot 7 inches tall.

    11. If something is **beneficial** to your health, it is good for you.

    12. If you believe something **initially**, you will ~~always~~ believe it.

## > READ AGAIN

Read "Bigger Is Better, Except When It's Not" again and complete the comprehension exercises. As you work, keep the reading goal in mind.

> **READING GOAL:** To understand the relationship between body shape and size and sports performance

## Comprehension Check

**A.** Check (✓) the main idea of "Bigger Is Better, Except When It's Not."

_____ **1.** Dr. Joyner was a very good runner, but he was too tall and heavy to become an elite runner.

_____ **2.** Body size and shape are important in sports, but motivation is also important.

_____ **3.** If you have the right body size and shape for a particular sport, you will do well in that sport.

**B.** Complete the sentences. Write the letter of the clause or phrase next to the correct sentence.

**Sentences**

_____ **1.** Water holds the boat up, so

_____ **2.** Big muscles are strong because of

_____ **3.** Big muscles can store a lot of glycogen, so

_____ **4.** When you swim, your body is horizontal in the water, so

_____ **5.** The young athlete was small and light, so

_____ **6.** Because running requires that you lift your body off the ground with each step,

_____ **7.** As a result of his injury,

_____ **8.** Dr. Joyner chose swimming because

_____ **9.** Dr. Joyner started swimming late in life, so

**Clauses/Phrases**

**a.** the coach told him to try running.

**b.** muscular athletes have energy for short, intense spurts of activity.

**c.** tall swimmers have an advantage over short swimmers.

**d.** runners with heavy, muscular legs are slower than runners with slim bodies and light legs.

**e.** he will never be an elite swimmer.

**f.** rowers can be heavy.

**g.** Dr. Joyner stopped running.

**h.** he is very tall.

**i.** their large cross-sections.

C. Check (✓) the body shape and size of each type of athlete.

| | tall | short | muscular | light and slim body | slim legs | long, powerful legs |
|---|---|---|---|---|---|---|
| Swimmer | ✓ | | ✓ | | | |
| Rower | ✓ | | ✓ | | | |
| Long-distance runner | | | | ✓ | ✓ | |
| Long-distance cyclist | | | ✓ | | | |

> DISCUSS

Work in small groups. Using what you have learned from the article and your own ideas, check (✓) the body shape and size for each type of athlete. Add a category (other), if you like.

| | tall | short | muscular | light and slim body | slim legs | long, powerful legs | other |
|---|---|---|---|---|---|---|---|
| Soccer player | ✓ | ✓ | | | ✓ | ✓ | |
| Short-distance sprinter (runner) | ✓ | | ✓ | | | | |
| Basketball player | | | | | | ✓ | |

# VOCABULARY SKILL BUILDING

*(ex-, dis-, un-)*

## Vocabulary Skill: The Prefix *cross-*

The prefix *cross-* means *across; going from one side of something to the other.*

**EXAMPLE:**

*cross-country* = a sport in which you run across fields, not along roads or a track

Some of the nouns that have *cross-* as a prefix are hyphenated, such as *cross-country*. Others are one word compounds, such as *crossword*. If you are not sure whether a word is hyphenated, check your dictionary.

Add the prefix *cross-* to the words in the list to make new words. Then write the letter of each definition next to the correct word. When you finish, check your answers in a dictionary.

Prefix: *cross-*

___b___ 1. _____ cross walk     *pedestrian(s)*     *walking*

___c___ 2. _____ training

___e___ 3. _____ section

___f___ 4. _____ reference

___a___ 5. _____ fire

___d___ 6. _____ cross roads

a. the area where bullets from two or more directions cross

b. a specially marked place for people to cross a street

c. the activity of practicing and preparing to play more than one sport in the same period of time

d. a place where two roads meet and cross each other

e. the place where two sections meet and overlap to make two layers

f. a note that tells the reader of a book to look in another place in the book for more information

# Learn the Vocabulary

**A.** Read the explanations. Look at the target words on pages 20 and 27. Write each word in the space after the explanation that matches your purpose for learning that word.

1. **Learning the meaning**

   <u>Purpose</u>: You want to learn the meaning of a word that is new to you.

   *Words from this unit:*

   _____

   <u>How to make the card</u>:

   • Write the word or expression on one side of the card.

   • Write the translation, a simple English definition, and/or draw a picture of the word on the other side of the card.

   • Include an example sentence under the word.

2. **Learning other forms of the word (for example, you know the noun form, but not the adjective form)**

   <u>Purpose</u>: You know one form of the word pretty well and want to learn other word forms.

   *Words from this unit:*

   _____

   <u>How to make the card</u>:

   • Write the known form of the word on one side of the card.

   • Write the other forms of the word on the other side of the card with their parts of speech written next to them.

3. **Learning the pronunciation of a known word**

   Purpose: You know the meaning of the word but have trouble pronouncing it or recognizing it when other people say it.

   *Words from this unit:*

   _____

   How to make the card:

   - Write the word on one side of the card.

   - Write the pronunciation on the other side of the card. Use the pronunciation symbols from the dictionary or your own system for remembering the correct pronunciation.

   - If the word has more than one syllable, clearly mark the stressed syllable.

**B.** Make cards for the words you wrote under each explanation. Follow the *How to make the card* instructions for each type of card.

**C.** Go back to the vocabulary list at the beginning of each chapter. What did you learn about the target words? Add numbers to the lists.

---

**Vocabulary Practice 2,** see page 235

# Doing Real Business in the Virtual World

## > THINK BEFORE YOU READ

**A.** Work with a partner. Look at the pictures. Ask and answer the questions. If you don't know a word in English, ask your partner or look in your dictionary. Then write your new words on page 232.

1. What are the people in the pictures doing?

2. What is happening in all of the pictures? What do all of them have in common?

**B.** Work with a partner. Ask and answer the questions.

1. Which of the activities in the pictures did you enjoy when you were a child?

2. Read the chapter titles and look at the pictures on pages 37 and 43. What do you think the unit is about?

# Your Second Life = virtual life

## PREPARE TO READ

**A.** Look at the words and phrases in the list. Write the number(s) next to each word to show what you know. You may be able to write more than one number next to some of the words. You will study all of these words in this chapter.

**1.** I can use the word in a sentence.

**2.** I know <u>one meaning</u> of the word.

**3.** I know <u>more than one meaning</u> of the word.

**4.** I know how to pronounce the word.

**B.** Work with a partner. Look at the picture. Ask and answer the questions. If you don't know a word in English, ask your partner or look in your dictionary. Then write your new words on page 232.

**1.** What does the woman in the picture look like? How is she dressed?

**2.** What are the differences between the woman and her picture on the computer?

_____ as far as
                 we know

_____ creature

_____ digital

_____ exchange

_____ expense

_____ income

_____ merge

_____ property

_____ range

_____ roughly

_____ toy

_____ virtual

*Process* is a common type of text organization. To understand a process, you need to understand the steps and the order of each step. Sometimes a writer does not list every step, so you have to imagine the missing step(s).

**C.** Preview the newspaper article "Your Second Life." What process does it explain? Check (✓) it.

_____ **a.** how to be a successful fashion designer

_____ **b.** how to make money by playing a virtual reality game

_____ **c.** how to design a virtual reality game

 **READ**

Read "Your Second Life." Check your answer from Exercise C.

# *Your Second Life*

1　As far as we know, humans are the only **creatures** on Earth with the ability to imagine lives that are different from the ones we have. Some people enter the world of imagination
5　through books and stories. Others watch television or movies. Children bring their **toys** to life with the power of their imagination. Today, the Internet makes it easier than ever for both children and adults to enter imaginary
10　worlds. But what happens when the real world and the world of the imagination start to **merge**? To find out, all you need to do is go on the Internet and enter the **virtual** world of Second Life.
15　First of all, to understand Second Life, let's meet someone who lives and works there, Nyla Cheeky. Cheeky is a fashion designer. She designs and makes women's clothing, and then sells it in her own
20　stores. Cheeky's clothes are surprisingly inexpensive. Her original designs **range** in price from 25¢ to $6. How can she afford to sell things at such low prices? She has an enormous number of customers. In fact,
25　thousands of people visit her stores every day.

Now meet Canadian fashion designer Nyla Kazakoff. Kazakoff's designs are very similar to Cheeky's. However, they cost significantly more. For example, both designers sell a
30　similar dress. Cheeky's dress costs about $5.35. Kazakoff's costs $1,500. Kazakoff needs to sell her designs at high prices because she can create and sell only a few of them every month.

Have you guessed the secret of the two
35　Nylas yet? They are both the same person. Nyla Kazakoff is a real-life fashion designer. Nyla Cheeky is a fashion designer, too, but she doesn't live in the real world. She lives in the online world of the virtual reality game Second Life.
40　The clothes in her stores are virtual, not real. But the money she makes is undeniably real.

To play Second Life, you create a computer character, or *avatar*, as it is called in the gaming world. Nyla Cheeky is Nyla Kazakoff's avatar.
45　When your avatar enters Second Life, he or she does many of the same things people do in the real world. For example, avatars go to nightclubs, drive cars, and play games. And like people in the real world, avatars love to shop.
50　This is where fashion designer Nyla Kazakoff

comes in. Designer fashions are very popular among Second Life avatars. The real world Nyla Kazakoff creates online **digital** copies of her real world clothes. Then Second Life Nyla
55 Cheeky sells the virtual clothing in stores that she rents in Second Life. Customers pay for her designs with money called Lindens. Second Life players **exchange** real money for Lindens.

Up to this point, Second Life might not
60 sound very different from other online games. But this is where things get interesting. The unique thing about Second Life is that players like Kazakoff create things and sell them in Second Life. They then exchange the Lindens
65 that they make for real money. For example, imagine that someone buys one of Kazakoff/Cheeky's designs for 500 Lindens. Those Lindens go into Kazakoff/Cheeky's Second Life account. After Kazakoff/Cheeky pays Second
70 Life **expenses** such as the rent on her stores, any remaining Lindens are hers. She can then exchange them for real dollars.

Currently, Kazakoff is making **roughly** two-thirds of her **income** from real-world sales of
75 her designs, and one-third from Cheeky's sales in Second Life. And Kazakoff isn't the only one making real money in the virtual world. Some Second Life players have done so well that they have given up their real-life careers. In fact,
80 there is at least one Second Life player who has become rich developing[1] and then selling **property** such as land, homes, and office buildings in Second Life.

But wait a minute! Why would anyone pay
85 real money for imaginary clothing or property? Probably for the same reason that a little girl saves her birthday money to buy clothing and a house for her favorite doll[2]. She dresses her doll in clothing that she can't wear in real life
90 and puts her in a house where adults can't tell her what to do. Through her doll, the little girl experiences a reality that is different from her own. The same is true of adults playing Second Life. Through their avatars, they have a chance
95 to experience a "second life." And they are happy to pay real money to bring that imaginary world to life.

---

[1] **develop (property):** to buy a building or land and then fix it or build on it in order to resell it and make money.

[2] **doll:** a toy that looks like a baby or small person

## Vocabulary Check

Look at the boldfaced words in the reading and try to guess the meaning. Then read the sentences and circle the letter of the correct answer to complete each sentence.

1. When you say "**As far as I know**," you are _____ of the facts.
   **a.** 100 percent sure      **b.** somewhat sure      **c.** not at all sure

2. When two things **merge**, _____.
   **a.** they become one      **b.** each one grows      **c.** they are very similar

3. If I go to a store to **exchange** a computer game I bought, I want to return the game and get _____.
   **a.** my money back      **b.** a different one      **c.** a receipt

*(continued on next page)*

**4.** When you have a job, you _____ an **income**.

    **a.** earn            **b.** don't need         **c.** pay

**5.** If your income **ranges** from $35,000 to $50,000, it _____.

    **a.** never changes     **b.** is often more      **c.** can vary by $15,000
                               than $50,000

**6. Creatures** are _____.

    **a.** animals           **b.** plants             **c.** avatars

**7.** It is difficult to _____ when your **expenses** are high.

    **a.** get up           **b.** save              **c.** work

**8.** Most children like to _____ **toys**.

    **a.** design           **b.** merge           **c.** play with

**9.** A **digital** camera does not use _____.

    **a.** film             **b.** pictures        **c.** a flash

**10.** He has a lot of **property** in the city, including _____.

    **a.** two jobs         **b.** an apartment    **c.** many friends
                          building

**11.** A **virtual** friend is a friend that you meet _____.

    **a.** frequently       **b.** online           **c.** with another friend

**12.** If you are making **roughly** $100,000 a year, _____.

    **a.** you are making    **b.** your job is      **c.** you earn about
      exactly $100,000       very difficult        $100,000

# ＞ READ AGAIN

Read "Your Second Life" again and complete the comprehension exercises on the next page. As you work, keep the reading goal in mind.

> **READING GOAL:** To understand how to play and make money in the virtual reality game Second Life

# Comprehension Check

**A.** Read the statements about the reading. Write *T* (true) or *F* (false). If it is not possible to tell, write *?*. For the statements you mark *T* and *F*, write the number of the paragraph where you found the answers.

_____ **1.** Nyla Kazakoff is a real person.

_____ **2.** Nyla Cheeky is a real person.

_____ **3.** Nyla Kazakoff designs clothes for famous people.

_____ **4.** Second Life players create a character to represent them in the game.

_____ **5.** Some Second Life players create digital clothing, houses, land, or other things and sell them to other players.

**B.** How does Second Life work? Put the steps in order for playing the game and for making money in the game. Write *1* for the first step, *2* for the second step, and so on. Some of the steps are stated directly in the reading; for others, you will need to use your imagination.

**How to Play the Game**

_____ **a.** Buy Lindens.

_____ **b.** Create an online avatar to use in Second Life.

_____ **c.** Register on Second Life's Web site.

_____ **d.** Dress your avatar in new clothes and go to a virtual nightclub.

_____ **e.** Go shopping for clothes for your avatar in virtual stores.

_____ **f.** Pay for your avatar's virtual clothes with Lindens.

**How Nyla Kazakoff Started Making Real Money in the Game**

_____ **a.** She exchanged dollars for Lindens and rented a store.

_____ **b.** She registered on Second Life's Web site and created an avatar named Nyla Cheeky.

_____ **c.** She set up an account on Second Life to deposit the Lindens that she would make from selling virtual clothing in her store.

_____ **d.** She made digital copies of her real world designs and put them in her store.

_____ **e.** She exchanged the Lindens in her account for real money.

_____ **f.** She started selling her designs to other players' avatars.

**C.** Write an explanation of how to play Second Life. You may review the reading and the steps on page 41 before you start writing, but once you have started writing, do not look at the reading or the exercises.

_____

_____

_____

_____

_____

_____

**D.** When you finish, compare your explanation to a classmate's. Whose explanation is more accurate?

 **DISCUSS**

Work in small groups. Ask and answer the questions.

**1.** Have you ever played Second Life or another similar online game? If you haven't, would you like to?

**2.** Do you think that playing a game such as Second Life is a useful way to spend your time? Explain your opinion.

**3.** How do adults use their imaginations in their work and personal lives?

# Virtual Reality: A Powerful Tool

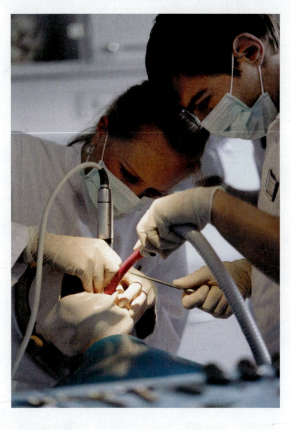

## > PREPARE TO READ

**A.** Look at the words in the list. Write the number(s) next to each word to show what you know. You may be able to write more than one number next to some of the words. You will study all of these words in this chapter.

   **1.** I can use the word in a sentence.

   **2.** I know <u>one meaning</u> of the word.

   **3.** I know <u>more than one meaning</u> of the word.

   **4.** I know how to pronounce the word.

**B.** Work with a partner. Look at the picture. Ask and answer the questions. If you don't know a word in English, ask your partner or look in your dictionary. Then write your new words on page 232.

   **1.** Who are the people? Where are they?

   **2.** What is happening?

_____ absorbed
_____ ancient
_____ attractive
_____ destroy
_____ likely = probably
_____ model = example
_____ mostly
_____ operation
_____ perform = act
_____ spot
_____ swallow
_____ vehicle = transport

## Reading Skill: Preparing a Graphic Organizer or Outline to Study From

If you know that you will be tested on the material from a reading, it is useful to make a graphic organizer or an outline. An outline serves the same purpose as a graphic organizer, but it looks a little different. Compare:

**GRAPHIC ORGANIZER**

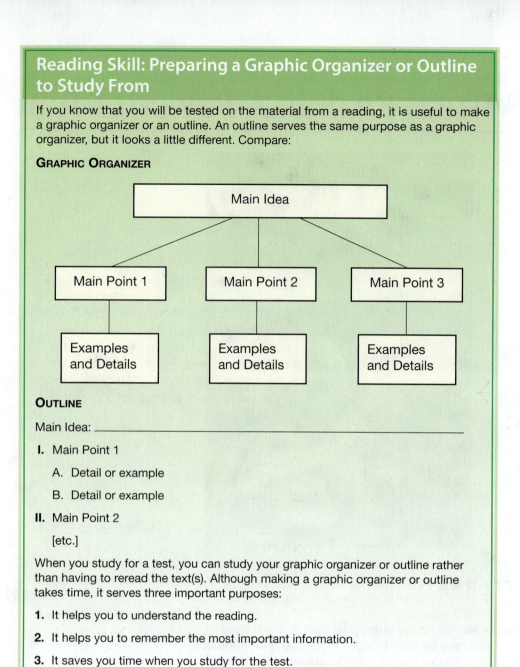

**OUTLINE**

Main Idea: _____

**I.** Main Point 1

   A. Detail or example

   B. Detail or example

**II.** Main Point 2

   [etc.]

When you study for a test, you can study your graphic organizer or outline rather than having to reread the text(s). Although making a graphic organizer or outline takes time, it serves three important purposes:

**1.** It helps you to understand the reading.

**2.** It helps you to remember the most important information.

**3.** It saves you time when you study for the test.

**C.** Preview the magazine article "Virtual Reality: A Powerful Tool" on the next page. Check (✓) the statement that best describes how the reading is organized.

_____ **1.** The writer introduces a technological problem and presents a solution. (problem/solution)

_____ **2.** The writer introduces a kind of technology and lists different uses of it. (simple listing)

_____ **3.** The writer compares and contrasts several different kinds of technology. (compare/contrast)

> **READ**

Read "Virtual Reality: A Powerful Tool." Check your answer from Exercise C.

# Virtual Reality: A Powerful Tool

1    Many people think of virtual reality (VR) as a toy. However, to many professionals today, VR is not a game. It is one of their most important tools. In fact, VR has become
5    as important to some professionals as a stethoscope[1] is to a doctor or scissors are to a hairdresser.

   Let's start with how doctors use VR. VR is used in many ways in medicine. With one VR
10    tool, doctors can practice difficult **operations** before they **perform** them on real people. For example, in 2001 doctors in Singapore used a VR tool to plan a very complex and dangerous operation. Twin baby girls were born with their
15    heads joined together. The doctors operated to separate them. The operation was a success, **mostly** because the doctors were able to perform the operation virtually before they tried it on their real patients.

20    Another medical use of VR is to help patients control their pain. One VR program is especially helpful for people with serious burns. It helps patients escape from their pain for a while. They go on exciting adventures
25    such as a deep-sea dive[2], a trip to the moon, or a ski trip. Using the program "was like watching a movie," one burned teenager said. "I got totally **absorbed** in my virtual world and forgot about the pain."

30    VR also has important uses in the business world. Several European automakers, including the makers of Jaguar Formula One racing cars, use VR to design their **vehicles**. Mercedes-Benz uses its VR center in Stuttgart, Germany both
35    to design and to crash-test vehicles. Results from these virtual crashes are 98 percent accurate. The virtual testing saves money because no vehicles are **destroyed**. Also, the computer shows what happens to each part
40    of the vehicle. The computer can **spot** many things that testers might not see in a real crash test.

   VR is also very useful for architects[3]. They use it to create virtual **model** homes. "By
45    bringing the floor plans[4] to life, buyers get a better understanding of what it would be like to actually live in this house," says Mitchell C. Hochberg, president and CEO[5] of Spectrum Skanska, a company that designs and builds
50    homes. Such virtual tours are much cheaper to make than real model homes. Hochberg calls the VR tours "our single most important marketing tool."

   Scientists use VR in a variety of ways.
55    Meteorologists (scientists who study weather and climate) use VR to enter hurricanes. Chemists and drug designers use VR to look at the shape of complex molecules[6] and build

*(continued on next page)*

---

[1] **stethoscope:** the instrument that a doctor uses to listen to your heart

[2] **deep-sea dive:** a dive far beneath the surface of the ocean

[3] **architect:** someone whose job it is to design buildings

[4] **floor plan:** a drawing that shows the shape of a room or rooms from above

[5] **CEO:** Chief Executive Officer (of a company); the head or president of the company

[6] **molecule:** one or more atoms that form the smallest unit of a particular substance

new ones. Paleontologists (scientists who study **ancient** forms of life such as dinosaurs) use VR to travel back in time. Entomologists (scientists who study insects) use VR to create life-size models of creatures such as grasshoppers. "You can even get **swallowed** by a grasshopper and find yourself in its abdomen[7]," says entomologist Alexie A. Sharov.

Now you've seen how doctors and other professionals use VR to do some very important work. But VR is also used for less serious purposes. For example, people in the beauty industry use VR programs, too. Some hairdressers use VR programs to make a digital copy of a client's head from a photograph.

They can then show clients what they will look like with a different hairstyle or color. Dentists can use VR to show people what they will look like with a more **attractive** smile. VR gives these dentists and hairdressers a significant edge over businesses that don't have VR.

Of course, none of these VR programs is cheap. However, as more and more people begin to use VR, prices are **likely** to come down. And for many professionals, the expense is small when compared to the benefits. The popularity of VR today, both as a toy and a tool, makes it clear that it is here to stay. In the future, we might be spending more time working and playing in the virtual world than we do in the real one.

---

[7] **abdomen:** stomach; front part of an animal, between the chest and the legs

## Vocabulary Check

Complete the sentences with the boldfaced words from the reading. Use the correct form of the word.

1. That is a great haircut. You look very _____attractive_____ with that hairstyle.

2. Cars, buses, and trucks are _____vehicles_____.

3. I can't show you the house today because it isn't ready to be shown. However, I can show you the _____ home. It is very similar to the one that is for sale.

4. Oh no!!! A fly fell in my coffee and I _____ it!

5. I don't want another dog. My last dog _____ my furniture.

6. It was a long _____. The doctors worked on the patient for ten hours.

7. Sadly, the doctor who _____ the operation couldn't save the patient.

8. Take an umbrella. It is _____likely_____ to rain later.

**9.** She was so ___Absorbed___ in her work that she did not even hear the telephone.

**10.** We cannot know exactly how people lived in _____ times, but with virtual reality we can experience how it probably felt to live centuries ago.

**11.** He was very sick, but he got better, _____ because of his wife's support.

**12.** We were in the forest for a long time, but we didn't _____ any birds.

## > READ AGAIN

**Read "Virtual Reality: A Powerful Tool" again and complete the comprehension exercises. As you work, keep the reading goal in mind.**

📖 **READING GOAL:** To prepare an outline of the reading

## Comprehension Check

**A.** Check (✓) the uses of virtual reality that are mentioned in the reading.

_____ **1.** as entertainment

_____ **2.** as a stethoscope

_____ **3.** to help doctors plan operations

_____ **4.** to help the sick and elderly at home

_____ **5.** to sell things

_____ **6.** in automobile safety tests

_____ **7.** to learn more about the natural world

_____ **8.** to learn about the past

_____ **9.** to distract people who are in pain

**B.** What is the writer's opinion of VR? Circle the letter of the correct answer.

   **a.** It should be used to help people, not as a toy, but most people don't understand that.

   **b.** It is an amazing tool and toy that will become more common in the future.

   **c.** It is interesting, but it won't become common anytime soon because of the expense.

**C.** Complete the outline of the reading.

> Main Idea: _____
>
>   **I.** _____
>
>     **A.** doctors can practice difficult operations
>
>     **B.** pain control: patients go on VR adventure
>
>  **II.** Business World
>
>     **A.** architects: design VR model homes
>
>     **B.** _____ crash a test
>
> **III.** _scientist_
>
>     **A.** meteorologists: experience dangerous weather conditions
>
>     **B.** _____
>
>     **C.** _____ travel back in time
>
>     **D.** paleontologists: create life-size models of creatures.
>
>  **IV.** Beauty Industry
>
>     **A.** hairdressers: make a digital copy of their head from a photograph
>
>     **B.** dentists: give you a more attractive smile

**D.** Compare your outline with a classmate's. Have you and your partner included the most important information?

## ▷ DISCUSS

Work in small groups. Ask and answer the questions.

**1.** Have you ever used virtual reality, either as a toy or as a tool? Explain.

**2.** What kind of job do you have or do you want to have in the future? Do you know if VR is used in that kind of job? If so, how? If not, imagine a use for it in that kind of job.

**3.** Do you know of any uses of VR other than those mentioned in the article? Describe them.

# VOCABULARY SKILL BUILDING

## Vocabulary Skill: Collocations

It is useful to learn the words that go together with, or *collocate* with, new words that you learn. For example, in the reading, the adjective *virtual* collocates with the noun *reality* to form *virtual reality*.

**A.** Skim "Virtual Reality: A Powerful Tool" for collocations that use the words on the left. Then match the words in the columns to form collocations. The numbers in parentheses are the paragraphs in the reading where you can find the words.

**Words from the reading**

_____ **1.** perform (2)

_____ **2.** model (5)

_____ **3.** life-size (6)

_____ **4.** beauty (7)

_____ **5.** prices (8)

**New words**

**a.** home

**b.** industry

**c.** model

**d.** come down

**e.** an operation

**B.** Complete the sentences with the collocations from Exercise A.

**1.** It is more difficult for doctors to _____ on a very young child than on an adult.

**2.** If you show customers a nice _____, they are more likely to buy a real home.

**3.** We can't afford a new house right now. We need to wait until the

_____.

**4.** The _____ is getting bigger and bigger. Every year, people spend billions of dollars on products to make themselves look more attractive.

**5.** At the Museum of Science they have a _____ of an enormous dinosaur. It's amazing.

# Learn the Vocabulary

### Finding the Core Meaning of Words: Example Sentences

In English there is often more than one meaning for a word. However, most of the meanings are actually based on one core meaning of the word. If you understand what the *core meaning* is, then you will be able to understand the word when it is used in many different contexts.

You can discover the core meaning of a word by looking at several sentences that contain the word. To find sentences containing a particular word, you can use an online tool called a *concordance*. When you enter a word into a concordance, it will give you sentences containing that word. To find a concordance, enter "word concordance" into the search box of your Internet browser and follow the links. Here are some sentences containing the target word *absorbed*:

EXAMPLE:

*The poison is **absorbed** by small organisms in the water, which are eaten by fish, which are eaten by larger fish.*

*As a boy in a local school, he was shy and solitary, **absorbed** in nature.*

*People who are self-**absorbed** do things mostly for their own benefit, putting their own feelings first.*

After reading these sentences, you might come up with this explanation of the core meaning of **absorbed**: When something or someone is absorbed, it is taken so deeply inside someone or something that it becomes a part of that person or thing.

**A.** Work in small groups. Read the sets of sentences and discuss the core meanings of the boldfaced words.

1. perform

   **a.** With one VR tool, doctors can practice difficult operations before they **perform** them on real people.

   **b.** Using the latest technology, the modern farmer can now **perform** the work of six men.

   **c.** The student orchestra **performs** several times a year at campus events. *play instruments*

   **d.** Physicists need to **perform** many experiments to test their theories.

   Core meaning of *perform*: _____

   *check*

   *coke*

**2.** virtual

    **a.** To find out, all you need to do is go on the Internet and enter the **virtual** world of *Second Life*.

    **b.** After the snowstorm, there was **virtually** no one on the street for days.

    **c.** The newspaper reports made him look like a **virtual** criminal, when in fact he had done nothing wrong.

    **d.** Costa Rica is a **virtual** paradise for nature lovers.

Core meaning of *virtual*: _____

**3.** crash

    **a.** Mercedes-Benz uses its VR center in Stuttgart, Germany, for both designing and **crash**-testing.

    **b.** I heard a **crash** and ran upstairs to see what had happened.

    **c.** He lost his life savings in the stock market **crash**.

    **d.** She took a **crash** course in Italian two weeks before her trip.

Core meaning of *crash*: _____

**B.** Use an online concordance to get sentences containing the target words below. Read the sentences and try to come up with the core meaning.

| | Core meaning |
|---|---|
| **1.** model | |
| **2.** swallow | |
| **3.** operation | |

**C.** Work in small groups. Compare your answers from Exercise B. Did you come up with similar core meanings?

**D.** Make cards for the words in the Learn the Vocabulary box and Exercises A and B. Put the core meaning on the card under the translation, English definition, or picture.

**E.** Go back to the vocabulary list at the beginning of each chapter. What did you learn about the target words? Add numbers to the lists.

**Vocabulary Practice 3,** see page 236

# FLUENCY PRACTICE 1

## Fluency Strategy

To improve your reading speed and fluency, time yourself as you read something that is easy for you. *Easy* means:

- You know all or almost all of the words (98–100%).
- The sentences are easy to understand.
- You can read quickly and still understand.
- Reading feels natural and relaxed.

Always read a text more than one time. Push yourself to read faster each time. It might seem strange, but reading faster will help you understand better. If you read too slowly, you might forget the beginning of a story, paragraph, or even sentence before you finish it.

Keep a record of your reading speed and comprehension. That way you will see your improvement. You will be surprised at how much both your speed and comprehension improve over time.

## > READING 1

### Before You Read

**A.** Read the words and their definitions. You will see these words in the reading.

> **hit:** a movie, song, play, etc. that is very successful
> **low-budget movie:** a movie that does not cost a lot to make

**B.** Preview "Sleeper Hits." Answer the questions.

**1.** A "sleeper" is a movie that is _____.

   **a.** expensive to make but boring to watch

   **b.** very good but not very popular

   **c.** inexpensive to make but very successful

**2.** Two things that make a movie a sleeper are _____.

   **a.** keeping it a secret and a lot of luck

   **b.** college students and creative marketing

   **c.** it costs a lot to make and millions of people watch it

## Read

**A.** Read "Sleeper Hits." Time yourself. Write your start and end times and your total reading time. Then calculate your reading speed (words per minute) and write it in the progress chart on page 246.

**Start time:** _____    **End time:** _____    **Total time:** _____ (in seconds)

**Reading speed:**

513 words ÷ _____ (total time in seconds) x 60 = _____ words per minute

# Sleeper Hits

1    The 1999 horror movie *The Blair Witch Project* took audiences by surprise. It told a story about three students lost in a forest. At the time, no one had ever seen anything
5   like it before. The film also surprised movie companies. Expenses to make the movie barely reached $22,000, but the income from ticket and DVD sales was (and continues to be) enormous. *The Blair Witch Project* is an example
10   of a sleeper. Sleepers are films that are made for very little money, but are enormously successful. Were the makers of *The Blair Witch Project* just lucky? Or are there secrets to making a sleeper hit?
15   Marketing experts say that for a movie to become a sleeper, it has to appeal to college students. College students are important for two reasons. First, they do not pay much attention to media reviews of movies. Instead, they listen to
20   their friends' opinions. Because of the Internet, the average college student today has hundreds of "friends." And those friends have hundreds of friends, and so on. That is why college students play such an influential role in the success or
25   failure of low-budget films. An example is the 1997 comedy *Austin Powers*. *Austin Powers* was a low-budget film. Initially, ticket sales were low, and the movie made very little money. But after it came out on video, it became enormously
30   popular on college campuses. In the end, *Austin Powers* made more money from video and DVD sales than it did in theaters.

   Another secret to sleepers is creative marketing, which also involves the Internet.

35   Internet marketing is cheap, and it can reach a specific audience. When director David Twohy filmed the science fiction movie *Pitch Black* in the late 1990s, for example, he needed an inexpensive way to promote the film. So Twohy went on
40   the Internet and visited science fiction chat rooms. He had conversations with people about his movie. Slowly, science fiction fans became interested in the film. In the end, "Internet buzz helped make it a success," says Twohy.

45   College students and Internet marketing were both important to the success of *The Blair Witch Project*. The filmmakers designed a Web page for the movie. It said that *The Blair Witch Project* was a true story (it wasn't). It
50   also said the three students in the film had disappeared (they hadn't). Soon, college students were talking about whether the movie was real or not. Many of them wanted to see for themselves. On the day of the film's release,
55   theaters were completely sold out. Today, many film studios follow the *Blair Witch Project* model when promoting their films.

   Of course, to make money, sleepers also need to be good films. The makers of *The*
60   *Blair Witch Project* never saw themselves as marketing experts. As Robin Cowie, who worked on *The Blair Witch Project*, says, "We never meant to change things. We set out to make a scary movie." Similarly, the makers of *Austin*
65   *Powers* set out to make a funny movie. And as millions who have seen the films would agree, they succeeded.

**B.** Read "Sleeper Hits" again, a little faster this time. Write your start and end times and your total reading time. Then calculate your reading speed (words per minute) and write it in the progress chart on page 246.

**Start time:** _____     **End time:** _____     **Total time:** _____ (in seconds)

**Reading speed:**
513 words ÷ _____ (total time in seconds) x 60 = _____ words per minute

## Comprehension Check

**A.** Check your answers to the Before You Read questions on page 52. Are they correct? If not, correct them.

**B.** Read the statements about the reading. Write *T* if the statement is true and *F* if the statement is false.

_____T_____ **1.** The *Blair Witch Project* was a sleeper hit.

_____F_____ **2.** The *Blair Witch Project* cost a lot to make.

_____ **3.** Sleepers are usually horror movies.

_____T_____ **4.** Marketing to college students is very important to the success of movies that become sleeper hits.

_____F_____ **5.** College students often read movie reviews in newspapers.

_____T_____ **6.** Sleeper hits make a lot of money.

_____T_____ **7.** *Austin Powers* was not very popular when it was in theaters.

_____ **8.** The Internet is a very important marketing tool for sleeper hits.

_____ **9.** The makers of the *Blair Witch Project* created a new way to market movies.

_____ **10.** *Austin Powers* and *The Blair Witch Project* made a lot of money, but they are not very good movies.

**C.** Complete the summary of "Sleeper Hits." Use the words in the list.

| | | | | |
|---|---|---|---|---|
| college students | good | Internet | marketing | surprised |
| creatively | inexpensive | likely | successful | video |

Sleepers are movies that are very (1) _____ to make, so everyone is (2) ___surprised___ when they make a lot of money. There are several things that can make a movie a sleeper hit. First of all, if the movie is not successful initially but it becomes popular with

(3) _____, it can become very successful when it is released

on (4) _____. Second, if the filmmakers use the

(5) _____ to market the movie (6) _____, they

can create a sleeper. One example of creative (7) _____ is

when the filmmakers visit Internet chat rooms to talk about their new movies

with people who are (8) _____ to be interested. Finally, in

order for a movie to become a sleeper, it has to be (9) _____.

If it isn't, it will never be (10) _____.

**D.** Check your answers for the comprehension questions in the Answer Key
on page 247. Then calculate your score and write it in the progress chart
on page 246.

_____ (my number correct) ÷ 20 x 100 = _____%

## ▷ READING 2

### Before You Read

**A.** Read the definition. You will see this word in the reading.

> scholarship = an amount of money that is given to someone
> by an organization to help pay for his or her education

**B.** Preview "A Tall Order" on the next page. Write three questions that you
think the text will answer.

1. _____

2. _____

3. _____

## Read

**A.** Read "A Tall Order." Time yourself. Write your start and end times and your total reading time. Then calculate your reading speed (words per minute) and write it in the progress chart on page 246.

**Start time:** _____ **End time:** _____ **Total time:** _____ (in seconds)

**Reading speed:**

770 words ÷ _____ (total time in seconds) x 60 = _____ words per minute

# A Tall Order

1 His full name is Dikembe Mutombo Mpolondo Mukamba Jean-Jacques Wamutombo. Friends call him "Deke." He once hoped to be called Dr. Mutombo. But life gave him another way to help
5 people—basketball.

### A Mind for Medicine, a Body for Basketball

Dikembe Mutombo was born in 1966 in the African city of Kinshasa, in Zaire (known today as the Democratic Republic of the Congo.) His
10 father, Samuel, was the head of a school in Kinshasa. He had studied at a famous university in France. His mother, Marie, was a homemaker. In addition to their own ten children, Samuel and Marie took care of several of their relatives'
15 children. They believed strongly that children were the responsibility of the entire community. They also believed that a good education was very important.

Young Dikembe Mutombo dreamed of becoming
20 a doctor. He planned to study in the United States and then return home to help the people in his country. He also enjoyed sports, especially soccer. He was a very good soccer player. But his parents wanted him to try basketball. They felt
25 that he had the perfect body for the game.

Many people in the Mutombo family were tall, but no one was as tall as Dikembe. At 13 years old, he was already 7 feet tall and still growing. That was when he first touched a basketball.
30 Initially, Dikembe disliked basketball. He played only because his parents pushed him to do so. Soccer was much more appealing to him.

In Dikembe's first basketball game, he fell down and cut his face. He wanted to quit, but his
35 parents wanted him to keep playing. After many arguments, Mutombo returned to the basketball court. He played on the Zaire national basketball team for two years. However, he still dreamed of becoming a doctor.

40 Dikembe was a pretty good basketball player, but he was an excellent student. In 1985, he won an academic scholarship to Georgetown University in Washington, D.C. Soon, he was on a plane to the United States.

45 ### A Difficult New Life

At first life in the United States was difficult for Dikembe. He knew how to speak several languages, but English was not one of them. He didn't have the money to call his family in
50 Africa. He often felt sad and lonely. During his first year, he did not play on the university basketball team. He focused on learning English. The pressure was intense, but Dikembe did well.

55 The university's basketball coach spotted the 7'2" Dikembe on the Georgetown campus. He invited him to play on the university team. At first, Dikembe mostly practiced with the team. He rarely played in a game. He made a lot of
60 mistakes, but he trained rigorously. With the help of Georgetown's top-ranked coaches, he made dramatic progress.

Dikembe graduated from Georgetown in 1991. Almost immediately, he became a player for the National Basketball Association (NBA). He exchanged his dream of becoming a doctor for a career as a professional basketball player.

**Dikembe's Big Promise**

By 1997, Dikembe was a basketball legend. He had won many awards and had a multi-million dollar income. Then one morning he received a phone call that changed his life. His mother had died in Africa. Suddenly ill, she couldn't get to a hospital in time to save her life. Dikembe remembered his dream of becoming a doctor. At that moment, he made a promise to his mother. He would build a hospital in his hometown of Kinshasa.

Over the next ten years, Dikembe continued to play basketball. In 2006, at age 40, he became the oldest player in the NBA. Each year his knees hurt more. At times he wanted to quit. But the memory of his mother motivated him. He saved money for the hospital. He also convinced other NBA players to give money. Finally, in 2007, his sixteenth year in the NBA, Dikembe's dream came true. The Biamba Marie Mutombo Hospital and Research Center opened in Kinshasa.

Today, Dikembe has great appreciation for his parents. They pushed him to get an education—and to play basketball. As a star NBA player, he is able to help many more people than he ever could have as a doctor. He has his own foundation, the Dikembe Mutombo Foundation (DMF). The DMF's goal is to improve the health, education, and quality of life for people in the Democratic Republic of the Congo.

Dikembe often uses this African saying to talk about his life: "When you take the elevator up to the top, don't forget to send it back down so that someone else can take it to the top."

**B.** Read "A Tall Order" again, a little faster this time. Time yourself. Write your start and end times and your total reading time. Then calculate your reading speed (words per minute) and write it in the progress chart on page 246.

**Start time:** _____   **End time:** _____   **Total time:** _____ (in seconds)

**Reading speed:**
770 words ÷ _____ (total time in seconds) x 60 = _____ words per minute

# Comprehension Check

**A.** Check the questions you wrote in Before You Read on page 55. Did you find the answers? If so, underline them in the text.

**B.** Answer the questions.

1. When Dikembe was young, what did he dream of?

   _____

2. How old was Dikembe when he played basketball for the first time?

   _____

3. Why did his parents want him to play basketball?

   _____

4. Did he like basketball at first? Why or why not?

   _____

5. What kind of scholarship did Dikembe get?

   _____

6. Where did he go to university?

   _____

7. When did he become an NBA player?

   _____

8. Why did Dikembe decide to build a hospital in his hometown?

   _____

**C.** Read the summary of "A Tall Order" and correct the mistakes. There are eight mistakes, including the example.

Dikembe Mutombo was born in Africa. When he was young, he dreamed
of becoming a ~~basketball player~~ *doctor*. His parents pushed him to play basketball

because he was so smart. He played on the Zaire national team for two

years. In 1985, he won a basketball scholarship to study at Georgetown

University in the United States.

At Georgetown, Dikembe became a great basketball player. Before he graduated, he started playing for the NBA. He stopped dreaming of becoming a doctor.

Dikembe became rich and famous as a professional basketball player. Then one day his father died because he could not get to a hospital in Kinshasa. Dikembe made a promise. He would build a hospital in his hometown. In 1997, Dikembe's dream came true when the Biamba Marie Mutombo Hospital and Research Center opened in Washington, D.C.

Dikembe didn't become a doctor. However, he is helping more people in his country than he could help if he were a doctor. He believes that it is important for successful people to help others to become successful, too.

**D.** **Check your answers for the comprehension questions in the Answer Key on page 247. Then calculate your score and write it in the progress chart on page 246.**

_____ (my number correct) ÷ 14 x 100 = _____%

# Checking Out

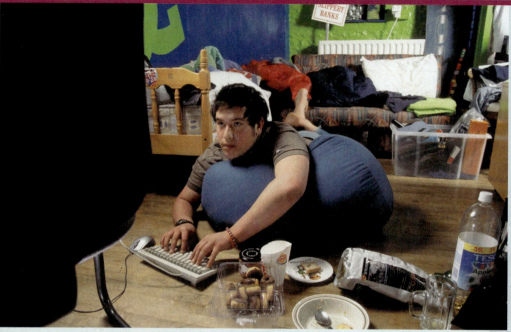

## ▶ THINK BEFORE YOU READ

**A.** Work with a partner. Look at the picture. Ask and answer the questions. If you don't know a word in English, ask your partner or look in your dictionary. Then write your new words on page 232.

1. What is the young man in the picture doing?

2. What kind of life do you think he has? Is it a traditional life? A happy life? Explain your answer.

**B.** Work with a partner. Complete the tasks.

1. The phrasal verb *check out* can have many meanings. Read the three below.

   **a.** to pay the bill and leave a hotel

   **b.** to examine something closely

   **c.** to choose not to participate in an activity or a lifestyle

2. Preview the unit. Which meaning of *check out* do you think the unit title refers to?

_____

# CHAPTER 7

# Choosing to Be Different

## > PREPARE TO READ

**A.** Look at the words and phrases in the list. Write the number(s) next to each word to show what you know. You may be able to write more than one number next to some of the words. You will study all of these words in this chapter.

1. I can use the word in a sentence.

2. I know <u>one meaning</u> of the word.

3. I know <u>more than one meaning</u> of the word.

4. I know how to pronounce the word.

**B.** Work with a partner. Look at the pictures. Ask and answer the questions. If you don't know a word in English, ask your partner or look in your dictionary. Then write your new words on page 232.

1. What do you see in each picture? Who are the people? Where are they?

2. What kind of lifestyle do you think the people in each picture have? In what ways do you think their lifestyles might be similar?

_____ accumulate

_____ carefree

_____ claustrophobic

_____ disturb

_____ fate

_____ isolation

_____ leisure

_____ reject

_____ retirement

_____ senior citizen

_____ set apart from

_____ uneasy

_____ withdraw

## Reading Skill: Writing a Summary

To check your understanding of a reading, it can be useful to write a summary of it. A summary is much shorter than the original reading. It includes only the main idea, the main points, and one or two of the most important details or examples. Follow these steps when you write a summary:

1. Underline the sentence or sentences in the reading that contain the main idea.

2. Underline the sentences that contain the main points.

3. Underline the most important example or detail for each main point.

4. Complete a graphic organizer of the reading (see page 44 for an example). Write notes, not full sentences. Express the ideas in your own words as much as possible.

5. Write your summary by looking at your graphic organizer. Do not look back at the text when you write.

6. Reread the original text and compare it to your summary. Make sure you have accurately expressed the main idea and the main points in your own words.

**C.** Preview the magazine article "Choosing to Be Different" on the next page and answer the questions.

1. Is there a hook? _____

2. Which paragraph contains the main idea? _____

3. What is the main idea? Copy it here. _____

4. How many main points are there? _____

5. Which pattern of organization does the writer use? Check (✓) it.

_____ **a.** cause/effect

_____ **b.** compare/contrast

_____ **c.** exemplification

_____ **d.** problem/solution

# READ

**Read "Choosing to Be Different." Check your answers from Exercise C.**

# Choosing to Be Different

1    In northern Iran, nomads walk their goats from winter quarters[1] in the desert to a summer home high in the Zagros Mountains. In a small bedroom in Tokyo, a young man plays
5    computer games by night and sleeps by day. He has not left his bedroom in over a year. In the middle of a large city, several families eat well but never go to a supermarket. They have cars and electricity but never need to go to a gas
10   station or pay an electric bill. In **retirement** communities throughout the United States, **senior citizens** live a **carefree**, child-free existence in gated[2] neighborhoods sometimes referred to as "Disney for adults."

15   These people all come from very different backgrounds. The motivation for their behavior is also quite varied. Some are escaping from the present. Others are returning to the past. Still others are preparing for the future.
20   However, they all have one thing in common. They have chosen lifestyles that **set them apart from** others.

## STAYING WITH TRADITIONS

In many parts of the world, there are
25   people who know about modern life but are not interested in being a part of it. Roughly a third of the Bakhtiari nomads of Iran have chosen not to go to cities, attend schools, or get jobs. During the twentieth century,

30   the Shah of Iran[3] tried to make the Bakhtiari give up their nomadic traditions. After the Shah was overthrown[4], however, the Bakhtiari returned to their traditional nomadic life. Every spring they pack up their animal-hair tents
35   and everything that they own. They leave the desert on foot, traveling 200 miles to their summer home high in the mountains. In the fall, they pack everything up again and return to the desert.

## WITHDRAWING

40   Rather than following traditions, some people **reject** them. The Hikikomori of Japan are one example. Hikikomori are young people, usually young men, who do not follow the
45   usual path of education, career, marriage, and family. Unlike the Bakhtiari, they do not leave the cities physically. Instead, they **withdraw** into their own **claustrophobic** worlds. They spend all of their time in their bedrooms.
50   They never leave. They don't attend school or even share family meals. They order take out or someone leaves food for them, which they eat alone. Dirty dishes **accumulate**, as the teenagers will not leave their rooms or allow
55   anyone else to enter. The number of Hikikomori is not very large, but their existence makes many people in Japan **uneasy**. Are the Hikikomori mentally ill? Or is their rejection of

*(continued on next page)*

---

[1] **quarters:** the house, room, or place where you live

[2] **gated:** enclosed, usually with a guard at the entrance

[3] **Shah of Iran:** Mohammad Reza Pahlavi, ruler of Iran from 1941 until 1979

[4] **overthrown:** removed from power by force

the typical Japanese lifestyle a sign of a wider
60 social problem?

## SEARCHING FOR A BETTER WAY

Another group includes those who are
concerned about the environment. They
believe that the **fate** of the planet depends
65 on the creation of new ways of living. They
call themselves *urban homesteaders*. Urban
homesteaders live in the middle of large cities.
However, they stay away from supermarkets,
malls, and gas stations. They grow fruit and
70 vegetables. They raise animals in their small
urban backyards. They use wind and solar
power to produce their own electricity. They
raise sheep and make cloth from the wool[5].
They make their own biofuel[6] to power their
75 cars and trucks. They collect rainwater for
washing. If they need something that they
cannot make or grow, they get it by bartering[7]
with other homesteaders. Urban homesteaders
don't give up all modern conveniences. Rather,

80 they look for ways to enjoy life in the twenty-
first century without harming the environment.

## LIVING THE DREAM

The final group is larger than the others.
It is made up of Americans fifty-five years of
85 age and older living in retirement communities
in the southern United States. In these
communities, the sun is always shining, the
streets are safe and clean, the golf courses are
always green, and the seniors' sleep is never
90 **disturbed** by crying children or loud teenagers.
Children can visit, but only for a few days. This
applies to anyone under the age of eighteen—
even the residents' own grandchildren. To
many residents, the "no-children" rule is the
95 best thing about their new lives. Free from
the stress of work and raising children, these
retirees choose to live their golden years
in happy **isolation**. They spend their days
enjoying their favorite **leisure** activities in
100 their own child-free "Disneyland."

---

[5] **wool:** soft thick hair of a sheep, used for making cloth or yarn

[6] **biofuel:** a substance produced from plants or other natural matter that can be used as fuel for a car or truck

[7] **barter:** to exchange goods or services to get what you need instead of using money

# Vocabulary Check

**A.** Read the definitions. Write the boldfaced word from the reading next to the correct definition.

1. _____ = without any problems or worries

2. _____ = to not accept someone or something

3. _____ = to stop participating in an activity or a group

4. _____ = worried and anxious because you think something bad might happen

5. _____ = the period of time after you stop working (usually because of old age)

**B.** Complete the sentences with the words from the list. Be careful. There are five extra answers. The boldfaced words are the target words.

| | | | |
|---|---|---|---|
| bad | moment | often | throw away |
| different | more | reason | without |
| elevators | no | retired | young |
| good | | | |

1. That movie **disturbed** me. I had _____ dreams after I saw it.

2. You will have _____ **leisure** time after **retirement**.

3. When something **sets you apart from** other people, you feel _____.

4. I am **claustrophobic**, so _____ make me feel very **uneasy**.

5. He lived in **isolation** for a year, _____ talking to his family or friends.

6. If you believe in **fate**, you think that bad things happen for a(n) _____.

7. Many **senior citizens** are _____.

8. It's hard for children to _____ anything, so sometimes toys **accumulate** in their rooms.

## > READ AGAIN

Read "Choosing to Be Different" again and complete the comprehension exercises. As you work, keep the reading goal in mind.

> 📖 **READING GOAL:** To write a one paragraph summary of "Choosing to Be Different"

## Comprehension Check

**A.** Underline the sentences in paragraphs 3–6 of the reading that contain the five main points.

**B.** On a separate piece of paper, draw a graphic organizer. Use the graphic organizer on page 44 as a model. Include only the most important information: the main idea, the main points, and the most important examples and details.

**C.** Work with a partner. Compare your graphic organizers. Do they contain similar information? Did you leave out any important information? Did you include any unnecessary information? Make any necessary changes.

**D.** Use the information from your graphic organizer to write a one-paragraph summary of the reading. Do not look back at the reading.

_____

_____

_____

_____

_____

_____

## > DISCUSS

Work in small groups. Ask and answer the questions.

**1.** Are there groups of people in your home country who are similar to the ones described in the reading? Why do you think they choose to live the way they do? Are their reasons the same or different from the reasons given in the text?

**2.** Would you like to live a nontraditional lifestyle? Why or why not?

**3.** How does the writer feel about each of the lifestyles described in the reading? Add check marks (✓) to the chart. Refer to the reading when explaining your answers.

| Lifestyle | Positive | Negative | Neutral (not positive or negative) |
|---|---|---|---|
| Bakhtiari nomads | | | ✓ |
| Hikikomori | | ✓ | |
| Urban homesteaders | | | ) |
| Americans in retirement communities | ✓ | | |

# > VOCABULARY SKILL BUILDING

## Vocabulary Skill: The suffix *-free*

The suffix *-free* means without. It is added to some nouns to form an adjective.

**EXAMPLES:**

*carefree* = without cares (worries)

*child-free* = without children

Most adjectives with the suffix *-free* are hyphenated.

Complete the sentences with a hyphenated adjective ending in *-free*. Use the boldfaced words to form the adjectives.

**1.** He does not have **cancer** any more. He has been _cancer-free_ for ten years.

**2.** Many products today do not contain **fat**. They are _____.

**3.** This software will not give you any **trouble**. It is _____.

**4.** He can't eat **salt**. He is on a _salt-free_ diet.

**5.** You are not allowed to **smoke** anywhere in this hotel. The entire building is _smoke-free_.

**6.** **Stress** is a natural part of life. It is not possible to live an entirely _____ life.

# CHAPTER 8

# Welcome to Leisureville

## > PREPARE TO READ

**A.** Look at the words and phrases in the list. Write the number(s) next to each word to show what you know. You may be able to write more than one number next to some of the words. You will study all of these words in this chapter.

1. I can use the word in a sentence.

2. I know <u>one meaning</u> of the word.

3. I know <u>more than one meaning</u> of the word.

4. I know how to pronounce the word.

**B.** Work with a partner. Look at the picture. Ask and answer the questions. If you don't know a word in English, ask your partner or look in your dictionary. Then write your new words on page 232.

1. Read the billboard in the picture. What does it advertise?

2. What are the people on the left doing?

3. The title of the reading is "*Welcome to Leisureville*." Do you think Leisureville is the name of a real town? Why or why not?

_____ catch up on

_____ excerpt

_____ facility

_____ gossip

_____ keep time

_____ permanent

_____ pinch

_____ ponder

_____ slogan

_____ sting

_____ widow

## Reading Skill: Recognizing Point of View

It is important to be able to recognize a writer's opinion or attitude. We call this the writer's *point of view*. Sometimes a writer will state his or her point of view directly, but often the reader must infer it. To discover a writer's point of view, look at the way he or she uses language. Do the writer's words help you form a positive or negative idea about the topic? Or does the writer use neutral words? Is the writer using words ironically? That is, does the writer say one thing but really mean the opposite?

**C.** Skim the excerpt from the book *Welcome to Leisureville*. Then read the questions and circle the answers.

1. What is the main topic?
   **a.** retirement communities in the United States
   **b.** senior citizens in the United States
   **c.** how people spend their leisure time in the United States

2. What is the writer's point of view?
   **a.** positive
   **b.** negative
   **c.** neutral

 READ

Read the excerpt from *Welcome to Leisureville*. As you read, circle any words or expressions that are positive. Underline any words or expressions that are negative.

# Welcome to Leisureville

In this **excerpt** from the book *Leisureville: Adventures in America's Retirement Utopias*[1], author Andrew D. Blechman describes visiting two friends and former neighbors at their new home in a retirement community called The Villages.

1  The Villages is located roughly in the center of Florida, about an hour north of Orlando International Airport. On the sides of the road there are billboards advertising retirement
5  communities. Photos of seniors playing golf and relaxing in pools are covered with **slogans** such as "Life is lovelier," "On top of the world," and "Live the life you've been waiting your whole life for!"
10  I turn on the radio and tune into WVLG AM640, The Villages's own radio station. "It's a beautiful day in The Villages," the DJ[2]

*(continued on next page)*

---

[1] **utopia:** an imaginary, perfect world where everyone is happy

[2] **DJ:** a disc jockey; someone who plays records on the radio or at a party

announces. "Aren't we lucky to live here? OK folks, here is a favorite I know you're going to love. 'The Candy Man Can.' C'mon, let's sing it together."

I listen to Sammy Davis, Jr.,[3] feeling slightly claustrophobic and uneasy about living in a gated retirement community for the next month.

A few miles later, I drive by a hospital, an assisted care[4] **facility** and a large Catholic church. Then I pass some faux[5]-Spanish fort ruins[6] and suddenly I'm in the "town" of Spanish Springs. I spot Betsy outside a Starbucks, standing beside her shiny red sports car, dressed attractively in pale pink slacks[7] and a white sweater. She greets me with a relaxed smile and a friendly hug, and insists on buying me a much-welcomed cup of iced coffee.

"Isn't it nice?" she asks. "People call it 'Disney for adults,' and I'm beginning to understand why. I just can't believe I'm here. I've met people that have been here for five years, and they're still **pinching** themselves. It's like being on a **permanent** vacation."

Betsy and I take our coffee to the central square, and sit on a bench beside the Fountain of Youth, which is peppered with lucky coins. We **catch up on** neighborhood **gossip**, the miserable New England weather, and the uncertain fate of our neighborhood park. Betsy is left **pondering** her incredible luck. "If we were still living up north, those problems would be our problems." Although it isn't meant to, her comment **stings**. But she's got a point; her life down here promises to be a lot more carefree than it was back home.

We walk around the square and then enter the western-motif saloon, Katie Belle's, which is for residents and their guests only. Inside the saloon the walls are covered in dark wood, and heavy drapes hang from several large windows. There are two dozen line dancers **keeping time** to a country and western[8] tune. I look at my watch. It's just past two in the afternoon.

"Line dancing is very popular here because you can do it without a partner," Betsy explains. "They say the only problem with being a **widow** in The Villages is that you're so busy you forget you are one."

"They call it 'Florida's Friendliest Hometown'—and that's just what it is," Betsy says as she gets into her shiny red sports car. "Everyone's so friendly because everyone is so happy. So make yourself comfortable at our house and enjoy your stay."

---

[3] **Sammy Davis, Jr.:** American singer and entertainer (1925–1990)

[4] **assisted care:** residence for people who cannot live independently

[5] **faux:** (French) imitation; not real

[6] **ruins:** the part of a building that is left after the rest has been destroyed or fallen down

[7] **slacks:** pants or trousers

[8] **country and western:** a popular style of music from the southern and western United States

# Vocabulary Check

Complete the sentences with the boldfaced words from *Welcome to Leisureville*. Use the correct form of the word.

1. If you haven't seen someone for a long time, it is common to take some

   time to _____ each other's lives.

2. You might want to read a short _____ from the book

   before you decide whether or not to buy it.

3. When you dance with a partner, it is important to ____keep time____ to the music. Otherwise, you might step on your partner's toes!

4. On average, women live longer than men. That is why there are a lot of ____widows____ in retirement communities.

5. In advertising, having a good ____slogan____ is very important. It can help people to remember your product and can lead to higher sales.

6. I believe in fate, so I think it is a waste of time to ____ponder____ the future. Thinking and worrying about the future will not change it.

7. He lives in a special ____facility____ for senior citizens. There are doctors and nurses in the building twenty-four hours a day in case of emergency.

8. She's a(n) ____permanent____ resident. She will live in this facility for the rest of her life.

9. I was really tired when I was driving home last night. I had to keep _____ myself to stay awake.

10. I don't like to listen to ____gossip____. I don't think it's good to talk about people behind their backs.

11. When someone says something unkind to you, it ____stings____. You feel hurt.

## > READ AGAIN

Read the excerpt from *Welcome to Leisureville* again and complete the comprehension exercises on the next page. As you work, keep the reading goal in mind.

> 📖 **READING GOAL:** To understand the writer's point of view

# Comprehension Check

**A.** Read the sentences taken from the reading. What do these sentences indicate about the author's point of view? Circle the letter of the correct answer.

Then I pass some faux-Spanish fort ruins, and suddenly I'm in the "town" of Spanish Springs.

"They say the only problem with being a widow in The Villages is that you're so busy you forget you are one."

"People call it 'Disney for adults'. . . ."

We . . . enter the western-motif saloon, Katie Belle's . . . There are two dozen line dancers keeping time to a country and western tune. I look at my watch. It's just past two in the afternoon.

The writer thinks that life at The Villages is _____.

   **a.** artificial      **b.** comfortable      **c.** normal      **d.** exciting

**B.** Look at the list of descriptive words from the reading. Do they have positive or negative meanings? Write each one in the appropriate column.

| | | | |
|---|---|---|---|
| ~~attractively~~ | friendly | miserable | sting |
| ~~claustrophobic~~ | happy | nice | uncertain fate |
| comfortable | lovely | problem | uneasy |
| enjoy | lucky | relax | |

| Positive | Negative |
|---|---|
| *attractively* | *claustrophobic* |
| | |
| | |
| | |
| | |
| | |
| | |
| | |
| | |

**C.** Circle the words from Exercise B that have very general meanings. Underline the words that have more specific meanings.

**D.** Answer the questions about the writer's word choice.

1. Which words are more specific—the positive or the negative?

   _____

2. What words are more powerful—the positive or the negative?

   _____  *powerful to feel than more*

3. What does the writer's choice of words reveal about his point of view? Circle the letter of the correct answer.

   He _____ The Villages.

   **a.** approves of

   **b.** disapproves of

   **c.** does not have a strong opinion about

# > DISCUSS

**Work in small groups. Ask and answer the questions.**

1. At what age do most people in your home country retire? What do they do after retirement?

2. In general, how are senior citizens treated in your home country? Who takes care of them if they can't live alone?

3. What kinds of facilities are there for senior citizens in your home country? Are there communities such as The Villages?

4. What do you think about life at The Villages? Would you like to live in a similar community when you are a senior citizen? Why or why not?

# Learn the Vocabulary

**A.** Work in small groups. Read the definitions and the example sentences and complete the tasks. Then decide on a core meaning.

| | Definitions | Example sentences | Tasks |
|---|---|---|---|
| *sting* | 1. If an insect or a plant stings you, it causes a sharp pain, and that part of your body swells. | 1. *Henry was stung by a bee at the picnic.* | 1. Name several plants or insects that sting. |
| | 2. If something that someone says stings, it makes you feel upset and embarrassed. | 2. *Nathan was stung by the teacher's criticism of his paper.* | 2. Describe the last time that you were stung by something that someone said. |
| Core meaning of *sting*: | | | |
| *roughly* | 1. not exactly; approximately | 1. *Martin makes roughly $150,000 a year.* | 1. Name a country that is roughly the same size as your home country. |
| | 2. not gently or carefully | 2. *He spoke to her very roughly.* | 2. Talk about a time when someone treated you roughly. |
| Core meaning of *roughly*: *not completely* | | | |
| *disturbed* | 1. worried or upset | 1. *Some Japanese are disturbed that so many young people are withdrawing from society.* | 1. Give examples of things that people in your home country today are disturbed about. |
| | 2. not behaving in a normal way because of mental or emotional problems | 2. *We never listen to what he says because we know that he is disturbed.* | 2. Give examples of things that a disturbed person might do. |
| Core meaning of *disturbed*: | | | |

**B.** Look up the words that were new to you when you started the unit. Include target words and words that you wrote on page 232. If the word has more than one definition, read all of the definitions, and try to come up with the core meaning. Work with a partner. Compare your core meanings.

**C.** Make cards for the words from Exercise B. Write the core meaning under the translation, picture, or English definition of each word. When you review your cards, try to recall the core meaning as well as the definition, translation, or picture.

**D.** Go back to the vocabulary list at the beginning of each chapter. What did you learn about the target words? Add numbers to the lists.

---

**Vocabulary Practice 4,** see page 237

# Great Minds

## > THINK BEFORE YOU READ

**A.** Work with a partner. Look at the pictures. Ask and answer the questions. If you don't know a word in English, ask your partner or look in your dictionary. Then write your new words on page 232.

   **1.** What is happening in the pictures? What are the people doing?

   **2.** What do all of the pictures have in common?

**B.** Work with a partner. Ask and answer the questions.

   **1.** Which of your five senses do you use the most in your daily life: hearing, sight, smell, taste, or touch?

   **2.** Which of your five senses is most important to you personally, and why?

   **3.** If you had to lose one of your senses, which one would you choose? Explain your choice.

# CHAPTER 9

# Reading Colors

A B C D E F G H I J K L M
N O P Q R S T U V W X Y Z

**Karen's colors**

A B C D E F G H I J K L M
N O P Q R S T U V W X Y Z

**Carol's colors**

 **PREPARE TO READ**

**A.** Look at the words in the list. Write the number(s) next to each word to show what you know. You may be able to write more than one number next to some of the words. You will study all of these words in this chapter.

1. I can use the word in a sentence.

2. I know <u>one meaning</u> of the word.

3. I know <u>more than one meaning</u> of the word.

4. I know how to pronounce the word.

_____ activate

_____ default

_____ defective

_____ endeavor

_____ hesitate

_____ hook

_____ incorporate

_____ intentionally

_____ perceive

_____ sensation

_____ simultaneously

_____ wear off

**B.** Look at the two sets of colored letters on page 77 and read the excerpt from an essay by a woman named Karen Chenausky. Ms. Chenausky and another woman, Carol Steen, have an unusual *neurological** condition. As you read, try to understand what the condition is.

In my quiet moments, sitting at my desk writing in the small pool of yellow light from my desk lamp, my letters' colors leap to mind most vividly. Some letters have colors I like, some have colors I don't; but I love that all my letters have a color.

Carol Steen [another woman with the same condition] and I can describe our [condition]; we can make lists of our colors and letters—but what we can't [communicate] . . . is the pleasure we feel when we experience it. . . . Each [letter] is unique . . . They all have different shapes and colors. And even though each letter of a word is colored differently, a word's color isn't simply made up of the colors of its component letters. The shades combine, bleed into each other, change slightly depending on their neighbors. A word's color is more influenced by the colors of its initial letters than by the colors of its final letters.

---

*A *neurological condition* is one that affects the body's nervous system. The nervous system includes the nerves, brain, and spinal cord, through which your body feels pain, heat, etc. and controls your movements.

**C.** Work with a partner. Ask and answer the questions. If you don't know a word in English, ask your partner or look in your dictionary. Then write your new words on page 232.

1. What happens when Carol and Karen read or write? What do they see when they look at individual letters? What do they see when they look at words?

2. How do they feel about the way that they experience letters and words?

3. Do Carol and Karen see the same colors?

**D.** Read the introduction to the article "Reading Colors." What analogy does the writer use to help the reader understand what *synesthesia* is? Check (✓) it.

_____ **1.** The writer compares the familiar experience of hearing a doorbell to the unfamiliar experience of seeing the color blue.

_____ **2.** The writer compares the familiar experience of reading a poem to the unfamiliar experience of hearing a color.

_____ **3.** The writer compares the familiar experience of seeing a color to the unfamiliar experience of hearing a color.

 **READ**

Read "Reading Colors." Find another analogy and underline it.

# Reading Colors

In the following excerpt from the Web site of a research lab at the Massachusetts Institute of Technology, you will read the stories of two women with a rare neurological condition called *synesthesia*.

In most people's brains, each of the senses is activated separately. That is, when you hear something, your sense of hearing is **activated**; when you see something, your sense of sight is activated, and so on. In the brain of someone with synesthesia, however, two or more senses are activated **simultaneously**. For example, a synesthete's sense of sight and hearing might be **hooked** together; as a result, whenever the synesthete hears a particular sound, she or he also sees a particular color. Thus, the synesthete might say that the sound of a doorbell is blue. This is not the same as a poet using language **intentionally** to excite the imagination of the reader. The synesthete is not making it up. The **sensation** of "hearing" a color is as real to the synesthete as seeing a color is to you. The brain of a synesthete is not **defective** in any way. It is just different from most people's brains.

1    Carol Steen is an artist who lives and works in New York City. She has experienced synesthesia for as long as she can remember,

5    **perceiving** colors in numbers, letters, and when hearing certain sounds. Carol has **incorporated** elements of what she sees

*(continued on next page)*

synesthetically in both her past work, painting, and current **endeavor**, sculpture.[1]

10 Karen Chenausky is a language researcher and project manager living in Boston. Her synesthesia also dates back to childhood and involves the perception of colors when viewing text or hearing spoken words.

Here Carol and Karen describe what it is like 15 to have synesthesia.

## CAROL

### *"I came back from college on a semester break."*

I came back from college on a semester 20 break and was sitting with my family around the dinner table, and—I don't know why I said it—but I said, "The number five is yellow." There was a pause, and my father said, "No, it's yellow-ochre[2]." And my mother and my brother 25 looked at us like, "This is a new game, would you share the rules with us?"

And I was dumbfounded.[3] So I thought, "Well." At that time in my life I was having trouble deciding whether the number two was 30 green and the number six blue, or just the other way around. And I said to my father, "Is the number two green?" and he said, "Yes, definitely. It's green." And then he took a long look at my mother and my brother and became 35 very quiet.

Thirty years after that, he came to my loft in Manhattan and he said, "You know, the number four is red, and the number zero is white. And the number nine is green." I said,

40 "Well, I agree with you about the four and the zero, but nine is definitely not green!"

### *"Orange is my default color for pain."*

I had to have a root canal[4] done once (not my favorite game) but you know, sometimes 45 when you have a tooth pain you're not quite sure which tooth it is?

The dentist said, "I can't really say that you need a root canal in this tooth."

I said, "This tooth is orange; please do it." 50 And he **hesitated**. I said, "Look. If I'm wrong, this tooth will never need a root canal." So he went ahead and he did it.

And sure enough, when the nerve was out, and the anesthesia[5] had **worn off**, there was 55 no more orange. It's like orange is my default color for pain.

## KAREN

### *"Linguistics is a grayish-purple-blue word."*

Well, when I was first doing science, when 60 I was first in graduate school right out of college, I had a really hard time deciding what kind of project to work on within linguistics.[6] But I knew that I liked linguistics because it's sort of a grayish-purple-blue word. And I really 65 didn't think that I wanted to work in speech at all, because "speech" is so yellowy and orange, and I don't really like those colors as much.

And what's funny is that I work in speech now, and I find it very interesting—but I 70 also know that I've come to like yellows and oranges better. You know, I like a kind of a

---

[1] **sculpture:** the art of making solid objects out of stone, wood, clay, etc.

[2] **yellow-ochre:** a greenish-yellow color

[3] **dumbfounded:** too surprised to speak

[4] **root canal:** dental treatment in which the diseased root of the tooth is removed

[5] **anesthesia:** medicine that stops pain or puts a person to sleep

[6] **linguistics:** scientific study of language systems

goldenrod[7], let's say, or a—you know, those sort of Mediterranean oranges and yellows.

***"I first realized it when I was about eleven."***

75    I was telling Carol that it's kind of like figuring out that you have a belly button.[8] You know, at some point you just notice and start playing with it!

Then, for a while, you get really into it: 80 "Wow, a belly button! Ooh, this is cool!" And after a while you get bored with it because, after all, it's still there, and then you realize everyone has one. Except that not everyone has synesthesia.

---

[7] **goldenrod:** yellow-orange color (from a plant with small yellow flowers)

[8] **belly button:** (informal) navel; the small hollow or raised place in the middle of your stomach

## Vocabulary Check

Circle the letter of the correct answer to complete each sentence. The boldfaced words are the target words.

1. When you **activate** something, you turn it _____.

   **a.** on                 **b.** over                 **c.** around

2. If you are wearing perfume and it **wears off**, the smell _____.

   **a.** disappears         **b.** gets on              **c.** gets stronger
                                 someone else

3. When you do something **intentionally**, you _____ what you are doing.

   **a.** know               **b.** like                 **c.** don't think about

4. When you **perceive** something, you _____ it.

   **a.** feel               **b.** know                 **c.** read

5. When two things are **hooked**, they are _____.

   **a.** connected          **b.** merged               **c.** set apart

6. When you **hesitate** to activate something, you _____.

   **a.** forget to turn it on    **b.** pause before     **c.** turn it on immediately
                                      turning it on

7. Two things that occur **simultaneously** happen _____.

   **a.** at the same time   **b.** in the same          **c.** to the same people
                                 place

8. If you **incorporate** an ingredient into a recipe you are making, you _____ it.

   **a.** absorb             **b.** add                  **c.** exchange

*(continued on next page)*

9. If the **default** setting for your computer screen is blue, your screen will be blue _____.

   **a.** automatically   **b.** intentionally   **c.** permanently

10. If you have the **sensation** that someone is looking at you, you _____ that it is actually happening.

   **a.** are sure   **b.** feel   **c.** understand

11. Your **endeavors** are the things that you _____.

   **a.** are good at   **b.** are trying to do   **c.** have succeeded at

12. If your computer is **defective**, it _____.

   **a.** doesn't work correctly   **b.** cost a lot   **c.** is old

## > READ AGAIN

Read "Reading Colors" again and complete the comprehension exercises. As you work, keep the reading goal in mind.

> 📖 **READING GOAL:** To explain in your own words what synesthesia is

## Comprehension Check

**A.** Check (✓) the excerpt from the text that contains an analogy.

_____ **1.** I came back from college on a semester break, and was sitting with my family around the dinner table, and—I don't know why I said it—but I said, "The number five is yellow." There was a pause, and my father said, "No, it's yellow-ochre."

_____ **2.** And what's funny is that I work in speech now, and I find it very interesting—but I also know that I've come to like yellows and oranges better. You know, I like a kind of a goldenrod, let's say, or a—you know, those sort of Mediterranean oranges and yellows.

_____ **3.** I was telling Carol that it's kind of like figuring out that you have a belly button. You know, at some point you just notice, and start playing with it! Then, for a while, you get really into it: "Wow, a belly button! Ooh, this is cool!" And after a while you get bored with it because, after all, it's still there, and then you realize everyone has one.

**B.** Circle the letter of the correct answer to complete each sentence.

1. Carol sees colors when she _____.
   **a.** hears certain sounds   **b.** sees certain letters and numbers   **c.** both a and b

2. Karen sees colors when she _____.
   **a.** hears certain words   **b.** reads certain words   **c.** both a and b

3. Carol has experienced synesthesia _____.
   **a.** her whole life   **b.** since college   **c.** since her father visited her in Manhattan

4. Carol's _____ is synesthetic, too.
   **a.** brother   **b.** father   **c.** mother

5. Carol's family did not realize that she was synesthetic until she _____.
   **a.** started to read   **b.** was in college   **c.** was living in Manhattan

6. Carol sees the color orange when she _____.
   **a.** sees a particular number   **b.** goes to the dentist   **c.** is in pain

7. In graduate school, Karen did not want to do a project on _____ because she didn't like the color of that word.
   **a.** linguistics   **b.** speech   **c.** goldenrod

8. Karen disliked the color yellow _____ she started a project involving speech.
   **a.** because   **b.** before   **c.** so

9. Today, Karen _____.
   **a.** dislikes the color yellow   **b.** researches language and speech   **c.** both a and b

10. Karen has experienced synesthesia since _____.
    **a.** she discovered her belly button   **b.** she was a child   **c.** she met Carol

11. Both Carol and Karen have a type of synesthesia that involves their senses of _____.
    **a.** touch and sound   **b.** sight and sound   **c.** taste and sound

**C.** Write a definition of synesthesia. Include an example or make an analogy to make your definition clear. Do not look back at the reading. Then share your definition with the class. Who has the best definition?

_____

_____

_____

 ## DISCUSS

Work in groups. Imagine three different people with synesthesia. Describe how each of these people might experience the world. Then share your description with the rest of the class.

**EXAMPLE:**

<u>Synesthete (Karen)</u>: sight and sound

<u>Karen's experience of the world</u>: Whenever she hears or sees a word, she also sees a particular color or combination of colors. For example, she always sees the word *linguistics* in a grayish-purple-blue color.

| Person | Senses that are hooked |
|---|---|
| Synesthetic A: | smell and sound |
| Synesthetic B: | sight and taste |
| Synesthetic C: | taste and touch |

 ## VOCABULARY SKILL BUILDING

### Vocabulary Skill: Adverb Placement: Adverbs That Modify Verbs

Adverbs of manner—adverbs that describe the way that something is done—end in *-ly*. They are placed immediately after the main verb *or* at the end of the sentence if the main verb has an object immediately after it. If there is an auxiliary verb (for example *have* or *be*) in front of the main verb, it is sometimes possible to place the adverb of manner between the auxiliary and the main verb. However, adverbs of manner are never placed in front of the auxiliary verb. Look at the examples.

**EXAMPLE:**

CORRECT: In most people's brains, each of the senses <u>is</u> <u>activated</u> <u>separately</u>.
          **aux. main verb  adverb**

CORRECT: In most people's brains, each of the senses <u>is</u> <u>separately</u> <u>activated</u>.
          **aux. adverb   main verb**

INCORRECT: In most people's brains, each of the senses <u>separately</u> <u>is</u> <u>activated</u>.
          **adverb  aux. main verb**

**A.** Scan the excerpt from the essay on page 78 and the reading "Reading Colors" on pages 79–81 for the sentences containing the adverbs below. Write the main verb next to the adverb that modifies it.

| Adverb | Main verb |
|---|---|
| **1.** separately | *activated* |
| **2.** vividly | _____ |
| **3.** differently | _____ |
| **4.** slightly | _____ |
| **5.** simultaneously | _____ |
| **6.** intentionally | _____ |
| **7.** synesthetically | _____ |

**B.** Complete the sentences with the adverbs from the list. Then circle the verb that each adverb modifies.

| | | | |
|---|---|---|---|
| hesitantly | intensely | permanently | simultaneously |
| horizontally | intentionally | separately | virtually |

**1.** He is speaking _____ because he does not have a lot of confidence or experience performing in front of a large group.

**2.** The boy was punished for having _____ hurt his little sister.

**3.** Many young people can _____ talk to one friend and send text messages to another.

**4.** They arrived at the party together, but they left _____.

**5.** The student driver practiced for the real driving test by first taking the test _____ on a computer.

**6.** She was looking at me so _____ that I began to feel uneasy.

**7.** His back was _____ damaged in the accident. He will never walk again.

**8.** That painting should be hung _____, not vertically.

# Not Enough Points on the Chicken

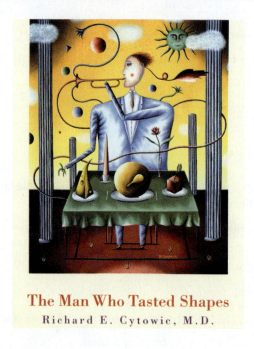

**The Man Who Tasted Shapes**
Richard E. Cytowic, M.D.

## > PREPARE TO READ

**A.** Look at the words in the list. Write the number(s) next to each word to show what you know. You may be able to write more than one number next to some of the words. You will study all of these words in this chapter.

1. I can use the word in a sentence.

2. I know <u>one meaning</u> of the word.

3. I know <u>more than one meaning</u> of the word.

4. I know how to pronounce the word.

**B.** Work with a partner. Look at the picture. Ask and answer the questions. If you don't know a word in English, ask your partner or look in your dictionary. Then write your new words on page 232.

1. What do you see in the picture? Find at least one example for each of the categories and point to it.

   something pointed

   something round

2. Considering what you learned about synesthesia in Chapter 9, the picture above, and the title of the reading, what do you think the article will be about?

_____ conflict

_____ conservative

_____ course

_____ diagnosis

_____ flow

_____ grasp

_____ grin

_____ identify with

_____ illusion

_____ rub

_____ stir up

_____ sweep

_____ sympathetic

_____ texture

**C.** Read the first two paragraphs of the book excerpt "Not Enough Points on the Chicken." Then read the last sentence of the excerpt. Check (✓) the statements that are true about the narrator (the person who is telling the story).

| | | | |
|---|---|---|---|
| _____ | **1.** He is a doctor. | _____ | **4.** He is a professional artist. |
| _____ | **2.** He is a neurologist. | _____ | **5.** He has synesthesia. |
| _____ | **3.** He likes art. | _____ | **6.** He does research on the brain. |

> **READ**

Read "Not Enough Points on the Chicken." Check your answer from Exercise C.

The following material has been adapted from the original and does not represent Dr. Cytowic's exact wording.

## ഌ **Not Enough Points on the Chicken** ൙

1    "Keep me company while I finish the sauce," Michael said, pulling me away from the other guests. I followed, examining the unusual layout[1] of his home. His house had no inside walls. Its "rooms" **flowed** into one another instead of keeping to well-defined spaces as rooms in most homes do.

5    I quickly **identified with** the atmosphere of Michael's house, an attraction that **stirred up** an old **conflict**. As a doctor, I was expected to be **conservative**, yet the house spoke to the artist in me, too. I was glad Michael had invited me to dinner. I had long preferred the company of creative people to the company of serious medical types.

10    I sat nearby while he stirred the sauce he had made for the roast chicken. "Oh, dear," he said tasting a spoonful, "there aren't enough points on the chicken."

"Aren't enough what?" I asked.

He froze and turned red. "Oh, you're going to think I'm crazy," he said. "I hope no one else heard," he said, quickly glancing at the guests in the far corner.

15    "Why not?" I asked.

"Sometimes I blurt these things out[2]," he whispered, leaning toward me. "You're a neurologist, maybe it will make sense to you. I know it sounds crazy, but I have this thing, see, where I taste by shape." He looked away. "How can I explain?" he asked himself.

20    "Flavors have shape," he started. "I wanted the taste of this chicken to be a pointed shape, but it came out all round." He looked up at me, still blushing[3]. "Well, I mean it's nearly spherical," he added. "I can't serve this if it doesn't have points."

*(continued on next page)*

---

[1] **layout:** the way in which a house, building, or town is arranged

[2] **blurt out:** to speak quickly without thinking

[3] **blush:** to turn red in the face, usually because you are embarrassed

A strange **diagnosis** came to mind, but I wanted to hear more in Michael's
own words to be sure. "It sounds like nobody understands what you're talking
about," I finally said.

"That's the problem. Nobody's ever heard of this. They think that I'm making it
up. That's why I never intentionally tell people about my shapes. It's so perfectly
logical that I thought everybody felt shapes when they ate. If there's no shape,
there's no flavor."

I tried not to show any surprise. "Where do you feel these shapes?" I asked.

"All over," he said, "but mostly I feel things **rubbed** against my face or sitting
in my hands."

I kept my poker face[4] and said nothing.

"When I taste something with an intense flavor," Michael continued, "the
feeling **sweeps** down my arm into my fingertips. I feel it—its weight, its **texture**,
whether it's warm or cold, everything. I feel it like I'm actually **grasping**
something." He held up his hands. "Of course, there's nothing really there," he
said, staring at his hands. "But it's not an **illusion** because I feel it."

One more question, to be certain. "How long have you tasted shapes?"

"All my life," he said. "But nobody ever understands . . . Am I a hopeless case,
Doc?"

"Not at all," I answered. Just as there were no walls between the rooms of
his house, I knew that Michael had no walls between his senses. Just as his
rooms flowed into each other, so too taste, touch, movement, and color flowed
together in his brain. For Michael, sensation was simultaneous, like a jambalaya[5],
instead of a meal served in neat, separate **courses**. Still, my self-satisfaction at
recognizing one of the rarest of medical conditions must have been perfectly
clear.

"What are you **grinning** about?" Michael asked. "I thought you would be
**sympathetic**!"

"I'm not making fun of you," I laughed. "I'm just delighted to know someone
with synesthesia. I've never met anyone who had it."

"Synesthe . . ."

"Synesthesia," I repeated. "It's Greek. *Syn* means 'together' and *aisthesis* means
'sensation.' Synesthesia means 'feeling together,' just as *syn-chrony* means at the
same time, or *syn-thesis* means different ideas joined into one, or *syn-opsis* means
to see all together. You've never heard the word?" I asked.

"You mean there's a name for this? Is that why you're grinning?"

"Sure, and I know a little about it. People with synesthesia have their senses
hooked together," I started to explain. "They can hear colors or feel sounds. Yours
is—well, it looks like you taste shapes."

"You mean I'm normal?"

"Normal is such a relative[6] term. Let's just say that you're a rare bird[7]," I
suggested. "Different, but not unheard of."

And with that roast chicken dinner started a research effort and a friendship
that has lasted for many years.

---

[4] **poker face:** showing no expression on your face

[5] **jambalaya:** a dish from the southern United States, containing a mix of things including fish and rice

[6] **relative:** having a particular quality when compared with something else

[7] **rare bird:** unusual person

# Vocabulary Check

**A.** Complete the sentences with the boldfaced words from the reading. Use the correct form of the word.

1. Parents and grandparents do not always agree about the best way to raise children. They often get into _____ about this issue.

2. When she is happy, she _____ and shows all of her teeth.

3. I have never made much money, so it is difficult for me to _____ people with very high incomes.

4. I like the taste of this, but I don't like the way it feels in my mouth. It has a very strange _____.

5. He thought he saw a ghost, but it was just a(n) _____. What he really saw was light that was reflected off the water.

6. Water never goes up a hill. It naturally _____ downhill.

**B.** Read the statements about the reading. Write *T* (true) or *F* (false). Then correct the false statements to make them true. The boldfaced words are the target words.

_____ 1. A **conservative** person enjoys experiencing new things.

_____ 2. When your doctor doesn't know what is wrong with you, he or she gives you a **diagnosis**.

_____ 3. The last **course** of a meal is usually dessert.

_____ 4. You **rub** your hands together when you wash them.

_____ 5. When you **grasp** something, you drop it.

_____ 6. If people are **sympathetic** to your situation, they will probably reject you.

_____ 7. If a man is married and is often seen with a woman who is not his wife, he will probably **stir up** gossip.

_____ 8. When a feeling **sweeps** over you, you feel a strong sensation all over your body.

## ▷ READ AGAIN

Read "Not Enough Points on the Chicken" again and complete the comprehension exercises. As you work, keep the reading goal in mind.

> 📖 **READING GOAL:** To understand and remember the details of an unusual story

## Comprehension Check

**A.** Underline the two analogies that the writer uses in "Not Enough Points on the Chicken."

**B.** Answer the questions in your own words. Do not copy from the text.

**1.** What does Michael's house look like? Describe it.

_____

**2.** Why was the narrator happy when Michael invited him for dinner?

_____

**3.** What does the narrator discover about Michael, and how does he discover it?

_____

**4.** Which of Michael's senses are hooked together?

_____

**5.** This excerpt is the first chapter of a book. What do you think the rest of the book is about?

_____

**C.** Work with a partner. Compare your answers from Exercise B. Then reread the text and check your answers. Next to each question in Exercise B, write the number of the paragraph(s) where you found the answer.

## ▷ DISCUSS

Work in small groups. Ask and answer the questions.

**1.** Synesthesia affects only a very small number of people. Why do you think neurologists are so interested in studying people with synesthesia?

**2.** In what ways might having synesthesia be difficult or cause a problem for the person with the condition?

**3.** What professions do you think someone with synesthesia might be good at?

**4.** Would you like to have synesthesia? If you had synesthesia, which of your senses would you like to have hooked together? Explain.

90    UNIT 5 ■ Great Minds

# Learn the Vocabulary

## Strategy

### Guessing Meaning from Context

When you are reading, don't use your dictionary to look up every new word. That will interfere with your fluency and make it difficult for you to remain engaged in the text. Instead, either skip the word if you can understand the sentence without it or use the *context* (the other words and sentences near the new word) to guess the meaning.

Usually it is not necessary to understand exactly what an unfamiliar word means—a general idea is enough. Then later you can look the word up in your dictionary to get a more exact definition.

Use your common sense to help you figure out the meaning of unfamiliar words. Ask yourself, "What does what to what?" Also, pay attention to examples and the relationship between the unfamiliar word and words that you already know. Look at the examples.

**EXAMPLE:**

*I sat nearby while he **stirred** the sauce he had made for the roast chicken. "Oh, dear," he said tasting a spoonful.*

To guess the meaning of *stir,* you might ask yourself, "What do cooks do to a sauce before they taste it?"

**EXAMPLE:**

*"You mean I'm normal?"*

*"Normal is such a relative term. Let's just say that you're a **rare bird**," I suggested. "Different, but not unheard of."*

To guess the meaning of the expression *rare bird,* read the whole sentence. The explanation/definition of "rare bird" is at the end of the statement: "different, but not unheard of."

**A.** Read the sentences. Guess the meaning of the boldfaced words. Underline the words in the context that help you understand the meaning.

1. Then, for a while, you **get really into** it: "Wow, a belly button! Ooh, this is cool!" And after a while you get bored with it because, after all, it's still there, and then you realize everyone has one.

   *Get into (something)* probably means _____.

2. I've come to like yellows and oranges better. You know, I like a kind of a **goldenrod,** let's say, or a—you know, those sort of Mediterranean oranges and yellows.

   *Goldenrod* probably means _____.

3. The synesthete is not **making it up**. The sensation of "hearing" a color is as real to the synesthete as seeing a color is to you.

   *Make something up* probably means _____.

*(continued on next page)*

4. "**Keep me company** while I finish the sauce," Michael said, pulling me away from the other guests.

   *Keep someone company* probably means _____.

5. For Michael, sensation was simultaneous, like a ***jambalaya***, instead of a meal served in neat, separate courses.

   *Jambalaya* probably means _____.

6. "Flavors have shape," he started. "I wanted the taste of this chicken to be a pointed shape, but it came out all round." He looked up at me, still blushing. "Well, I mean it's nearly **spherical,**" he added. "I can't serve this if it doesn't have points."

   *Spherical* probably means _____.

**B.** Look up the boldfaced words from Exercise A in a dictionary. Compare your definitions to the ones in the dictionary. Are your definitions similar?

**C.** Go back to the vocabulary list at the beginning of each chapter. What did you learn about the target words? Add numbers to the lists.

**Vocabulary Practice 5,** see page 238

# Creature Feature

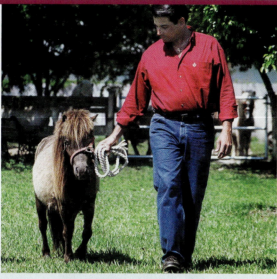

## > THINK BEFORE YOU READ

**A.** Work with a partner. Look at the pictures. Ask and answer the questions. If you don't know a word in English, ask your partner or look in your dictionary. Then write your new words on page 232.

   **1.** What are the animals in the pictures?

   **2.** Which of the animals are useful to humans? How are they useful?

   **3.** Which of the animals is the most intelligent? The least intelligent?

**B.** Complete the sentences with the animals from Exercise A. More than one animal might be possible.

   **1.** _____
     can use tools.

   **2.** _____
     can form close relationships with humans.

   **3.** _____
     can be trained to help the disabled (for example, people who are blind or who cannot walk).

   **4.** _____
     can live for more than thirty years.

# Crows' Brains and Geckos' Feet

## ▶ PREPARE TO READ

**A.** Look at the words in the list. Write the number(s) next to each word to show what you know. You may be able to write more than one number next to some of the words. You will study all of these words in this chapter.

1. I can use the word in a sentence.

2. I know <u>one meaning</u> of the word.

3. I know <u>more than one meaning</u> of the word.

4. I know how to pronounce the word.

**B.** Work with a partner. Look at the picture. Ask and answer the questions. If you don't know a word in English, ask your partner or look in your dictionary. Then write your new words on page 232.

1. What kind of bird is in the picture? What is it holding?

2. Do you have a lot of these birds in your home country or city? Do you like them? Why or why not?

3. Is this type of bird intelligent?

_____ accommodate

_____ bend

_____ cautious

_____ colleague

_____ genius

_____ instinctively

_____ intersection

_____ obligation

_____ partnership

_____ primate

_____ suburb

_____ thrive

_____ widespread

**C.** Read the questions. Then scan the newspaper article "Crows' Brains and Geckos' Feet" and write the answers.

1. Which animals are mentioned in the article? _____

2. Who is Betty? _____

3. Who is Joshua Klein? _____

4. What kind of animal is Klein interested in? _____

5. Who is Robert Fuller? _____

6. What kind of animal does Fuller study? _____

## ▶ READ

Read "Crows' Brains and Geckos' Feet." Check your answers from Exercise C.

# Crows' Brains and Geckos' Feet

1    Betty, a New Caledonian[1] crow living in a research lab, was hungry. She could see a piece of meat at the bottom of a glass test tube[2], but she could not reach it. In the wild, crows use
5    twigs to dig into trees to get insects. There were no twigs in Betty's cage, but that didn't stop the hungry crow. She found a straight piece of wire[3] that someone had left in the cage. She picked it up with her beak. Then she stuck the
10    wire under some sticky tape[4] that was also in her cage, and **bent** the wire. Finally, she used her new tool to remove the piece of meat from the test tube. The scientists in the lab watched in amazement as she popped the piece of meat
15    in her mouth. They knew crows could use tools, but could they make them? That was something new. Clearly crows were more intelligent than they had thought.
     In another show of intelligence, a group of
20    crows in a Tokyo **suburb** have learned a new way to get lunch. They fly over **intersections** and drop nuts in front of cars. The cars drive over the

nuts, and the crows wait for the light to change. When the light turns red, the **cautious** crows fly
25    down and eat the nuts without fear of being run over. The behavior has become **widespread** as more and more crows teach it to others.
     After observing crow behavior in the laboratory and in the wild, scientists now
30    believe that the birds are not just acting **instinctively**. They believe that crows have the intellectual capacity to plan, solve problems, and teach new behaviors to others. The obvious implication is that crows, like **primates** and
35    dolphins, are highly intelligent.
     These stories of crow **genius** attracted the attention of a writer named Joshua Klein. To find out if crows could be trained, Klein designed an experiment. He built a vending
40    machine[5] for crows. Inside the machine were nuts. He knew that crows were attracted to shiny things, so he put coins on the ground around the machine. At first, the crows just picked up the coins. By chance, a few crows dropped some

*(continued on next page)*

---

[1] **New Caledonia:** several islands in the South Pacific, belonging to France
[2] **test tube:** small glass container shaped like a tube, used in scientific experiments
[3] **wire:** metal in the form of a long thin thread
[4] **tape:** narrow length of sticky material used to stick things together
[5] **vending machine:** a machine that you can get candy, drinks, etc., from by putting in coins or bills

45 coins into the machine and were rewarded with a nut. Soon, the crows appeared to understand the relationship among the coins, the machine, and the nuts. Klein watched in amazement as they started intentionally dropping the coins into
50 the machine to get the nuts.

Klein's experiment, along with other research, shows how well crows can adapt to new challenges. They are also good at taking advantage of new resources. This is particularly
55 useful in large cities, where the environment is constantly changing. And as anyone who lives in a city knows, crows **thrive** in cities. In fact, many city residents see crows as a problem. The birds make a mess and are very noisy. But Klein
60 thinks we could find ways to **accommodate** crows and even give them useful work. After all, he reasons, if crows can use a vending machine, why can't we train them to do more useful things? For example, why can't we train
65 them to pick up garbage or search for survivors of a natural disaster?

As Klein and others continue to study crow intelligence, a scientist at the University of California at Berkeley is looking at the

70 usefulness of animals in a different way. The biologist, Robert Fuller, can tell you a lot about a small lizard[6] called a gecko. He has several of them in his lab. Geckos have an amazing ability to climb on any surface. Using his knowledge
75 of geckos, Fuller worked with engineers to design an extremely strong dry adhesive[7]. It is so strong that a human could use it to climb up the side of a building like a comic book superhero—or like a gecko. But Fuller's work
80 did not stop there. He and his **colleagues** have built a robot gecko. It climbs walls and enters places that are impossible for humans to enter.

Fuller believes that **partnerships** between biologists and engineers will become more
85 common in the future. Partnerships between animals and humans are also becoming more common. Every day, animal researchers are discovering more about the intelligence and natural abilities of animals. However,
90 such partnerships will only work if humans recognize their **obligation** to protect the environment of the geckos, crows, and other creatures that share the planet.

---

[6] **lizard:** a reptile that has rough skin, four short legs, and a long tail

[7] **adhesive:** a substance such as glue that is used to stick things together

## Vocabulary Check

**A.** Complete the sentences with the words from the list. Be careful. There are three extra answers. The boldfaced words are the target words.

| birds | easy | ponder | steel | wire |
|-------|------|--------|-------|------|
| carefree | humans | similar | uneasy | |

1. Both _____ and chimpanzees are **primates**.

2. It is not possible to **bend** _____ with your hands.

3. When you do something **instinctively**, you do not _____ it before doing it.

**4.** A **cautious** child will probably feel _____ in an unfamiliar place.

**5.** When you form a **partnership** with someone, you should have _____ goals.

**6.** When a business is **thriving**, it is _____ to make money.

**B.** Write the letter of the correct definition next to the target word. Be careful. There are two extra definitions.

_____ **1.** accommodate

_____ **2.** colleague

_____ **3.** intersection

_____ **4.** obligation

_____ **5.** suburb

_____ **6.** widespread

**a.** existing or happening in many places or among many living things

**b.** an area away from the center of a city, where a lot of people live

**c.** to motivate

**d.** a moral or legal duty to do something

**e.** the place where two or more lines, roads, etc., meet and cross each other

**f.** occurring in one place at a time

**g.** to try to meet the needs of people or animals, especially if their needs are different from yours

**h.** someone you work with

Read "Crows' Brains and Geckos' Feet" again and complete the
comprehension exercises. As you work, keep the reading goal in mind.

📖 **READING GOAL:** To understand the relationship between main points
and the examples and details that illustrate them

## Comprehension Check

**A.** In each set of sentences, write *MP* next to sentences containing the main
point and *I* next to sentences that illustrate the main point.

1. _____ **a.** She found a straight piece of wire that someone had left in
the cage and picked it up with her beak.

_____ **b.** They knew crows could use tools, but could they make
them?

_____ **c.** Then she stuck the wire under some sticky tape that was also
in her cage, and bent the wire.

2. _____ **a.** A group of crows in a Tokyo suburb have learned a new way
to get lunch.

_____ **b.** The behavior has become widespread as more and more
crows teach it to others.

_____ **c.** They believe that crows have the intellectual capacity to plan,
solve problems, and teach new behaviors to others.

3. _____ **a.** Klein built a vending machine for crows.

_____ **b.** Klein watched in amazement as they started intentionally
dropping the coins into the machine to get the nuts.

_____ **c.** Klein's experiment, along with other research, shows that
crows are able to adapt to new challenges.

_____ **d.** And as anyone who lives in a city knows, crows thrive in
cities.

4. _____ **a.** But Klein thinks we could find ways to accommodate crows
and even give them useful work.

_____ **b.** Why can't we train them to pick up garbage or search for
survivors of a natural disaster?

5. _____ **a.** A scientist at the University of California at Berkeley is looking
at the usefulness of animals in a different way.

_____ **b.** Using his knowledge of geckos, Fuller worked with engineers
to design an extremely strong dry adhesive.

**B.** Find examples and details from the reading that illustrate the intelligence and abilities of crows. On a separate piece of paper, list the headings below. Then write the examples and details under the correct heading. Some examples and details fit under more than one heading.

Making tools                Using tools
Learning                    Planning
Solving problems            Adapting to new situations and environments

**C.** Work with a partner. Discuss what scientists have learned from studying geckos and what they are doing with that knowledge.

> ## DISCUSS

Work in groups. Complete the chart with animals that you are familiar with. Then share the information in your chart with the class.

| Animal | The ability or characteristic that makes this animal useful to humans |
|--------|------------------------------------------------------------------------|
|        |                                                                        |
|        |                                                                        |
|        |                                                                        |
|        |                                                                        |

# Creature Comforts

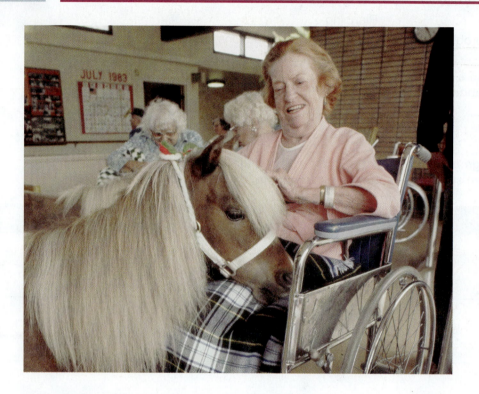

## ▷ PREPARE TO READ

**A.** Look at the words in the list. Write the number(s) next to each word to show what you know. You may be able to write more than one number next to some of the words. You will study all of these words in this chapter.

1. I can use the word in a sentence.

2. I know <u>one meaning</u> of the word.

3. I know <u>more than one meaning</u> of the word.

4. I know how to pronounce the word.

**B.** Work with a partner. Look at the picture. Ask and answer the questions. If you don't know a word in English, ask your partner or look in your dictionary. Then write your new words on page 232.

1. What is the animal in the picture?

2. Why is it with the woman, in the room?

_____ anxiety

_____ barely

_____ breed

_____ costume

_____ disability

_____ lawsuit

_____ mild-mannered

_____ miniature

_____ privilege

_____ suspicion

_____ tap

_____ threatening

Compare/contrast is a common type of text organization. When writers compare, they discuss the similarities between two people, places, things, or ideas. When they contrast, they discuss the differences. Often writers will both compare and contrast in the same reading.

There are many common signal words for comparing and contrasting. Certain grammar patterns are also used. Often the writer states one side of the comparison or contrast directly using signal words or grammatical patterns and assumes that readers will figure out the other side of the comparison or contrast for themselves.

| Signal words: Comparison | Grammar pattern: Comparison | Signal words: Contrast | Grammar pattern: Contrast |
|---|---|---|---|
| *similar to,* *like,* *similarly,* *likewise,* *in the same way* | *as ... as ...* *the same ... as ...* *both ... and ...* *not only ... but* *also ...* | *but,* *different from,* *unlike,* *in contrast,* *on the other hand,* *however* | *more (or -er) ... than* *not as ... as ...* *less/fewer ... than ...* |

**C.** Skim "Creature Comforts." Then answer the questions.

   **1.** Which words and grammar patterns does the writer use to signal comparisons and contrasts? Underline them in the text.

   **2.** What does the writer compare and contrast in the article?

      _____ *creature guide* _____

## ▶ READ

Read "Creature Comforts." Was your answer from Exercise C, question 2 correct?

# Creature Comforts

1    On Halloween night in a suburb of Albany, New York, a group of children dressed as vampires[1] and witches[2] ran past a middle-aged woman in plain clothes. She was holding a
5    leather harness—like the kind used for seeing-eye dogs. In the harness was a small black-and-white horse **barely** tall enough to reach the woman's hip[3].

    "Cool **costume**," one of the kids said. But it
10  wasn't a costume. The woman, Ann Edie, was

*(continued on next page)*

---

[1] **vampire:** an imaginary creature: looks like a person and sucks people's blood by biting their necks

[2] **witch:** a woman who is believed to have magic powers, especially evil powers

[3] **hip:** the part of the body where the legs join the body

simply blind, and out for an evening walk with Panda, her guide **miniature** horse.

There are no sidewalks in Edie's neighborhood, so Panda led her along the side of the street. At one point, Panda paused, waited for a car to pass, then walked into the road to avoid a group of children running toward them. She led Edie to a traffic pole at a busy intersection. There she stopped and **tapped** her hoof.[4]

"Find the button," Edie said. Panda raised her head inches from the pole so Edie could run her hand along Panda's nose to find and press the "walk" signal button.

Edie isn't the only blind person who uses a guide horse instead of a dog—there's actually a Guide Horse Foundation that's been around for almost ten years. The obvious question is why? In fact, Edie says, there are many reasons: Miniature horses are **mild-mannered**, trainable, and less **threatening** than large dogs. They're naturally cautious and have excellent vision, with eyes set far apart for nearly 360-degree range. Plus, they're herd[5] animals, so they instinctively match their movements to others'. But the biggest reason is age: Miniature horses can live and work for more than thirty years. In that time, a blind person typically has five to seven guide dogs. That can be difficult both emotionally and economically. It can cost up to $60,000 to **breed**, train, and place each dog in a home.

"Panda is almost eight years old," her trainer, Alexandra Kurland, told me. "If Panda were a dog, Ann would be thinking about retiring her soon, but their relationship is just getting started. They're still improving their communication and learning to read each other's bodies. It's the difference between dating for a few years and being married so long you can finish each other's sentences."

Edie has nothing against service dogs—she has had several. One worked beautifully. Two didn't—they dragged her across lawns[6] chasing cats and even pulled her into the street chasing dogs in passing cars. Edie doesn't worry about those sorts of things with Panda because miniature horses are less aggressive[7].

Still, she says, "I would never say to a blind person, 'Run out and get yourself a guide horse,' because there are definite limitations." They eat far more often than dogs and go to the bathroom about every two or three hours. (Yes, Panda is house-trained.[8])

Plus, they can't lie down in small places, which makes going to the movies or riding in airplanes a challenge. (When miniature horses fly, they stand in first class or bulkhead[9] because they don't fit in standard coach.)

After the first shock of seeing a horse walk into a café or ride in a car, watching Edie and Panda work together makes the idea of guide miniature horses seem completely logical. Even normal. So normal, in fact, that people often find it hard to believe that the United States government is considering forcing Edie and many others like her to stop using their service animals. But that's exactly what's happening. A growing number of people believe the world of service animals has gotten out of control: First it was guide dogs for the blind; now it's monkeys for quadriplegia,[10] guide miniature horses, parrots for psychosis,[11] and any number of animals for **anxiety**, including cats, pigs,

---

[4] **hoof:** the hard foot of an animal such as a horse or cow

[5] **herd:** a group of a particular type of animal that lives together

[6] **lawn:** the area of ground in a yard or park that is covered with short grass

[7] **aggressive:** forceful and showing that you are determined to have your own way

[8] **house-trained:** an animal that is trained to use a litter box or go to the bathroom outside

[9] **bulkhead (seat):** the first row of seats, usually in a plane, with a wall but no seats in front of it

[10] **quadriplegia:** the condition where someone is completely paralyzed and cannot move their arms or legs

[11] **psychosis:** serious mental illness that changes your character and makes you unable to behave normally

85 and a duck. They're all showing up in stores and in restaurants. This is perfectly legal because of the Americans with **Disabilities** Act (A.D.A.). The Act requires that service animals be allowed wherever their owners want to go.

90 Some people enjoy running into an occasional primate or farm animal while shopping. Many others don't. This has resulted in a growing debate over how to handle these animals. There is also widespread **suspicion**

95 that people are abusing the law[12] to get special **privileges** for their pets. Increasingly, business owners, landlords, and city officials are refusing to accommodate non-canine[13] service animals. Animal owners are responding

100 with **lawsuits**. These cases are raising questions about how to balance the needs and rights of people who rely on these animals, of businesses obligated by law to accommodate them, and of everyday people who—because

105 of health and safety concerns or just general discomfort—don't want monkeys or ducks walking the aisles of their grocery stores.

---

[12] **abuse the law:** to deliberately use the law for the wrong purpose

[13] **non-canine:** not dogs

## Vocabulary Check

Look at the boldfaced words in the reading and try to guess the meaning. Then read the sentences and circle the letter of the correct answer to complete each sentence.

1. You **breed** an animal because you want it to _____.
   a. have babies      b. lose weight      c. be healthy

2. She is **barely** sixteen. Her birthday was _____.
   a. a year ago      b. late      c. yesterday

3. His **anxiety** makes it _____ for him to relax.
   a. common      b. difficult      c. fun

4. She's wearing a **costume**. She's probably going to _____.
   a. a party      b. school      c. work

5. She is **mild-mannered**. She is _____ angry.
   a. always      b. rarely      c. sometimes

6. He talked to her in a **threatening** way, but _____.
   a. he didn't hurt her      b. she didn't laugh      c. she felt uneasy

7. You cannot _____ someone based on your **suspicions**. First you need proof.
   a. accommodate      b. arrest      c. threaten

*(continued on next page)*

8. **Lawsuits** are handled by _____.
   a. courts          b. colleagues          c. partnerships

9. She _____ when he **tapped** her on the shoulder.
   a. was injured          b. fell down          c. turned around

10. He has special **privileges**. He _____.
    a. can't walk          b. doesn't have to          c. is not allowed inside
                              pay to enter

11. He has a **disability**, _____ he can do almost everything that other
    people can do.
    a. because          b. so          c. but

12. **Miniature** horses are _____.
    a. disabled          b. very small          c. threatening

## ▶ READ AGAIN

Read "Creature Comforts" again and complete the comprehension
exercises. As you work, keep the reading goal in mind.

> 📖 **READING GOAL:** To learn about an unusual type of service animal

## Comprehension Check

**A.** Read the statements about the reading. Write *T* (true) or *F* (false). If it is
not possible to tell, write *?*. Then correct the false statements to make
them true.

_____ **1.** Guide miniature horses are common in the United States today.

_____ **2.** Miniature horses are better service animals than dogs.

_____ **3.** Guide miniature horses cannot go on airplanes or in movie

theaters.

_____ **4.** The Americans with Disabilities Act does not protect people who

suffer from anxiety.

_____ **5.** Some restaurant and store owners do not allow people with

guide dogs to enter their place of business.

_____ **6.** Some people would like the government to prevent certain types

of service animals from entering public places.

_____ **7.** Some of the disabled are going to court to protect their right to

take unusual service animals with them wherever they go.

**B.** Complete the graphic organizer with information about guide dogs and guide miniature horses.

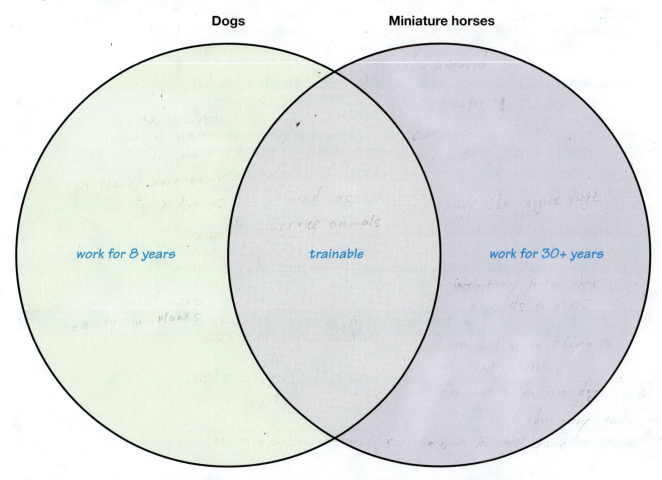

Dogs        Miniature horses

work for 8 years     trainable     work for 30+ years

used as service animals

**C.** On a separate piece of paper, use the information in the graphic organizer to summarize the similarities and differences between dogs and miniature horses. Write two paragraphs—one about the similarities and the other about the differences. Use appropriate signal words and grammatical patterns. Do not look back at the text.

**D.** Exchange summaries with a partner. Did you and your partner include the same information?

> **Vocabulary Skill: Understanding the Meaning of Compound Words**

Compound words are common in English. A compound word is made up of two or more different words. Compound words in English can be one word, two words joined by a hyphen (-), or two separate words. The word compound has its own particular meaning that often goes beyond the meaning of its two separate parts.

**EXAMPLE:**

| | | | |
|---|---|---|---|
| widespread | wide + spread | = | Something that is widespread starts in one area and then spreads to another area; as a result, it affects a large or wide area. |
| mild-mannered | mild + mannered | = | A mild-mannered person or animal is mild or gentle in behavior or manner; it is not aggressive. |
| service animal | service + animal | = | A service animal is an animal that is trained to serve or assist people in some way. |

Some compound words have their own entry in a dictionary. Other compound words are listed within the entry for one of the words that make up the compound. If you are not sure whether a word compound is one word, two words, or hyphenated, look in your dictionary.

**A.** Break the compound words into their separate parts and write a definition for each one.

| Compound word | Parts | Definition |
|---|---|---|
| **1.** lawsuit | | a ... that a person or organization brings to a court |
| **2.** house-trained | house | |
| **3.** seeing-eye dog | | ... for blind people |
| **4.** test tube | | ... that is shaped like a tube and ... |
| **5.** vending machine | machine | a machine ... you can get cigarettes, chocolate, drinks etc. |

**B.** Work with a partner. Compare your definitions. Then look up the words in an English/English dictionary and compare your definitions to the dictionary definitions.

# Learn the Vocabulary

## Strategy

### Using the Keyword Technique

There are many ways to remember the meaning of a new word. Research on language learners shows that the keyword technique works well for many learners. Here's how it works:

1. Look at the new word, and choose a *keyword*. A keyword is a word in your native language that sounds similar to the beginning or all of the new word in English. Look at the example from a native speaker of Spanish.

**EXAMPLE:**

New word = *costume*

Keyword (Spanish word that sounds similar) = *casa* (= *house* in English)

2. Imagine a picture where the meaning of the new word and the meaning of the keyword are connected in some way. The connection can be strange. In fact, strange pictures are often easier to remember!

**EXAMPLE:**

3. To remember the word *costume* in English, think of the image of the clown dressed in a *costume* standing on the roof of the *casa* (house).

*(continued on next page)*

**4.** If you like to draw, you can draw the picture on the back side of your word card, with the English word on the front side.

*costume*
*('kastum)*

**A.** Think of keywords for five target words from the unit, and write them below.

| New word | Keyword |
|----------|---------|
| 1. _____ | _____ |
| 2. _____ | _____ |
| 3. _____ | _____ |
| 4. _____ | _____ |
| 5. _____ | _____ |

**B.** Now imagine a picture to connect the new word and the keyword for each of the new words in Exercise A. Draw the picture on one side of a word card. Write the new word on the other side of the card.

**C.** Show your cards to a classmate. Explain your pictures by pronouncing the keywords and telling your partner the meaning.

**D.** Go back to the vocabulary list at the beginning of each chapter. What did you learn about the target words? Add numbers to the lists.

**Vocabulary Practice 6,** see page 239

# FLUENCY PRACTICE 2

 ## READING 1

## Before You Read

Read the questions. Then scan "Can't Name That Tune?" to find the answers.

1. What does "amusic" mean?

   _____

2. What percentage of the population is amusic?

   _____

3. What does music sound like to someone who is amusic?

   _____

4. How old is Margaret? What did she recently discover?

   _____

## Read

**A.** Read "Can't Name That Tune?". Time yourself. Write your start and end times and your total reading time. Then calculate your reading speed (words per minute) and write it in the progress chart on page 246.

**Start:** _____   **End:** _____   **Total time:** _____ (in seconds)

**Reading speed:**
509 words ÷ _____ (total time in seconds) x 60 = _____ words per minute

# Can't Name That Tune?

Music is everywhere. It is played at parties and sporting events. It is an important part of TV advertising and movies. We hear it in elevators and in doctors' and dentists' offices.
5 And these days more and more people take their music with them wherever they go. Just look around you. Almost everyone is listening to music on a personal electronic device such as an MP3 player or an iPod®. It seems that
10 music is more a part of contemporary life than at any other time in human history.

For some people, however, music is no fun at all. About four percent of the population is what scientists call "amusic." People who are amusic
15 are born without the capacity to recognize or reproduce musical notes. As a result, amusic people often cannot tell the difference between two songs. Two totally different songs, such as "Happy Birthday" and "Yesterday," by the
20 Beatles, may sound the same.

Many people can't sing well. However, not being able to *make* music is very different from not being able to *perceive* music. Most people who can't sing or play a musical instrument
25 can still hear two musical notes and know which note is higher. However, amusics can only hear the difference between two notes if they are very far apart on the musical scale.

As a result, songs sound like noise to an
30 amusic. Many amusics compare the sound of music to pieces of metal hitting each other. "It sounds like you went in the kitchen and threw all the pots and pans on the floor," says one amusic woman.

35 Life can be hard for amusics. Their inability to enjoy music sets them apart from others. It can be difficult for other people to identify with their condition. In fact, most people cannot begin to grasp what it feels like to be amusic.
40 Just going to a restaurant or shopping mall can be uncomfortable or even painful. That is why many amusics intentionally stay away from places where there is music. However, this can result in withdrawal and social isolation. "I
45 used to hate parties," says Margaret, a seventy-year-old woman who only recently discovered that she was amusic. By studying people like Margaret, scientists are finally learning how to identify this unusual condition.

50 Scientists say that the brains of amusics are different from the brains of people who can appreciate music. The difference is complex, and it doesn't involve defective hearing. Amusics can understand other nonmusical
55 sounds perfectly well. They also have no problems understanding ordinary speech. Scientists compare amusics to people who just can't see certain colors.

Many amusics are happy when their
60 condition is finally diagnosed. For years, Margaret felt embarrassed about her problem with music. Now she knows that she is not alone. There is a name for her condition. That makes it easier for her to explain. "When
65 people invite me to a concert, I just say, 'No thanks, I'm amusic,'" says Margaret. "I just wish I had learned to say that when I was seventeen and not seventy."

**B.** Read "Can't Name That Tune?" again, a little faster this time. Write your start and end times and your total reading time. Then calculate your reading speed (words per minute) and write it in the progress chart on page 246.

Start: _____    End: _____    Total time: _____ (in seconds)

**Reading speed:**
509 words ÷ _____ (total time in seconds) x 60 = _____ words per minute

# Comprehension Check

**A.** Circle the letter of the correct answer to complete each sentence.

1. Amusics are people who _____.
   a. cannot hear music
   b. cannot recognize or reproduce musical notes
   c. do not like music very much

2. Two very different songs might sound _____ to an amusic.
   a. a little bit different
   b. the same
   c. very bad

3. For an amusic, listening to music can be _____.
   a. enjoyable
   b. interesting
   c. painful

4. Amusics sometimes avoid places where they _____.
   a. are likely to hear music
   b. do not know anyone
   c. feel uncomfortable

5. It is _____ for most people to understand what it is like to be amusic.
   a. uncomfortable
   b. lonely
   c. difficult

6. Being amusic can be compared to _____.
   a. not being able to hear
   b. not being able to see colors
   c. not being able to sing well

7. The brains of people who are amusic are _____.
   a. defective
   b. different
   c. creative

**B.** Complete the summary of "Can't Name That Tune?". You will need to write more than one word in many of the spaces. There is more than one correct way to complete the sentences.

Amusics do not have the capacity to (1) _____. It is difficult for people who are not amusic to (2) _____. To someone who is amusic, music sounds like (3) _____. That's why amusics often (4) _____. As a result, (5) _____. Being diagnosed as amusic can (6) _____.

**C.** Check your answers for the comprehension questions in the Answer Key on page 247. Then calculate your score and record it in the progress chart on page 246.

_____ (my number correct) ÷ 13 x 100 = _____ %

# > READING 2

## Before You Read

**A.** Read the words and their definitions. You will see these words in the reading.

> **moth:** an insect similar to a butterfly, that usually flies at night, especially toward lights
> **butterfly:** an insect with large and usually colored wings
> **caterpillar:** a small creature with a long rounded body and many legs that develops into a butterfly or moth

**B.** Read the question. Then scan "The Language of Pheromones" to find the answers.

What are pheromones and what are two of their purposes?

_____

## Read

**A.** Read "The Language of Pheromones." Time yourself. Write down your start and end times and your total reading time. Then calculate your reading speed (words per minute) and write it in the progress chart on page 246.

**Start:** _____     **End:** _____     **Total time:** _____ (in seconds)

**Reading speed:**
550 words ÷ _____ (total time in seconds) x 60 = _____ words per minute

# The Language of Pheromones

1   Pheromones are chemicals that animals, including insects, produce. Plants also produce pheromones. Studies show that flowers use pheromones to attract bees. Pheromones play
5   a very important role in the natural world. For many creatures, life would not be possible without pheromones.

Moths are one insect that could not survive without pheromones. Moths have poor
10  eyesight, and most species cannot use sound to communicate. Instead, they communicate through pheromones. Female moths, for example, release pheromones from their legs and wings. A male moth can identify female
15  moth pheromones from as many as five miles away. And because the pheromones don't wear off for several hours, male moths have enough time to find the females and breed.

Ants have different pheromones for different
20  purposes. Like moths, ants use pheromones to find each other. They also use pheromones to find food. When an ant finds food, it takes a piece and returns to the nest. Along the way, it releases a trail of pheromones. Other ants
25  follow the trail to find the food. If something blocks the trail, the ants look for a new way to reach the food. When they find the shortest way, they produce a new trail of pheromones. In this way, pheromones help ants adapt to
30  changes in their environment.

When an ant is hurt or threatened, it produces an "alarm" pheromone. Other ants identify the alarm pheromone and immediately come to help. The more serious the threat, the
35  more alarm pheromones the ant produces. In this way, ants can quickly organize to fight insects hundreds of times their size.

Some species of ants use "trick" pheromones to stir up trouble and confuse their enemies.

40  Fire ants, for example, produce pheromones near the nests of other ants. Those ants become confused and begin to fight each other instead of attacking the fire ants.

Other insects use trick pheromones to
45  imitate another species. In some cases, this protects them from becoming the next course in another insect's meal. An interesting example is the Large Blue butterfly. During its caterpillar stage, this unusual insect releases
50  a pheromone similar to that of an ant. If ants find a Large Blue caterpillar in the forest, they carry it home. There, instead of eating it, they care for it—like a family member. The ants do not suspect that anything is wrong, even when
55  the caterpillar starts to eat their young! The caterpillar doesn't leave the nest until it has safely turned into a butterfly.

Yet another insect-like creature uses trick pheromones to attract its next meal. The bolas
60  spider, a species common in South America and Africa, releases a pheromone similar to that produced by a female moth. The spider then waits for a male moth to arrive. Instead of finding a female, the unsuspecting moth
65  becomes a tasty meal for the spider.

Because of examples like these, many biologists now believe that pheromones are the true language of spiders and insects. But pheromones are also important to plants
70  and other animals. Their significance in the natural world is undeniable. Some scientists even believe that humans, like other living creatures, use pheromones to attract members of the opposite sex. If that turns
75  out to be true, it might be more accurate to talk about "Love at first smell" than "Love at first sight!"

**B.** Read "The Language of Pheromones" again, a little faster this time. Write your start and end times and your total reading time. Then calculate your reading speed (words per minute) and write it in the progress chart on page 246.

**Start:** _____ **End:** _____ **Total time:** _____ (in seconds)

**Reading speed:**
550 words ÷ _____ (total time in seconds) x 60 = _____ words per minute

## Comprehension Check

**A.** Read the statements about the reading. Write *T* (true) or *F* (false).

_____ **1.** Bees use pheromones to attract flowers.

_____ **2.** Insects use pheromones to communicate.

_____ **3.** When a female moth releases pheromones, the pheromones stay in the air for only a few minutes.

_____ **4.** Without pheromones, some moths would not be able to breed.

_____ **5.** Ants release different pheromones in different situations.

_____ **6.** Fire ants release pheromones that confuse other ants.

_____ **7.** The Large Blue caterpillar has a unique way of protecting itself.

_____ **8.** The bolas spider uses pheromones to attract female moths.

_____ **9.** Many animals release pheromones, but humans do not.

**B.** Complete the chart with the names of the creatures mentioned in the reading. Some creatures will appear in more than one place in the chart.

| Insects | Function of pheromones |
|---|---|
| | to attract members of the opposite sex |
| | to tell others where to find food |
| | to warn others of danger |
| | to confuse its enemies |
| | to protect itself from being eaten |
| | to get another species to take care of it |
| | to get food |

**C.** Check your answers for the comprehension questions in the Answer Key on page 247. Then calculate your score and write it in the progress chart on page 246.

_____ (my number correct) ÷ 16 x 100 = _____ %

# Getting Away from It All

## > THINK BEFORE YOU READ

**A.** Work with a partner. Look at the pictures. Ask and answer the questions. If you don't know a word in English, ask your partner or look in your dictionary. Then write your new words on page 233.

1. What are the places in the postcards? What do you know about them?

2. Which of the three would you most like to visit? Why? Which wouldn't you want to visit? Why?

**B.** Work with a partner. Ask and answer the questions.

1. Do you enjoy traveling? Why or why not?

2. What is the most interesting place you've ever visited? What was interesting about it?

3. Which country or city would you most like to visit in the future? Why?

# Trends in Tourism

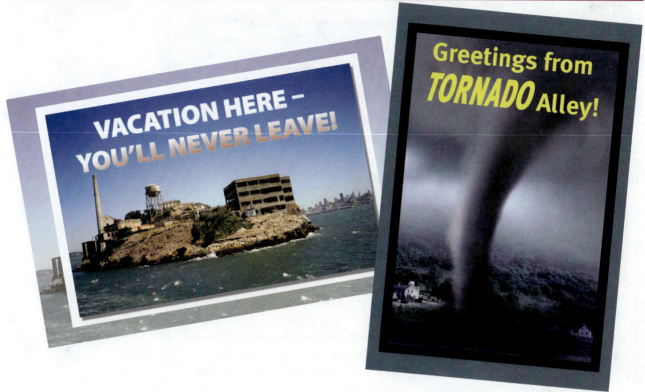

VACATION HERE – YOU'LL NEVER LEAVE!

Greetings from **TORNADO** Alley!

 **PREPARE TO READ**

**A.** Look at the words and phrases in the list. Write the number(s) next to each word to show what you know. You may be able to write more than one number next to some of the words. You will study all of these words in this chapter.

**1.** I can use the word in a sentence.

**2.** I know <u>one meaning</u> of the word.

**3.** I know <u>more than one meaning</u> of the word.

**4.** I know how to pronounce the word.

**B.** Work with a partner. Look at the postcards. Ask and answer the questions. If you don't know a word in English, ask your partner or look in your dictionary. Then write your new words on page 233.

**1.** What do the postcards show?

**2.** Why would either of these be a tourist attraction? Could you imagine either as a vacation for yourself?

_____ be associated with
_____ destination
_____ engulf
_____ fee
_____ first hand
_____ flood
_____ foresight
_____ man-made
_____ subscribe
_____ tuck in
_____ violent

## Reading Skill: Identifying Purpose

As you read, you should always consider the writer's purpose. In other words, why did the writer write the text? To understand the writer's purpose, you also need to think about the writer's audience. In other words, for whom was the text written? Look at the examples in the chart.

| Purpose | Audience | Possible text types |
|---|---|---|
| to convince the reader to buy something | the general public | an advertisement for a product or service |
| | people who like to read | a Web site that sells books |
| to entertain | the general public | comic strips in the newspaper |
| | people who like to travel or read about traveling | a travel diary |
| to inform | the general public | a newspaper article about a scientific discovery |
| | people who love movies | a Web site with movie reviews |
| to teach the reader how to do something | someone who just bought a computer | a computer instruction manual |
| | home cooks | a recipe |

Often a writer will have more than one purpose, and more than one audience. However, it is usually possible to identify the writer's main purpose and audience.

**C.** Skim the Web page "Trends in Tourism" on the next page. Then read the questions and check (✓) the correct answer.

   **1.** Who is the main audience? In other words, who would be most interested in reading this Web page?

   _____ **a.** people who like to visit unusual places

   _____ **b.** tourists with a lot of money

   _____ **c.** travel agents

   **2.** What is the main purpose of this Web page?

   _____ **a.** to convince the reader to buy something

   _____ **b.** to entertain

   _____ **c.** to inform

   _____ **d.** to teach the reader how to do something

Read the Web page "Trends in Tourism." Check your answers from Exercise C.

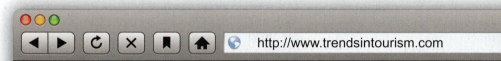

# TRENDS IN TOURISM

1     As travel professionals, you know that tourism has become a highly competitive business. How can you stay ahead of the competition? You need knowledge and

5  **foresight**. That is where we at Trends in Tourism can help.

    Trends in Tourism helps travel professionals get to the top and stay there. How? Our highly skilled researchers identify

10  the latest trends in tourism. They then make predictions about future growth areas and opportunities. For a small **fee**, we will share that valuable information with you. Here are just a few examples of the trends that our

15  researchers have identified.

## STORM CHASING

    The 1996 movie *Twister*, about tornado-chasing scientists, was an enormous success. After the movie came out, there

20  was a sudden increase in travel to places where **violent** storms are common. These storm-chasing tourists do not hesitate to pay thousands of dollars to experience a violent storm **first hand**.

25  ***Opportunities:*** Right now, there are only a few tour operators in the storm-chasing market. Most are located in the United States. Look for opportunities in other extreme weather **destinations** such as Australia and

30  Southeast Asia. The time is right to get in on this trend. A word of caution, however: There **are** real dangers **associated with** storm chasing. You should learn about the legal risks before jumping into this market.

35  ## DARK TOURISM

    Dark tourism is another growing trend. Dark tourists travel to the scene of both natural and **man-made** disasters. For example, dark tourists might travel to a

40  place like New Orleans, which was nearly destroyed by **flooding** during Hurricane Katrina. Or they might travel to the scene of a man-made disaster such as the Chernobyl nuclear power plant[1] in Russia.

45  They visit former prisons such as Alcatraz in San Francisco Bay. They tour "haunted"[2] houses or castles, such as Glamis Castle in Scotland. They visit the scenes of violent crimes on tours such as the Jack the Ripper[3]

50  walking tour of London. They wait in line for hours to enter attractions such as the London Dungeon.[4] Apparently, people will pay good money to be **engulfed** in scenes of violence, suffering, and death.

55  ***Opportunities:*** The number of dark tourists has grown significantly over the past few years. While some might find this trend disturbing, it will likely continue.

*(continued on next page)*

---

[1] **nuclear power plant:** a place where nuclear energy is used to produce electricity

[2] **haunted:** a place where the spirits of dead people are believed to live

[3] **Jack the Ripper:** a mass murderer in late nineteenth century London who was never caught

[4] **dungeon:** a dark prison, usually below the surface of the earth

## CULINARY TOURISM

60     Fewer people are eating and cooking at home. At the same time, culinary tourism is on the rise. People who never turn on the oven in their own homes are now traveling to distant lands to learn how to cook the
65 local food. Popular destinations include Italy, Thailand, and France. Culinary tourists happily pay thousands of dollars for the privilege of sweating over a hot stove and then **tucking in** to their own creations.

70 **Opportunities:** We expect that culinary tourism will become more widespread. Look for growth in travel to destinations such as Vietnam, West Africa, and the Middle East.

## EXTREME TOURISM

75     Extreme tourists risk their lives in exchange for an unforgettable adventure.

    Perhaps the most famous extreme tourist is Hungarian billionaire Charles Simonyi. For $25 million, Simonyi became the world's first
80 space tourist. He visited the International Space Station for the first time in 2007 and then again in 2009, at a cost of $35 million. Mountain climbing tours to destinations such as Mount Everest are another example
85 of extreme tourism. Clients on such tours pay tens of thousands of dollars for the experience of a lifetime.

**Opportunities:** Interest in extreme tourism remains high. There is a lot of room
90 for growth in this market. However, we advise caution, as there are legal risks associated with such extreme tours.

    Do you want to learn more about the latest trends in tourism? Click here to **subscribe** to
95 the Trends in Tourism e-newsletter.

## Vocabulary Check

**A.** Complete the paragraph with the boldfaced words from the reading. Use the correct form of the word.

    I almost never travel, but I love the idea of travel and everything that

(1)_____ it. I (2)_____ to

several travel magazines and love to be (3)_____

in the pictures and stories of those who spend their lives traveling

to exotic (4)_____. The subscription

(5)_____ for travel magazines are high, but the cost

is significantly lower than the expense of actually traveling. Maybe you'll

find me a little strange, but as much as I love to read about other peoples'

travel experiences, I have almost no desire to experience travel

(6)_____. I prefer to travel in my imagination, in the comfort

of my own home.

**B.** Read the statements about the reading. Write *T* (true) or *F* (false). Then correct the false statements to make them true. The boldfaced words are the target words.

_____T_____ **1.** A hurricane is an example of a **violent** storm.

_____F_____ **2.** Your house is built by the side of a river. You do not have to worry about **floods**.

_____F_____ **3.** Tornadoes and snowstorms are **man-made** events.

_____ **4.** If someone tells you to "**Tuck in**," they want you to start eating.

_____ **5.** Businesspeople with **foresight** are usually not surprised by changes in market trends.

## ▶ READ AGAIN

Read the "Trends in Tourism" Web page again and complete the comprehension exercises. As you work, keep the reading goal in mind.

> 📖 **READING GOAL:** To understand some unusual trends in tourism

## Comprehension Check

**A.** Without looking back at the Web site article, complete as many of the sentences as you can. Some sentences need more than one word. If you can't remember, leave that sentence blank.

**1.** Tourism is a highly _____competitive_____ industry.

**2.** Trips to places where both natural and man-made disasters have occurred are examples of _____Dark_____ tourism.

**3.** According to the information on the Web site, "dark tourists" enjoy being engulfed in _____scenens_____.  ⟨om⟩

**4.** There are a lot of opportunities for storm-chasing tours in _____Australia_____ ⟨ria⟩

**5.** Although it is possible to make a lot of money in _____storm_____ and _____ tourism, tour operators need to be cautious. There are serious risks associated with both of these types of tourism.

*(continued on next page)*

6. Culinary tourists learn _how to cook the local food_.

7. The Web site predicts that culinary tours will soon be available to
   destinations in ___Vienna___, ___West Africa___, and
   ___Middle East___.

8. Extreme tourist Charles Simonyi has paid ___$60 million___ so far for
   two trips to ___International Space Station___.

**B.** Scan the Web site to check your answers and complete Exercise A.

**C.** Read the trip descriptions. Which type of tourist would enjoy the trip?
Write the tourist type next to the correct trip description.

**Trip Description**                              **Type of Tourist**

1. a bicycle tour of the wine-growing regions     ___Culinary tourism___
   of France

2. a rafting trip down the Amazon River in Brazil ___Extreme___

3. a visit to the ancient city of Pompeii,        ___Dark___
   destroyed by a volcanic eruption in
   the year 79 C.E.

4. a twenty-six-day tour of active volcanoes      ___Storm chasing___
   around the world

**D.** First answer the questions in your notebook. Then discuss your answers
with a classmate.

1. Why do you think dark tourism is popular? Do you think there is anything
   wrong with dark tourism? Explain your answer.

2. Why do you think the Web site owners believe that culinary tourism is
   likely to grow and spread to more destinations?

3. What type of personality do you think most extreme tourists have? Do
   you know anyone who is an extreme tourist? What is he/she like?

4. Of the four types of tourism described on the Web page, which is the
   strangest, in your opinion? Explain.

# ▶ DISCUSS

First complete the checklist about yourself. Then work in groups.
Compare your answers.

When you travel, how important are the following things to you? Rank them.

| absolutely necessary | very important | somewhat important | not important |
|:---:|:---:|:---:|:---:|
| 1 | 2 | 3 | 4 |

_____ **a.** being able to speak the language

_____ **b.** good food

_____ **c.** warm weather

_____ **d.** good service

_____ **e.** good shopping

_____ **f.** excitement

_____ **g.** interesting history

_____ **h.** learning something new

_____ **i.** lots of attractions

_____ **j.** luxurious accommodations (hotels)

_____ **k.** meeting new people

_____ **l.** natural beauty

_____ **m.** nightlife

_____ **n.** relaxation

_____ **o.** visiting somewhere you've never been before

# Just Back: High Tide in La Serenissima

## > PREPARE TO READ

**A.** Look at the words in the list. Write the number(s) next to each word to show what you know. You may be able to write more than one number next to some of the words. You will study all of these words in this chapter.

1. I can use the word in a sentence.

2. I know <u>one meaning</u> of the word.

3. I know <u>more than one meaning</u> of the word.

4. I know how to pronounce the word.

**B.** Work with a partner. Look at the picture. Ask and answer the questions. If you don't know a word in English, ask your partner or look in your dictionary. Then write your new words on page 233.

1. What is the city in the photograph? Describe everything you see.

2. What is this city famous for? Why do people like to visit it?

3. Can you guess what serious problem this city is facing?

_____ antique

_____ captivating

_____ circuit

_____ crate

_____ dawn

_____ depth

_____ ferry

_____ invader

_____ retreat

_____ splash

_____ submerge

_____ tide

_____ wade

## Reading Skill: Understanding Descriptive Language

Good writers use words in the same way that artists use paint. That is, they use words to paint a picture for the reader. When describing a place, writers use words that help the reader "feel" the atmosphere of the place. For example, words such as *light*, *bright*, and *sunny* can create a warm, cheerful atmosphere. Words such as *midnight*, *shadows*, and *moon* can create a romantic or scary atmosphere. When you read a description, pay attention to how the descriptive words make you feel.

**C.** Skim the magazine article "Just Back: High Tide in La Serenissima" on the next page. Then read the questions and circle the letter of the correct answer.

1. Who is the main audience for this article? In other words, who would be most interested in reading this article?
   a. tourists looking for a good hotel in Venice
   b. engineers trying to solve the problem of sinking cities
   c. people who enjoy reading about travel

   *writer / describe his experience*

2. The writer uses a lot of _____.
   a. words related to the cold
   b. words related to darkness
   c. words related to light
   d. words related to water

3. *La Serenissima* is the Italian name for the Republic of Venice. In English, *La Serenissima* means "the most serene (peaceful)." What does this choice of a title tell you about the writer's attitude towards Venice?
   a. It is positive.
   b. It is negative.
   c. It is neutral.

 **READ**

Read "Just Back: High Tide in La Serenissima." Check your answers from Exercise C, questions 2 and 3, by circling the words the writer uses to create an atmosphere.

# Just Back: High Tide in La Serenissima

1  Waking to the air raid siren[1] I slowly realized that this would be no ordinary **dawn** in Venice. From the third-floor window of our hotel a few yards from St Mark's Square, we
5  could see two canals. Beside them, people were **splashing** their way along the pavements.

We had read about the *acque alte*, the high **tides** that briefly **submerge** parts of Venice in winter, and thought we knew what to expect.
10  But we were wrong. Slowly at first, then faster, the canals began to rise. On this, our first day in the city, the waters of the lagoon,[2] due to a full moon and a strong southeasterly wind out in the Adriatic, would rise up to engulf Venice
15  as no **invader** had in a thousand years.

It was not yet eight, and leaning from our window we watched as the waters rose, first to ankle height, then to full calf height, and finally beyond the knee. We decided it was time
20  to dive downstairs for breakfast.

The water was there before us, flooding the ground floor to a **depth** of perhaps 18 inches, and rising. It would be another three hours until high tide. Soft sofas were propped up on
25  milk **crates**. **Antique** sideboards[3] were raised on chests. On the last dry stairs sat a selection of boots for guests' use. There was even a pair for me, with my very large size 46 feet. These Venetians knew the meaning of "be prepared."

30  The concierge,[4] Barbara, asked if we would like "eggs, perhaps a little pancetta,[5] a few mushrooms?" We **waded** into breakfast, and were offered advice by Barbara's impeccably[6] dressed colleague, Gigi. The courtyard was
35  deeply submerged and leaving the hotel would be inadvisable before the tide had receded[7]— in five hours. Ah, well. Best tuck in.

Twenty minutes, some fine food and several coffees later, the lights went out and, finally,
40  the power. Leaving Gigi and Barbara to raise the furniture yet another 18 inches, we **retreated** upstairs to our room, where Venetian foresight (and separate **circuits**) had left us power, light, and heat. Outside, gondolas
45  could not pass under bridges. On the Web, the sinking of Venice was once again news.

Later, we would literally wade through an afternoon's sightseeing in this **captivating** city, surfacing only to cross the Grand Canal
50  by *traghetto* (the traditional gondola **ferry**). Streets filled with flotsam.[8] Seagulls bobbed[9] on squares. On our return to the hotel, though, only the tidemarks betrayed[10] the highest *acqua alta* in forty years. Had it all been a
55  dream? How could your very first morning in Venice be anything else?

---

[1] **air raid siren:** a piece of equipment that makes a very loud sound to warn of emergencies such as a fire or flood

[2] **lagoon:** an area of the ocean that is not very deep, and separated from the open sea by rock, sand, or coral

[3] **sideboard:** a piece of furniture used for storing plates, cups, glasses, etc.

[4] **concierge:** someone in a hotel whose job it is to help guests with problems

[5] **pancetta:** Italian ham

[6] **impeccably:** completely perfect and impossible to criticize

[7] **recede:** to move back from an area it was covering

[8] **flotsam:** broken pieces of wood, plastic, etc., floating in the ocean

[9] **bob:** to bounce up and down

[10] **betray:** to reveal a secret

# Vocabulary Check

**A.** Write the letter of the correct definition next to the target word. Be careful. There are two extra definitions.

_____ 1. antique

_____ 2. tide

_____ 3. circuit

_____ 4. crate

_____ 5. invader

**a.** the complete circle that an electrical current travels through

**b.** a flood

**c.** a wooden or plastic box used for packing or storing things in

**d.** someone who is part of an army that enters a town or country by force to take control of it

**e.** old and often valuable

**f.** the regular rising and lowering of the level of the ocean

**g.** a small pool of water

**B.** Read each question and circle the letter of the correct answer. The boldfaced words are the target words.

1. What happens when someone **splashes** you?
   **a.** You get wet.   **b.** You get sick.   **c.** You get tired.

2. What is the **depth** of that swimming pool?
   **a.** 80 degrees F   **b.** six feet   **c.** $5,000

3. What is a **ferry**?
   **a.** a boat   **b.** someone who lives on an island   **c.** a taxicab

4. In a war, who **retreats**?
   **a.** the side that is losing   **b.** the most powerful side   **c.** the side with more soldiers

5. When you **wade** in water, what do you do?
   **a.** sink   **b.** swim   **c.** walk

6. What happens at **dawn**?
   **a.** It rains.   **b.** The sun comes up.   **c.** The moon appears.

7. Why are the streets **submerged**?
   **a.** It's been raining for ten days.   **b.** There's no money to fix them.   **c.** There is a lot of traffic.

8. How does a **captivating** city make you feel?
   **a.** accurate   **b.** fascinated   **c.** claustrophobic

## > READ AGAIN

Read "Just Back: High Tide in La Serenissima" again and complete the comprehension exercises. As you work, keep the reading goal in mind.

> 📖 **READING GOAL:** To understand the atmosphere that the writer creates

## Comprehension Check

**A.** Read the statements about the reading. Write *T* (true) or *F* (false). If it is not possible to tell, write *?*. Then correct the false statements to make them true.

_____ **1.** This was the writer's first visit to Venice.

_____ **2.** The Italian words *acque alte* refer to the periodic flooding that

occurs in Venice.

_____ **3.** Weather forecasters had not predicted any flooding on that day.

_____ **4.** The writer was staying in a nice hotel.

_____ **5.** This was the first time the hotel had been flooded.

_____ **6.** The writer was upset by the situation. *He enjoy it.*

_____ **7.** The hotel workers were upset by the situation.

_____ **8.** There was no electricity in the hotel.

_____ **9.** Because of the flooding, the writer could not do much

sightseeing.

_____ **10.** The flooding at the time of the writer's visit was worse

than usual.

**B.** Check (✓) the statements that the writer would probably agree with.

_____ **1.** Venetians have easy lives.

_____ **2.** Venice is unlike any other city in the world.

_____ **3.** Venice is an uncomfortable place to visit.

_____ **4.** Venetians are very adaptable.

_____ **5.** Venice is a magical place.

_____ **6.** You should not visit Venice in the wintertime.

_____ **7.** Venice is a depressing city.

**C.** Circle the letter of the correct answer to complete the sentence.

With his words, the writer makes readers feel as if they are _____.

**a.** floating in a warm bath

**b.** in an underwater dream

**c.** trapped and drowning

**D.** Discuss your answers from Exercises B and C with a classmate. Support your answers by referring to specific sentences in the article.

## > DISCUSS

Survey your classmates about their attitudes towards travel. How many classmates agree with each statement? Record the numbers in the chart.

| Statement | Number of classmates who agree |
|---|---|
| **1.** Traveling to new places is exciting. | |
| **2.** Traveling makes me anxious. | |
| **3.** It is important to read a lot about your destination and plan your trip carefully before you go. | |
| **4.** I don't like to plan too much; I prefer to be spontaneous. | |
| **5.** When traveling, I want to see all of the famous attractions. | |
| **6.** Traveling helps me to appreciate the place where I live. | |
| **7.** I am often sad to go home at the end of a trip. | |
| **8.** I like to travel alone. | |
| **9.** I like to travel with a group. | |
| **10.** I learn a lot about myself when I travel. | |

### Vocabulary Skill: Core Meanings

As you learned in Units 3 and 4, most definitions of a word are actually based on one core meaning of the word. If you understand what the core meaning is, then you will be able to understand the word when it is used in many different contexts.

Look up the words in a dictionary. Identify the similarities in the definitions and example sentences for each word. Then discuss the core meaning of each word with a partner.

| | Similarities of definitions and example sentences | Core meaning |
|---|---|---|
| 1. splash | | |
| 2. circuit | | |
| 3. betray | | |
| 4. recede | | |

# Learn the Vocabulary

## Strategy

### Using a Dictionary to Find the Core Meaning of Related Words

As you learned in the Vocabulary Strategies for Units 3 and 4, learning the core meaning of a word with multiple definitions will make it easier for you to understand the word when it is used in a variety of contexts. You can also look at nearby entries in the dictionary to see if there are any other words that share the core meaning. Look at the example for the target word *destination*.

EXAMPLE:

**des·ti·na·tion** /ˌdɛstəˈneɪʃən/ *n.* [C] the place that someone or something is going to: *Allow plenty of time to get to your destination.* | *Maui is a popular tourist destination.*

**des·tined** /ˈdɛstənd/ *adj.* **1** [not before noun] seeming certain to happen at some time in the future: [+ **for**] *Beautiful and young, Carmen seemed destined for stardom on Broadway.* | [**be destined to do sth**] *Miyazawa was destined to succeed Toshiki Kaifu as Prime Minister.* **2** (**be**) **destined for sth** to be traveling or taken to a particular place: *The new trade rules do not apply to exports destined for Europe.*

**des·ti·ny** /ˈdɛstəni/ *n. plural* **destinies** **1** [C usually singular] the things that will happen to someone in the future, especially those that cannot be changed or controlled; FATE (1): *Nancy wondered whether it was her destiny to live in England and marry Melvyn.* **2** [U] the power that some people believe decides what will happen to them in the future; FATE (2)

The highlighted words in the dictionary entries are repeated or are related in meaning to one another. Thus, you should notice that the words *destined* and *destiny* share a common meaning with *destination*:

*future (going to, fate) + place + travel (going to, tourist)*

↓

**Shared core meaning** = *place you go or travel to in the future*

**A.** Look at the dictionary page that contains the entry for the target word **antique**. Then answer the questions.

> **an·ti·quar·i·an** /ˌæntɪˈkwɛriən/ *adj.* [only before noun] an antiquarian store sells old valuable things such as books
>
> **an·ti·quat·ed** /ˈæntɪˌkweɪtɪd/ *adj.* old-fashioned and not suitable for modern needs or conditions; OUTDATED: *antiquated laws*
>
> **an·tique**¹ /ænˈtik/ *adj.* **1** antique furniture, jewelry etc. is old and often valuable: *an antique rosewood desk* **2** LITERARY connected with ancient times, especially ancient Rome or Greece
>
> **antique**² *n.* [C] a piece of furniture, jewelry etc. that was made a long time ago and is therefore valuable: *The palace is full of priceless antiques.* | *an antiques dealer*
>
> **an·tiq·ui·ty** /ænˈtɪkwəti/ *n. plural* **antiquities** **1** [U] ancient times: *The common household fork was nearly unknown in antiquity.* **2** [U] the fact or condition of being very old: *the antiquity of Chinese culture* **3** [C usually plural] a building or object

1. Which words are repeated or related in meaning in the entries of both the target word *antique* and the entries nearby?

   _____

2. Based on your answer to question 1, which of the words on the page share a core meaning with *antique*?

   _____

3. What is the shared core meaning of the words you wrote in question 2?

   _____

**B.** Work with a partner. Compare your answers from Exercise A.

**C.** Make cards for the words that were new to you when you started the unit. Include target words and words that you wrote on page 233. Look up the words in a dictionary; read all of the definitions and example sentences to determine the core meaning of the word. Also check the nearby entries for words that might be related. Write the core meaning of the word on the back of the card under the translation, definition, or drawing.

**D.** Go back to the vocabulary list at the beginning of each chapter. What did you learn about the target words? Add numbers to the lists.

**Vocabulary Practice 7,** see page 240

# Civilized Dining

## ▶ THINK BEFORE YOU READ

**A.** Work with a partner. Look at the pictures. Ask and answer the questions. If you don't know a word in English, ask your partner or look in your dictionary. Then write your new words on page 233.

**1.** Describe the details of what you see in the two pictures.

**2.** How long do you think people have been cooking their food?

**B.** Work with a partner. Ask and answer the questions.

**1.** Imagine the very first cooked meal. How did someone suddenly get the idea to cook food rather than eat it raw? Or was it an accident? Describe what might have happened, and what food might have been served.

**2.** How important is food to you? Rate the statements according to how strongly you agree or disagree with them. Then share your answers with your partner.

| strongly agree | agree | disagree | strongly disagree |
|:---:|:---:|:---:|:---:|
| 1 | 2 | 3 | 4 |

\_\_\_\_\_ **a.** I spend a lot of time every day thinking about what I'm going to eat.

\_\_\_\_\_ **b.** If I have time, I prefer to cook rather than eat out.

\_\_\_\_\_ **c.** I eat more when I am depressed or upset.

\_\_\_\_\_ **d.** I eat to live; I don't live to eat.

# A Blossom Lunch

## > PREPARE TO READ

**A.** Look at the words and phrases in the list. Write the number(s) next to each word to show what you know. You may be able to write more than one number next to some of the words. You will study all of these words in this chapter.

1. I can use the word in a sentence.

2. I know <u>one meaning</u> of the word.

3. I know <u>more than one meaning</u> of the word.

4. I know how to pronounce the word.

**B.** Work with a partner. Look at the picture and label it with the words or phrases from the list. Then ask and answer the questions on the next page. If you don't know a word or phrase in English, ask your partner or look in your dictionary. Then write your new words and phrases on page 233.

_____ approach

_____ coat

_____ enhance

_____ flame

_____ gather

_____ pityingly

_____ scent

_____ slide

_____ stay put

_____ stem

_____ stroke

_____ terrace

_____ thrill

---

a. basil          c. green beans     e. herbs     g. salt and pepper     h. stem
                                                     grinder
b. blossom     d. head of celery     f. sage                                i. zucchini

---

1. Which of the things in the picture on page 134 have you eaten? Which do you like?

2. Do you like to cook? What do you know how to cook?

3. Do you know anyone who is a good cook? Who?

4. How does someone become a good cook?

## Reading Skill: Making Inferences

Writers do not always explain everything directly in a text. Instead, some texts are like a puzzle that readers have to put together for themselves. The writer expects the readers to pay attention to the details in the reading, and make reasonable conclusions based on that information. Those conclusions are called *inferences*. When you make an inference, you should be able to identify the information in the text that supports your inference.

**C.** Preview "A Blossom Lunch." What can you infer about the writer? Circle the answer(s).

The writer likes _____.

**a.** city life

**b.** cooking

**c.** eating

**d.** meat

**e.** vegetables

**f.** simple, fresh food

## > READ

Read "A Blossom Lunch." Check your answers from Exercise C by underlining the parts of the text that support your inferences.

# A Blossom Lunch

1    On the piazza[1] sits Sergio's fruit and vegetable shop, so we look about for things to **enhance** our blossom-lunch menu. Sergio suggests a stir-fry of vegetables and herbs. He
5    pulls out a handful of sage leaves, each one long and soft as a rabbit's ear, whacks[2] the leaves and small **stems** from a head of celery, picks through a basket of skinny green beans, and adds some to our pile. He asks if we like

10   potatoes but doesn't wait for us to answer before digging into a box of yellow-skinned ones, still covered in dirt, each no bigger than a cherry.[3] *every thing close = small town*
     Four steps away up toward the church and
15   the city hall is a *gastronomia* (Italian grocery store) where we buy flour and sea salt and peanut oil for frying. I ask for eggs, and the man looks **pityingly** on me, and says all I need

*(continued on next page)*

---

[1] **piazza:** public square or market place, especially in Italy

[2] **whack:** to hit something hard

[3] **cherry:** small dark red round fruit with a long stem and a large seed

to do is stop at the henhouse just down the
20 hill from our place.

   I have never before **gathered** eggs from under a hen. Fernando has never before
25 seen a hen. We bend low into the henhouse where there are a dozen or so fat lady birds. I **approach** one and ask her if she has an egg or two. Nothing. I ask in Italian. Still nothing. I ask Fernando to pick her up, but he's already outside the henhouse telling me he really doesn't like eggs at all and he especially
30 doesn't like frittata.[4] Both lies. I start to move the hen, uncovering the place where two lovely brown eggs sit. I take them, one at a time, bend down and put them in my bag. I want two more. I move on to another hen and this
35 time find a single, paler brown-shelled beauty. I take it and leave with an unfamiliar **thrill**. This is my first full day in Tuscany, and I've robbed a henhouse before lunch.

   *their own kitchen*  Back home in the kitchen I beat the eggs
40 with a few grindings of sea salt, a few more of pepper, adding a tablespoon or so of white wine and a handful of Parmigiano[5] cheese. I twirl[6] my frying pan to **coat** it with a few drops of my oil, and let it warm over a quiet **flame**. I
45 drop in the blossoms whole, flatten them a bit so they **stay put**, and leave them for a minute or so while I tear a few basil leaves and give the eggs another **stroke** or two. I throw a few fennel seeds[7] into the pan to **scent** the oil,
50 where the blossoms are now beginning to take color on their bottom sides. Time to increase the heat and add the egg batter.[8] I perform the motions necessary to cook the frittata without disturbing the blossoms, coating them in the
55 eggs. Next, I run the little cake under a hot grill to form a gold skin on top before **sliding** it onto a plate, sprinkling torn basil on top.

   Fernando and I batter and fry the sage leaves and celery tops, eating them right away
60 while standing in front of the stove. We fry only a few of the blossoms and all of the tiny potatoes and green beans and carry them out to the **terrace** with the frittata.

---

[4] **frittata:** egg dish, similar to an omelet

[5] **Parmigiano cheese:** Italian cheese, also called Parmesan

[6] **twirl:** to turn around and around

[7] **fennel seeds:** seeds from a pale green plant, often used as a spice for food

[8] **batter:** mixture of eggs or other ingredients, before it is cooked

## Vocabulary Check

**A.** Complete the paragraph with the boldfaced words from the reading. Use the correct form of the word.

   First, wash the (1)_____ of the celery in cold water, and cut them into one-inch pieces. Then (2)_____ a large saucepan with oil, and heat it for one minute over a medium (3)_____. Add the vegetables to the pan and cook for one to two minutes, giving them a couple of (4)_____ with a wooden spoon. When they start to feel a little soft, (5)_____ them carefully onto a heated plate. Serve immediately with a sprinkling of salt and pepper.

**B.** Complete the sentences with the boldfaced words from "A Blossom Lunch." Use the correct form of the word.

1. I love the _____ of baking bread. It smells like home!

2. She looked at me _____ when I told her I had not eaten a home-cooked meal in years. I could tell that she felt sorry for me.

3. The children _____ flowers from the garden to put on the dining room table.

4. It's a beautiful evening. Why don't we eat outside on the _____?

5. The right amount of salt will _____ the flavor of the meat.

6. "Children, please _____ until everyone has finished eating. Then you can leave the table and go outside to play."

7. The first time I prepared an entire meal by myself was a(n) _____. I felt very excited and proud of myself.

8. When the waiter _____ our table, we told him we weren't ready to order yet.

## > READ AGAIN

Read "A Blossom Lunch" again and complete the comprehension exercises on the next page. As you work, keep the reading goal in mind.

> **READING GOAL:** To make reasonable inferences based on the information in the text

# Comprehension Check

**A.** Check (✓) the answers that you can infer from the text. Support your inferences with details from the text.

1. Where does the story take place?

    __✓____ in a small town

    _____ in a large city

    _____ in the United States

    Details:

    _____

2. Who is Fernando?

    __✓____ a chef

    _____ the owner of a grocery store

    __✓____ the writer's husband  *we talking together*

    Details:

    _____

3. Why does the man in the *gastronomia* feel pity for the woman?

    _____ because she can't afford to buy eggs

    _____ because she doesn't know how to cook the local food

    __✓____ because she is an outsider and doesn't understand the local customs

    Details:

    _____

**B.** Read the statements about the reading. Write *T* (true) or *F* (false). Support your answers with details from the text.

_____ F **1.** The writer was born and raised in Italy.

Details: _____

_____ T **2.** Fernando is used to living in the city.

Details: _____

_____ T **3.** The writer appreciates simple food.

Details: _____ She was simple _____

_____ T **4.** The writer has invited a group of people for lunch.

Details: _____

_____ **5.** Fernando does not know how to cook.

Details: _____

_____ F **6.** The writer is visiting friends in Tuscany.

Details: _____

_____ T **7.** The writer and her husband have just moved to Tuscany.

Details: _____ 39 _____

_____ F **8.** The writer writes cookbooks.

Details: _____

**C.** Work with a partner. Compare your answers from Exercises A and B. Did you make the same inferences? Did you use the same details to support your inferences? If your answers are different, decide who has the correct answer by reviewing the information in the text.

# DISCUSS

Survey your classmates. Find out who has had experience growing, raising, finding, or catching their own food. Try to find at least one classmate who has experienced each activity.

| Classmates' names | Activity | Did it? Yes = ✓ No = X | Ate it? Yes = ✓ No = X | How did it taste? (compared to supermarket food) |
|---|---|---|---|---|
| | gathered eggs from a hen | | | |
| | milked a cow, goat, sheep, camel, or other animal | | | |
| | raised farm animals such as chickens or pigs for their meat | | | |
| | hunted wild animals such as birds, deer, etc. | | | |
| | caught fish or shellfish (shrimp, lobster, etc.) | | | |
| | gathered wild nuts, berries, mushrooms, etc. | | | |
| | grown vegetables, herbs, fruits, etc. | | | |
| | kept a honey beehive | | | |

# The First Home-Cooked Meal

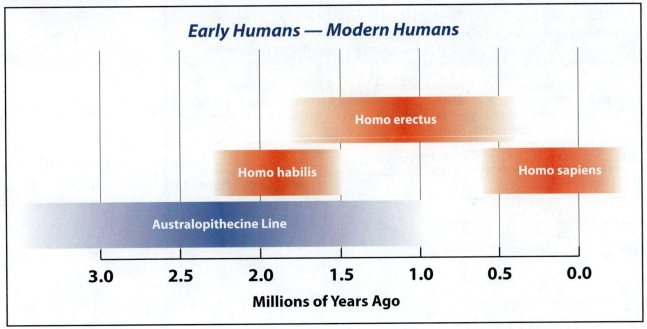

**Early Humans — Modern Humans**

Homo erectus

Homo habilis

Homo sapiens

Australopithecine Line

| 3.0 | 2.5 | 2.0 | 1.5 | 1.0 | 0.5 | 0.0 |

**Millions of Years Ago**

## ▶ PREPARE TO READ

**A.** Look at the words and phrases in the list. Write the number(s) next to each word to show what you know. You may be able to write more than one number next to some of the words. You will study all of these words in this chapter.

1. I can use the word in a sentence.

2. I know <u>one meaning</u> of the word.

3. I know <u>more than one meaning</u> of the word.

4. I know how to pronounce the word.

**B.** Work with a partner. Look at the timeline and ask and answer the questions. If you don't know a word in English, ask your partner or look in your dictionary. Then write your new words on page 233.

1. What is the name of the species that came before the *Homo* line?

2. According to the time line, which came first, *Homo erectus* or *Homo habilis*?

3. When did *Homo erectus* first appear?

4. What is the scientific name for modern humans (us!)?

_____ agriculture

_____ devote oneself to

_____ digest   消化する

_____ distinct   はっきりと異なる

_____ enable   ～を可能にする

_____ jaw   图 あご 動 小さく言う

_____ lead to

_____ mate   仲間

_____ nutritional

_____ profound   深い

_____ shift

*the movie has profound meaning*

## Reading Skill: Understanding the Relationships between Ideas—Cause and Effect

We often read to understand *why* something happens or is true. To understand *why*, we need to understand the relationship between *causes* and *effects*.

**EXAMPLE:**

*Cooked food is also softer than raw food, <u>so</u> the body uses less energy digesting it. <u>Thus,</u> cooking is vitally important to supporting the large human brain, which consumes a quarter of the body's energy.*

In the above sentences, the words *so* and *Thus* introduce effects. A graphic organizer can also help to understand the relationship between causes and effects. Often, the effect of one thing will become the cause of another. A graphic organizer can make these relationships clear.

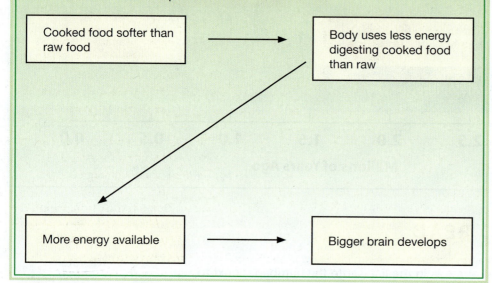

**C.** Read the first two paragraphs of the book review "The First Home-Cooked Meal" on the next page. Then check the diagram that matches the theory that Richard Wrangham presents in his new book.

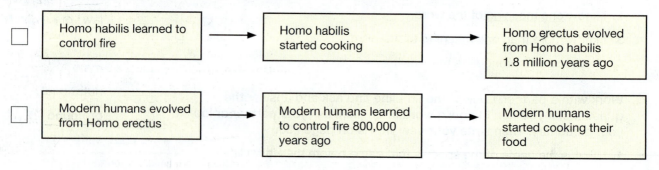

## READ

Read "The First Home-Cooked Meal." As you read, circle any words that
signal cause and effect relationships.

# The First Home-Cooked Meal

1 Have you ever wondered when early humans
first began cooking their food? Harvard
professor Richard Wrangham has some ideas.
His latest book, *Catching Fire: How Cooking*
5 *Made Us Human*, explores the role of cooking
in human evolution. In this fascinating and very
readable book, Wrangham challenges us to look
at one of the most common of human activities
in an entirely new way.

10 Scientists have found evidence of campfires
from 800,000 years ago. Archaeologists[1]
believe that humans first learned how to
control fire around that time. And because fire
is needed to cook, archaeologists reason that
15 the first home-cooked meal could not have
been served any earlier than 800,000 years
ago. But biological anthropologist[2] Wrangham
does not agree with those dates. He argues
that early humans started cooking long before
20 that. In fact, Wrangham believes that cooking
played an essential role in the evolution of our
ancestor, Homo erectus, 1.8 million years ago.
In other words, modern humans did not invent
cooking—cooking invented modern humans.

25 Most of us enjoy a hot, home-cooked meal,
but the idea that cooking is actually responsible
for our existence might be a bit hard to swallow.
Wrangham, however, makes a convincing
case for his unusual theory. And he does it in
30 language that even those without a scientific
background can understand.

Wrangham does not deny that the
archaeological evidence of cooking goes back
only 800,000 years. However, he uses the
35 evolutionary record, not the archaeological one,
to support his theory. In evolutionary biology, it
is widely accepted that modern humans' early
ancestor, Homo erectus, first appeared about
1.8 million years ago, when it evolved from an
40 earlier species, Homo habilis.

Homo habilis had larger stomachs, teeth,
and jaws than Homo erectus, but much smaller
brains. Why were their bodies like that?
Wrangham thinks it was because they ate raw
45 food. Those early human ancestors needed big
teeth and **jaws** to chew all that raw food. They
also needed large stomachs and intestines[3] to
**digest** it. And eating and digestion used up so
much energy that there wasn't enough energy
50 left to feed a large brain.

Wrangham argues that the **shift** from eating
raw to cooked food **enabled** the evolution
of the larger-brained Homo erectus. How?
Cooking makes more energy from food
55 available for the body to use. Cooked food is
also softer than raw food, so the body uses less
energy digesting what it takes in. Thus, cooking
is vitally important to supporting a large
brain, which consumes a quarter of the body's
60 energy. "It's hard to imagine the leap to Homo
erectus without cooking's **nutritional** benefits,"
writes Wrangham. "It's the development that
underpins[4] many other changes that have made
humans so **distinct** from other species."

65 Cooking also makes eating faster and easier.
Most of our primate relatives spend half the day

*(continued on next page)*

---

[1] **archaeologist:** a person who studies ancient societies by examining what remains of their buildings, tools, etc.

[2] **anthropologist:** a scientist who studies people, their societies, and cultures

[3] **intestines:** the long tube, consisting of two parts, that takes digested food from your stomach out of your
body

[4] **underpin:** to give strength or support to something and help it succeed

chewing tough raw food, such as the stems and roots of plants. Wrangham argues that because cooking freed early humans from all of that chewing, they could then **devote themselves to** more productive activities, such as the development of tools, **agriculture**, and social networks.

According to Wrangham, this newfound freedom had a **profound** effect on early human relationships. Males did not have to hunt as often, which meant they stayed put for longer periods of time. Staying at home and gathering around the fire became central to humanity. This **led to** paired **mating** and perhaps even traditional male-female household roles. Males entered into relationships to have someone to cook for them. This freed them up for socializing and other activities and enhanced their social position. Females benefited from the protection of the males they cooked for.

Many other scientists believe that eating meat, rather than cooking food, led to the evolution of Homo erectus. That might explain Homo erectus's large brains, but not their small jaws and teeth, argues Wrangham. Wrangham does not deny the significance of meat eating to human evolution. However, he believes that meat eating played a role in an earlier stage of evolution, from Australopithecines to Homo habilis—a species about the size of a chimpanzee, but with a larger brain.

Wrangham's book leaves at least one important question unanswered. Why isn't there any archaeological evidence of cooking until 800,000 years ago, at the earliest? Many scientists see this gap in the archaeological record as evidence against Wrangham's theory. They have a valid[5] point. Nevertheless, *Catching Fire: How Cooking Made Us Human* provides the reader with some very rich food for thought.

[5] **valid:** based on what is true or sensible, and therefore should be treated in a serious way

## Vocabulary Check

**A.** Read the definitions. Write the boldfaced word from the reading next to the correct definition.

1. _____ = make something possible

2. _____ = very significant and deep

3. _____ = not alike; different in nature or quality

4. _____ = be the cause of

5. _____ = put a lot of one's energy into something

**B.** Complete the sentences with the boldfaced words from "The First Home-Cooked Meal." Use the correct form of the word.

1. In the animal world, some creatures _____ just once for life. That is, they choose only one partner to bond with.

2. Animals with small teeth and _____ probably do not eat foods that are very hard and difficult to chew.

3. When you _____ the food you eat, the energy from the food becomes available for your body to use.

4. You can find out the _____ value of the food you buy by reading the information on the package.

5. After _____ was developed, people were able to eat a more nutritional diet consisting of vegetables, fruits, and grains, in addition to the meat they got from hunting.

6. At some point in history, there was a big change. There was a _____ from eating raw food to cooked food.

# > READ AGAIN

Read "The First Home-Cooked Meal" again and complete the comprehension exercises. As you work, keep the reading goal in mind.

> READING GOAL: To distinguish causes from effects in Wrangham's theory

## Comprehension Check

**A.** Answer the questions in your own words. Do not copy from the text.

1. Who is Richard Wrangham? Why is he famous?

2. What theory does Wrangham propose in his book?

3. What is the basic difference between Wrangham's theory and that of many other scientists?

4. The earliest evidence of fire and cooking that scientists have found dates back only 800,000 years. Does this evidence challenge or support Wrangham's theory? Explain.

**B.** Complete the diagram of the causes and effects in Wrangham's theory. Write each effect next to its cause.

**EFFECTS**
paired mating, male/female roles
food more nutritious and easier to digest
more energy for bigger brain
more time for productive activities such as tool making, agriculture, and social networking

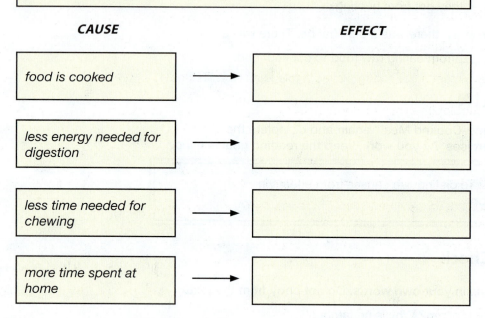

| CAUSE | | EFFECT |
|---|---|---|
| food is cooked | → | |
| less energy needed for digestion | → | |
| less time needed for chewing | → | |
| more time spent at home | → | |

**C.** Read the sentences taken from the reading. Circle the word(s) in the sentences that help you understand the relationship between causes and effects as they are explained in the book review. Then underline and label the cause and the effect in the sentence.

                    *cause*                                  *effect*

**1.** Cooked food is also softer than raw food, so the body uses less energy

    digesting it.

**2.** Wrangham argues that the shift from eating raw to cooked food enabled

    the evolution of the larger-brained Homo erectus.

**3.** Wrangham argues that because cooking freed early humans from all of that

    chewing, they could then devote themselves to more productive activities,

    such as the development of tools, agriculture, and social networks.

4. Males did not have to hunt as often, which meant they stayed put for longer periods of time.

5. Staying at home and gathering around the fire became central to humanity. This led to paired mating and perhaps even traditional male-female household roles.

6. Many other scientists believe that eating meat, rather than cooking food, led to the evolution of Homo erectus.

7. However, he believes that meat eating played a role in an earlier stage of evolution, from Australopithecines to Homo habilis.

## > DISCUSS

**Work in small groups. Ask and answer the questions.**

1. What is your opinion of Wrangham's theory? Do you think he could be right? Do you agree that cooking made us human? Why or why not?

2. The article makes a connection between the development of cooking and the development of traditional male/female household roles, but that connection is not fully explained in the article. For example, why was it the women who did the cooking? Come up with your own explanation for or against the connection.

# > VOCABULARY SKILL BUILDING

## Vocabulary Skill: Understanding Words That Signal Cause/Effect

There are many ways that writers express the relationship between causes and effects. Common signal words for cause and effect include *because, so, as a result, thus,* and *therefore.* Other words and grammar patterns also signal cause and effect. Look at the examples.

**EXAMPLE:**

(cause)
Wrangham argues that <u>the shift from eating raw to cooked food</u> **enabled**

(effect)
<u>the evolution of the larger-brained Homo erectus</u>.

(cause)
<u>Staying at home and gathering around the fire</u> became central to humanity, and

(effect)                                        (effect)
**led to** <u>paired mating</u> and perhaps even <u>traditional male-female household roles</u>.

**A.** Read the boldfaced sentences. The underlined words will help you identify the causes and effects. Then read the two sentences under each boldfaced sentence. Check (✓) the sentence that has the same meaning as the boldfaced sentence.

1. **The money from the government <u>enabled</u> the school to serve more nutritional meals.**

   _____ **a.** Because of the money from the government, the school was able to serve more nutritional meals.

   _____ **b.** The school was able to serve more nutritional meals, so the government gave the school money.

2. **The change in diet <u>led to</u> profound changes in early humans.**

   _____ **a.** The human diet changed. As a result, there were profound changes in early humans.

   _____ **b.** Because of profound changes in early humans, the human diet changed.

3. **Men did not have to hunt as often, <u>which meant</u> they spent more time gathered around the fire.**

   _____ **a.** Because they spent more time gathered around the fire, men did not have to hunt as often.

   _____ **b.** Not having to hunt as often enabled men to spend more time gathered around the fire.

4. **A lack of nutritious food in childhood <u>had a profound effect on</u> the boy's physical development, <u>leading to</u> his small size.**

   _____ **a.** He did not get enough nutritious food in childhood, and as a result, he did not grow as much as he should have.

   _____ **b.** Because of his small size, he probably didn't get enough nutritious food as a child.

5. **She quit her job <u>to</u> devote herself to her studies.**

   _____ **a.** She quit her job. As a result, she wanted to devote herself to her studies.

   _____ **b.** Quitting her job enabled her to devote herself to her studies.

6. **Poor nutrition <u>plays a significant role in</u> digestive problems.**

   _____ **a.** One of the causes of poor nutrition is digestive problems.

   _____ **b.** Poor nutrition can lead to digestive problems.

**B.** Complete the sentences with true information.

1. Learning English will **enable** me to _____.

2. The ability to speak English well can **lead to** _____.

3. Poor nutrition can **lead to** _____.

4. Having more money would **enable** me to _____.

# Learn the Vocabulary

## Strategy

### Using Word Cards: Changing Order, Grouping, and Spaced Learning

Using word cards offers several advantages that other vocabulary learning methods do not. Word cards make it easy to do the following:

**Avoid serial learning of words.**

Serial learning happens when you always study a group of words in the same order, such as when you study words in a list. Because you learn the words in order, it is difficult to remember just one of the words without remembering all of them. With word cards, it's easy to change the order and avoid serial learning. But make sure you change the order of your cards <u>every time</u> you study them.

**Change card groupings to match your learning goal.**

You can separate word cards into different groups for different purposes. For example, if you want to focus on the grammar of the words, group your word cards by part of speech (noun, verb, adjective, adverb). Later, if you want to focus on meaning, regroup the word cards by topic, such as food or travel.

**Space your learning.**

You can divide a large number of cards up into smaller, more manageable packets (fifty cards/packet maximum). Then you can space your review sessions depending on how well you know the words in the packet. Follow these steps:

1. Every day, make a new packet for words that you are having trouble remembering. Review that packet very frequently, for example three times/day.

2. When it is easy for you to remember a word, move that card to a packet of easier words. Review the easier packet only once a day.

3. Gradually lengthen the time between your review of the words in the easier packets. For example, review them once every other day, and then once every three days, and so on.

4. If you forget a word in the easier packet, move it back to the packet of words that you review more frequently (Step 1).

**A.** Make cards for the words that were new to you when you started the unit. Include target words and words that you wrote on page 233. Add them to your other vocabulary cards, and practice the strategies in the box. Remember: Change the order of your cards <u>every time</u> you review them.

**B.** Go back to the vocabulary list at the beginning of each chapter. What did you learn about the target words? Add numbers to the lists.

**Vocabulary Practice 8,** see page 241

**150    UNIT 8 ■ Learn the Vocabulary**

# Family Matters

## ▶ THINK BEFORE YOU READ

**A.** Work with a partner. Look at the picture. Ask and answer the questions. If you don't know a word in English, ask your partner or look in your dictionary. Then write your new words on page 233.

   **1.** Describe the people you see in the picture. How many generations are there? Who is related to whom? How are they related? Who are siblings? Parents and children? Husbands and wives?

   **2.** Do they look like a happy family to you? Why or why not?

**B.** Work with a partner. Ask and answer the questions.

   **1.** Who are you closest to in your family? Why are you close?

   **2.** Who do you resemble the most in your family, either in appearance, personality, or both?

   **3.** Do you have a large extended family? If so, how often do you see them? How important are they in your life?

   **4.** If you don't have a large family, do you wish you did? Why or why not?

# Widows

## > PREPARE TO READ

**A.** Look at the words and phrases in the list. Write the number(s) next to each word to show what you know. You may be able to write more than one number next to some of the words. You will study all of these words in this chapter.

1. I can use the word in a sentence.

2. I know <u>one meaning</u> of the word.

3. I know <u>more than one meaning</u> of the word.

4. I know how to pronounce the word.

**B.** Work with a partner. Look at the picture. Ask and answer the questions. If you don't know a word in English, ask your partner or look in your dictionary. Then write your new words on page 233.

1. Describe what you see in the picture. What are the women doing? Are they enjoying the game?

2. Think about some sisters you know. What kind of relationship do they have? Are they close? Competitive? Friendly? Supportive?

3. If you are a woman and have a sister, describe your relationship with her.

_____ be at it

_____ companionship

_____ dragging

_____ evaporate

_____ get used to

_____ insult

_____ make allowance for

_____ not give an inch

_____ object (of a game)

_____ opponent

_____ pastime

When you read a poem for the first time, it is often helpful to read it out loud. Poets indicate rhythm by where they break the lines in the poem and where they put punctuation. Sometimes these places are unexpected.

Try to read a poem the way that you might look at a painting. Although poets and artists have their own ideas about the meaning of their work, their ideas are always open to the reader or viewer's interpretation. Poets try to communicate a lot in very few words, so the words often have double or even triple meanings.

When you read a poem, appreciate the beauty of the language and form your own impression of its meaning. Your interpretation may even change over time as you read the poem at different stages in your life.

**C.** Preview the poem "Widows" on the next page by reading the title and the first stanza. Then complete the tasks.

1. Spite and Malice is the name of an actual card game. The goal of the game is to get rid of your cards so that the first player who has no cards is the winner. But the words *spite* and *malice* also have their own independent meanings. Look up *spite* and *malice* in your dictionary and copy the definitions or translations here.

   spite: _____

   malice: _____

2. What do you think the poem might be about? Don't worry about getting the "right" answer. Just write your first impressions and thoughts.

   _____

   _____

   _____

   _____

 **READ**

Read "Widows" and think about your answers from Exercise C.

# Widows
### BY LOUISE GLÜCK

1   My mother's playing cards with my aunt,
Spite and Malice, the family **pastime**, the game
my grandmother taught all her daughters.

   Midsummer: too hot to go out.
5   Today, my aunt's ahead; she's getting the good cards.
My mother's **dragging**, having trouble with her concentration.
She can't **get used to** her own bed this summer.
She had no trouble last summer,
getting used to the floor. She learned to sleep there
10  to be near my father.
He was dying; he got a special bed.

   My aunt does**n't give an inch**, doesn't **make
allowance for** my mother's weariness.[1]
It's how they were raised: you show respect by fighting.
15  To let up[2] **insults** the **opponent**.

   Each player has one pile to the left, five cards in the hand.
It's good to stay inside on days like this,
to stay where it's cool.
And this is better than other games, better than solitaire.[3]

20  My grandmother thought ahead; she prepared her daughters.
They have cards; they have each other.
They don't need any more **companionship**.

---

[1] **weariness:** extreme tiredness, especially because you've been doing something for a long time
[2] **let up:** to stop or become less serious
[3] **solitaire:** a game of cards for one player

All afternoon the game goes on but the sun doesn't move.
It just keeps beating down, turning the grass yellow.
25  That's how it must seem to my mother.
And then, suddenly, something is over.

My aunt's **been at it** longer; maybe that's why she's playing
    better.
Her cards **evaporate**: that's what you want, that's the **object**: in
30  the end,
the one who has nothing wins.

## Vocabulary Check

Read the definitions. Write the boldfaced words from the reading next to
the correct definitions.

1.  _____ = to adapt to something that was unfamiliar at first

2.  _____ = to say or do something that offends someone by
                        showing that you do not respect him or her

3.  _____ = final goal; the reason for playing

4.  _____ = the person you are playing against in a game or
                        competition

5.  _____ = to slowly disappear until nothing is left

6.  _____ = a close, friendly relationship with someone with
                        whom you feel very comfortable

7.  _____ = falling behind because of a lack of energy

8.  _____ = something you do in order to entertain yourself

9.  _____ = to persist in doing something, especially
                        something that is difficult or unpleasant in
                        some way

10. _____ = to refuse to negotiate or compromise with
                        someone

11. _____ = to consider someone else's situation and
                        change your own behavior to accommodate
                        him or her

## > READ AGAIN

Read "Widows" again and complete the comprehension exercises. As you work, keep the reading goal in mind.

> 📖 **READING GOAL:** To form and give reasons for your own interpretation of the poem

## Comprehension Check

**A.** Answer the questions. Remember that there are many ways of interpreting a poem, so don't worry about finding the "correct" answer. The important thing is to be able to explain your answers.

1. When the poet says . . . the game my grandmother taught all her daughters," what do you think she means by "game?"

_____

2. Why is the poet's mother having trouble concentrating on the game?

_____

3. How and why does the poet's aunt react to her sister's weariness?

_____

4. Why does the poet say that the game is better than solitaire?

_____

5. How did the poet's grandmother prepare her daughters, and what did she prepare them for?

_____

6. What does the poet mean when she says her aunt ". . . has been at it longer"? What does her aunt have more experience with?

_____

**B.** Discuss your answers from Exercise A with a partner. Explain your interpretation of the poem. Did you and your partner have a similar interpretation? If your interpretations were different, did you change your mind about any of your answers when you discussed them with your partner?

## > DISCUSS

**Work in small groups. Ask and answer the questions.**

1. Do you enjoy reading poetry in your native language? Why or why not?

2. Is it common in schools in your home country for children to memorize and recite poems? Is it a useful activity? Explain.

3. Have you ever memorized a poem, either in English or in your native language? If so, can you remember it?

## > VOCABULARY SKILL BUILDING

### Vocabulary Skill: Understanding Idioms

An *idiom* is a group of words with a special meaning. You cannot understand the meaning of an idiom just by understanding the meaning of each of the individual words.

It can be difficult to find idioms in your dictionary, so it is often easier to look them up online. Enter the idiom into the search box of your Internet browser. Make sure you put quotation marks around the idiom, like this: "not give an inch." After the idiom, type "definition."

**A.** Look up the meanings of the idioms online and write the definitions on a separate sheet of paper. (The idioms are from this and previous units.)

1. not give an inch

2. make allowance for

3. let up

4. give (someone) an edge

5. catch up on (something)

**B.** Complete the sentences with the idioms from Exercise A. Use the correct form of the verb in the idiom.

1. She could speak Spanish. That _____ over the other candidates for the job who couldn't speak any Spanish at all.

2. You need to _____ the fact that he has a serious disability. He has the capacity to do as well as or even better than his colleagues, but you need to give him extra time.

3. I did my best to convince the teacher to give me more time for my project, but she would _____.

4. We hadn't seen each other in years. We had a lot to _____. We stayed up all night talking.

5. The competition will be intense in the race tomorrow. If you _____ for even one minute, someone will pass you.

# Lost and Found

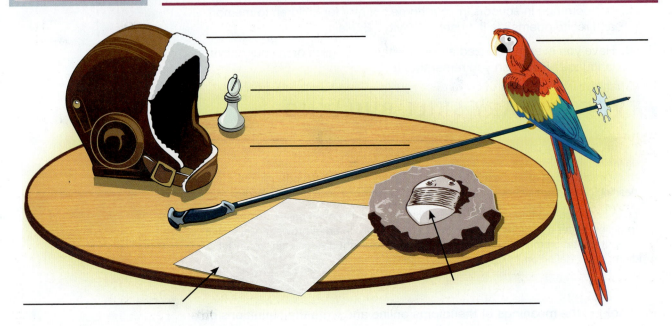

## ▶ PREPARE TO READ

**A.** Look at the words and phrases in the list. Write the number(s) next to each word to show what you know. You may be able to write more than one number next to some of the words. You will study all of these words in this chapter.

1. I can use the word in a sentence.

2. I know <u>one meaning</u> of the word.

3. I know <u>more than one meaning</u> of the word.

4. I know how to pronounce the word.

**B.** Work with a partner. Look at the picture. Ask and answer the questions. If you don't know a word in English, ask your partner or look in your dictionary. Then write your new words on page 233.

1. You are going to read the first chapter of a novel about a reality show called *Lost and Found*. In this reality show, the contestants have to find the items in the pictures. Find the words in the first paragraph of the reading on the next page and write the names of the objects next to the pictures above.

2. Do you know what a scavenger hunt is? If not, ask a classmate or look it up in your dictionary.

_____ chip

_____ decipher

_____ eliminate

_____ fragile

_____ freak out

_____ overflow

_____ provision

_____ qualify

_____ reunite

_____ rigid

_____ segment

_____ trail behind

_____ unison

In the first chapter of a novel, a writer often introduces the main characters and the conflict(s) that will be resolved in the novel. The writer usually gives readers enough information so that they are interested in the characters and the story without giving away too much information. At the end of the chapter, the writer hopes that readers will be trying to predict what will happen next. If the readers are making predictions, they are probably engaged and will want to continue reading.

**C.** Scan the first chapter of a novel called *Lost and Found*. As you scan, underline the names of the characters.

 **READ**

Read the excerpt from *Lost and Found*. Of the names that you underlined when you did Exercise C, predict which two are the main characters in the novel. Circle them.

## ✎ Excerpt from *Lost and Found* ✐
### by Carolyn Parkhurst

1   By the sixth leg[1] of the game, we have accumulated the following objects: a ski pole, a bishop from a crystal chess set, a sheet of rice paper, a trilobite fossil, an aviator's helmet, and a live parrot.
    Our backpacks are **overflowing**. I drop the chess piece into a sock to keep
5   it from bumping against anything and **chipping**. I fold the rice paper into a guidebook. The helmet I put on my head.
    I hand the ski pole to Cassie. "Ready?" I ask, picking up the parrot's cage.
    "Like I have a choice," she says. Our cameraman, Brendan, grins. I know he thinks Cassie makes great footage.[2]
10   "OK, then," I say. "We're off."
    We leave our hotel room and walk down the hall, Brendan walking backward so he can film us; our sound guy **trails behind**. In the elevator, the parrot squawks.[3]
    "We should give this guy a name," I say to Cassie, holding up the cage.
15   "How about Drumstick?[4]" Brendan smiles behind his camera. He's loving this.
    "How about Milton?" I try. "He looks kind of like a Milton, don't you think?"
    "Fine, Mom," Cassie says, staring up at the lighted numbers. "Whatever."
    The doors open onto the lobby, and we step out. There are only seven teams left, and the other six are already here. The only seat left is next to Betsy and
20   Jason, the former high school sweethearts who have recently been **reunited** after twenty years apart. They seem to be having a fight; they're sitting beside each

*(continued on next page)*

---

[1] **leg of the game:** part of the game

[2] **footage:** part of a film

[3] **squawk:** to make a sharp angry sound (usually used for animals)

[4] **drumstick:** the name we give to the leg of a chicken or other bird when we eat it

other, but his arms are crossed, and their commitment to not looking at each other is very strong. I sit down next to Betsy, balancing Milton's cage on my lap.

25 "Morning," Betsy says, turning her whole body away from Jason. "Did your parrot keep you guys up all night, too?"

"No, we just put a towel over his cage, and he went right to sleep."

"Lucky," she says. "We tried that, but it didn't work. Ours was **freaking out** all night. I think we got a defective one."

"A defective parrot. I wonder if there's any **provision** for that in the rules."

30 "Yeah, maybe they'll let us trade it in. Otherwise, I'm gonna put it in Barbara's room tonight."

There are two camera people filming this conversation.

One of the producers,[5] Eli, steps to the middle of the room and claps his hands. "Quiet, everyone," he says. "Here comes Barbara."

35 The front door opens and the host of the show, Barbara Fox, walks in with an entourage[6] of makeup artists and even more camera people. She's small and **rigid** with short blond hair and a frosty smile. She's one of the most unnatural people I've ever met. I don't know how she got a job on TV. We're not allowed to approach her.

40 "Good morning, everybody," she says, turning her glassy smile to each of us in turn.

"Good morning," we say like schoolchildren, except less in **unison**.

Her crew sets her up in front of a large mural[7] of the Sphinx.[8] Filming begins. "I'm Barbara Fox," she says, "and I'm standing in a hotel in Aswan, the

45 southernmost city in Egypt, with the seven remaining teams in a scavenger hunt that will cover all the corners of the earth. Ladies and gentlemen, this . . ." —dramatic pause here, and a strange little roll of her head— "is *Lost and Found*."

The rules of the game are simple. For each **segment**, they fly us to a new city where we follow a trail of clues through various exotic (and, presumably,

50 photogenic[9]) locations until we're able to **decipher** what item we're looking for. Then each team sets out to find an object that **qualifies**. Every item we find has to remain with us until the end of the game, so the items are usually heavy or **fragile** or unwieldy;[10] it adds to the drama. Losing or breaking a found object is grounds for disqualification. The last team to find the required object and make it

55 to the finish line gets sent home.

At the end of each leg, Barbara interviews the team that's been **eliminated**, and she asks the following question: "You've lost the game, but what have you found?"

I don't think there's much of a chance Cassie and I will win the game, but I don't really care. Secretly, this is the moment I'm looking forward to most, the

60 moment when Cassie and I stand before Barbara, and she asks me what I've found. Cassie and I will look at each other and smile; I'll reach out and touch her arm, or her hair, and she won't move away. I'll turn back to Barbara, and the cameras, and all the TV viewers of the world. I found my daughter, I'll say. I found my little girl.

---

[5] **producer:** the person in charge of a film; controls the budget

[6] **entourage:** a group of people who travel with an important person

[7] **mural:** a painting on a wall

[8] **Sphinx:** an ancient Egyptian statue of a lion with a human head, lying down

[9] **photogenic:** always looking attractive in photographs

[10] **unwieldy:** big, heavy, or difficult to carry or use

# Vocabulary Check

**A.** Circle the letter of the correct answer to complete each sentence. The boldfaced words are the target words.

1. If you **trail behind** a friend, your friend is _____.
   - **a.** slow
   - **b.** angry with you
   - **c.** ahead of you

2. When someone **freaks out**, he or she _____.
   - **a.** is calm
   - **b.** has a disability
   - **c.** loses control

3. If your backpack is **overflowing**, it is _____.
   - **a.** difficult to close
   - **b.** expensive
   - **c.** very wet

4. It is easy to _____ something that is **fragile**.
   - **a.** break
   - **b.** find
   - **c.** lose

5. If you **qualify** for a race, you _____.
   - **a.** are the best runner
   - **b.** can run in the race
   - **c.** choose the winner

6. When you **decipher** something, you _____.
   - **a.** don't understand it
   - **b.** destroy it
   - **c.** figure it out

7. He **chipped** his tooth when he _____.
   - **a.** fell down
   - **b.** found a good dentist
   - **c.** was brushing his teeth

8. If you want the job, one of the **provisions** is that you _____.
   - **a.** stop working
   - **b.** work weekends
   - **c.** will not be hired

**B.** Read the statements about the reading. Write *T* (true) or *F* (false). If it is not possible to tell, write *?*. Then correct the false statements to make them true. The boldfaced words are the target words.

_____ 1. The words *segment* and *excerpt* are similar in meaning.

_____ 2. A **rigid** person will not usually give an inch.

_____ 3. When two people sing in **unison**, they start singing on different notes.

_____ 4. If you follow the rules, you will be **eliminated** from the game.

_____ 5. When you **reunite** two people, you introduce them to each other for the first time.

## ▶ READ AGAIN

Read the excerpt from *Lost and Found* again and complete the comprehension exercises. As you work, keep the reading goal in mind.

📖 **READING GOAL:** To make predictions about what will happen in the novel

## Comprehension Check

**A.** Answer the questions.

1. Who is telling the story? _____

2. Where are the characters in the story? _____

3. What is the object of the reality show *Lost and Found*? How does someone win? How does someone get disqualified? Eliminated? _____

_____

_____

**B.** Read the sentences taken from the reading. What can you infer about the characters by reading the sentences? Circle the letter of the logical inference for each character. More than one answer is possible. The numbers in parentheses are the lines where you can find the sentences in the text.

**CASSIE**

"Like I have a choice." (8)

"How about Drumstick?" (15)

"Fine, Mom," Cassie says, staring up at the lighted numbers. "Whatever." (17)

I'll reach out and touch her arm, or her hair, and she (Cassie) won't move away. (61)

1. You can infer that _____.

   **a.** Cassie is excited about being on the reality show with her mother.

   **b.** Cassie has a sense of humor.

   **c.** Cassie and her mother are having problems in their relationship.

## CASSIE'S MOM (THE NARRATOR)

"We should give this guy a name," I say to Cassie, holding up the cage. (14)

I don't think there's much of a chance Cassie and I will win the game, but I don't really care. Secretly, this is the moment I'm looking forward to most, the moment when Cassie and I stand before Barbara, and she asks me what I've found. (58)

I found my daughter, I'll say. I found my little girl. (63)

2. You can infer that _____.

   a. Cassie's mom wants to have a better relationship with her daughter.

   b. Cassie's mom wants to lose the game.

   c. Cassie and her mom are close.

## BARBARA FOX

"Yeah, maybe they'll let us trade it in. Otherwise, I'm gonna put it in Barbara's room tonight." (30)

She's small and rigid with short blond hair and a frosty smile. She's one of the most unnatural people I've ever met. I don't know how she got a job on TV. We're not allowed to approach her. (36)

"Good morning, everybody," she says, turning her glassy smile to each of us in turn. (40)

"Good morning," we say like schoolchildren, except less in unison. (42)

3. You can infer that Barbara _____.

   a. thinks that she is a star

   b. is not well-liked by the contestants

   c. wants the contestants to like her

## BETSY AND JASON

They seem to be having a fight; they're sitting beside each other, but his arms are crossed, and their commitment to not looking at each other is very strong. I sit down next to Betsy, balancing Milton's cage on my lap. (21)

"Morning," Betsy says, turning her whole body away from Jason. "Did your parrot keep you guys up all night, too?" (24)

4. You can infer that Betsy and Jason _____.

   a. do not fight very often

   b. are going to win the game

   c. are having some problems in their relationship

**C.** Check (✓) the things that you think will happen in the rest of the novel. Add your own prediction(s) at the end. There are no correct or incorrect answers, but you should be able to explain your predictions.

_____ **1.** Cassie and her mother will win the game.

_____ **2.** Cassie and Barbara Fox will become friends.

_____ **3.** Cassie and her mother will become close.

_____ **4.** Betsy and Jason's parrot will die, and they will be disqualified.

_____ **5.** Betsy and Jason will win the game.

_____ **6.** Betsy and Jason will break up (end their relationship).

Other predictions? _____

**D.** Work with a partner. Discuss your answers from Exercises B and C.

## > DISCUSS

Work in small groups. Ask and answer the questions.

**1.** Why do you think reality shows are so popular these days?

**2.** Do you think that people find out important things about themselves when they participate in reality shows? What kinds of things? Explain.

**3.** Do you like to watch reality shows? If so, which ones do you watch?

**4.** If you had the chance, would you participate in a reality show? Why or why not?

# Learn the Vocabulary

## Strategy

### Using Word Cards: Adding Visual Images

Try using visual images to remember the meaning of words or idioms. When you add a visual image to a definition or translation, you are able to store and retrieve the word from your brain in two different ways: visually (with pictures) and verbally (in words). Using visual images can be particularly useful when learning idioms since they are often difficult or even impossible to translate.

**Adding visual images to word cards**

1. Form a picture of the word or idiom in your mind.

2. Draw a picture of the word or idiom on the back of your card, under the definition or translation.

   OR

3. Find a picture (in a magazine, newspaper, or on the Internet) and paste it onto your card.

NOTE: The picture does not need to be an exact representation of the meaning; it simply needs to be meaningful to you.

**A.** Find word cards for words from previous units that you are having difficulty remembering. Add visual images to those cards.

**B.** Make cards for the words that were new to you when you started the unit. Include target words and words that you wrote on page 233. Add visual images to the cards for words that are difficult for you.

**C.** Review all of your cards that have visual images on them with a classmate. See if your classmate can guess what word or idiom your visual images represent.

**D.** Go back to the vocabulary list at the beginning of each chapter. What did you learn about the target words? Add numbers to the lists.

**Vocabulary Practice 9,** see page 242

# FLUENCY PRACTICE 3

##  READING 1

### Before You Read

**A.** Read the words and their definitions. You will see these words in the reading.

> **journey:** a trip from one place to another, especially over a long distance
> **wandering:** walking slowly, without having a clear direction or purpose
> **servant:** someone who is paid to take care of someone else by cleaning that person's house, cooking food, etc.
> **cherry blossom:** a tree that produces cherry fruit and pink flowers in springtime
> **blossom:** to produce flowers

**B.** Preview "The Haiku Master" and answer the questions.

**1.** What is haiku?

_____

**2.** What is Basho famous for?

_____

**3.** Where was Basho born?

_____

**4.** When did he live?

_____

## Read

**A.** Read "The Haiku Master." Time yourself. Write your start and end times and your total reading time. Then calculate your reading speed (words per minute) and write it in the progress chart on page 246.

**Start:** _____  **End:** _____  **Total time:** _____ (in seconds)

**Reading speed:**
606 words ÷ _____ (total time in seconds) x 60 = _____ words per minute

### ✌ The Haiku Master ☙

1   In 1694, at the age of forty-nine, a remarkable Japanese poet died. Before his death, Matsuo Kinsaku, better known as "Basho," wrote this final poem:

_Fallen sick on a journey_
_my dream goes wandering_
5   _over a field of dried grass_

Basho's last poem, like much of his work, was a _haiku_—a traditional Japanese poetic form. Most haiku share certain characteristics. First, they are short: only three lines long. Second, they describe a profound moment in a few simple, yet vivid words. Third, they mention nature in some way. Haiku are often associated
10   with the changing of the seasons.

Basho was one of the greatest masters of haiku. He wrote over 1,000 of these small, surprising poems. His haiku reflect his life experiences.

Basho's life began in 1644 in Ueno, a small town in Iga Province. After the death of his father in 1656, Basho left home and became a servant. His master
15   was Todo Yoshitada, a wealthy young man. Todo and Basho quickly discovered that they both loved writing poetry. They became close companions. One of their favorite poetic subjects was an old cherry blossom tree in Todo's garden. Basho wrote many haiku about it, such as this one, from 1664:

_The old-lady cherry_
20   _is blossoming—in her old age_
_an event to remember_

Until 1666, Basho enjoyed a simple life devoted to work and poetry. Then Todo suddenly died. Basho lost his job and his best friend. Filled with sadness, he traveled to the capital of Edo (modern-day Tokyo) to start a new life. There, he
25   studied and wrote poetry. His poetry began to attract attention. Soon, Basho had his own school and many students. His life was comfortable again.

_(continued on next page)_

Inside, however, Basho felt empty. Although his friends liked the many shops and crowded streets of Edo, Basho could not get used to city life. He wanted a change. Looking for inspiration, he moved to a small, simple house outside of
30 Edo in the winter of 1680. In front of this simple house, he planted a banana tree, called a *basho* in Japanese. It became the subject of many haiku.

Because the poet loved his banana tree so much, his friends began calling him Basho. Then one cold winter day, a fire burned down his little house. For the third time in his life, Basho was without a home.
35 Feeling lost and without purpose, Basho set out to travel through the countryside of Japan. He planned to visit the twelve provinces between Edo and Kyoto, Japan's second largest city. Now forty years old, Basho knew the trip would be difficult and dangerous. He expected to die from illness or to be killed by violent criminals. But he traveled safely. Basho began to enjoy his long journey.
40 He met many people and made new friends. As he traveled, the topics of his haiku began to shift. He focused less on his feelings and more on nature. While on the road, Basho wrote some of his best haiku.

For the rest of his life, Basho traveled the Japanese countryside. He never stayed put for long. His travels took him east to the Pacific coast. He climbed the
45 mountains of Honshu in the north. He traveled west to the inland sea. His last journey was south to the city of Osaka, where he wrote his final poem. During his travels, he wrote many great books of poetry. Today, Basho's haiku inspire writers and readers from countries all over the world and enhance their appreciation for the natural world. His simple yet captivating poems help people see their lives
50 and the things around them in a new way.

**B.** Read "The Haiku Master" again, a little faster this time. Write your start and end times and your total reading time. Then calculate your reading speed (words per minute) and write it in the progress chart on page 246.

**Start:** _____  **End:** _____  **Total time:** _____ (in seconds)

**Reading speed:**
606 words ÷ _____ (total time in seconds) x 60 = _____ words per minute

## Comprehension Check

**A.** Scan "The Haiku Master" for the answers to the questions.

**1.** How many haiku did Basho write?

_____

**2.** Where was Basho born?

_____

**3.** When did Basho start working?

_____

**4.** Why did he leave his job?

_____

**5.** What was the city of Tokyo called during Basho's lifetime?

_____

**6.** What does _basho_ mean in Japanese?

_____

**7.** How did Basho get his name?

_____

**8.** How many times did Basho find himself without a home?

_____

**9.** How many provinces are there between Edo and Kyoto?

_____

**10.** In which city did Basho write his final poem?

_____

**B.** Read the summary of the important events in Basho's life. There is one mistake in each sentence, for a total of 14 mistakes. Find the mistakes and correct them.

The great Japanese poet, Matsuo Kinsaku, better known as "Basho," was born in 1644 in the large city of Ueno, Japan. When Basho was 12 years old, his father died, so he left home to study. He worked for a poor young man named Todo for ten years. Basho and Todo both loved to write poetry, but they were not close friends. When Todo died after a long illness, Basho lost his job and his home.

Basho then went to the capital city of Edo to work. His poems attracted attention, and he started to attend school. Basho was happy in Edo, but his friends were not, so he moved to the countryside. There he lived in a large house and planted a banana tree. He wrote many haiku about the tree, so his friends started to call him _Basho_, which means _blossom_.

One day, the house burned down, and for the second time in his life, Basho had nowhere to live. He then decided to travel to all twelve of the Japanese cities between Edo and Kyoto. For years, he traveled around Japan and wrote novels. He died when he was 40 years old in the city of Osaka.

**C.** Check your answers for the comprehension questions in the Answer Key on page 248. Then calculate your score and write it in the progress chart on page 246.

_____ (my number correct) ÷ 24 x 100 = _____ %

## > READING 2

### Before You Read

Preview "So You Want to Write Haiku?" and answer the questions.

**1.** What is the writer's purpose?

_____

**2.** What do you think you will learn from reading "So You Want to Write Haiku?" Write three questions that you think the reading will answer.

_____

_____

_____

### Read

**A.** Read "So You Want to Write Haiku?". Time yourself. Write your start and end times and your total reading time. Then calculate your reading speed (words per minute) and write it in the progress chart on page 246.

**Start:** _____    **End:** _____    **Total time:** _____ (in seconds)

**Reading speed:**
595 words ÷ _____ (total time in seconds) x 60 = _____ words per minute

## ⌘ So You Want to Write Haiku? ⌘

1    If you are interested in writing haiku, take a look at this famous example by Basho:

*The old pond*
*a frog jumps in*
*sound of water*
5              —Basho (translated by Robert Hass)

Notice how simple and direct the poem is. Other poets might go on and on about frogs singing, but Basho just describes the splash of a frog hitting the water. The poem clearly mentions nature. It also contrasts something—the quiet of the pond with the noise of the frog. Finally, it has a feeling of *sabi*, a Japanese word meaning something like "peaceful sadness." Basho's haiku creates a picture in your mind. You can easily imagine sitting alone by the pond, engulfed in the sounds of nature.

Haiku can be a lot of fun to write. In this simple, short poetic form, you can describe your environment, explain how you feel about something, or present a funny situation. To write your own haiku, just follow these steps.

**STEP 1:** First, decide what you want to write about. Traditional haiku focus on nature, but they can be about anything. It is best if you have first hand experience with the subject of your haiku. A lot of modern haiku discuss city life, work, or school. Take a look at these examples:

20    *Still in a meeting*
      *boss talks, nightfall approaches—*
      *dreams of the weekend*
                    —Sandra Duque

      *English class is here*
25    *my favorite time of day;*
      *chance for a nice nap*
                    —David Clayton

      You might want to write about something you love, something you hate, the things that thrill you or make you anxious, or anything else that you are thinking
30    about.

**STEP 2:** Decide on the form of your haiku. In Japanese, a haiku must have exactly seventeen *on*, or segments, of sound. To write haiku in English, many writers count each syllable as one segment of sound. The first line has five syllables. The second line has seven syllables, and the third line has five. Count
35    the syllables in the next example.

      *Summer has arrived*
      *see children running outside—*
      *fresh smell of cut grass*
                    —Jessica Andrea

40    **STEP 3:** The next step is the most challenging for many writers. You must include some kind of shift or contrast in your haiku. Look at the example haiku above. The haiku that begins *Still in a meeting* contrasts work with dreams of the weekend. *English class* contrasts something serious, a class, with a funny idea—taking a nap in school. *Summer has arrived* contrasts something that you see (children running)
45    with something that you smell (fresh cut grass). The contrast doesn't have to be big, but it needs to be there. Some writers use special punctuation, such as a dash (—) or semicolon (;) to show the contrast in their poem.

**STEP 4:** Include a season word, if possible. This word tells the reader what time of year it is in your poem. For example, if the haiku mentions "cherry blossoms,"
50    the reader knows it's spring. If the haiku mentions snow, the reader pictures winter. Depending on the topic you choose, you may want to eliminate this step.

**STEP 5:** Practice, practice, practice! The more haiku you write, the better you will get at it. It also helps to read a lot of haiku. Submerge yourself in haiku. Be sure to read a variety of types—traditional, contemporary, serious, sad, funny, and
55    so on.

**STEP 6:** Have fun with it! Don't worry if it is difficult at first. Just keep at it. With enough time and practice, you'll soon be able to write your own great haiku.

Read "So You Want to Write Haiku?" again, a little faster this time. Write your start and end times and your total reading time. Then calculate your reading speed (words per minute) and write it in the progress chart on page 246.

**Start:** _____     **End:** _____     **Total time:** _____ (in seconds)

**Reading speed:**
595 words ÷ _____ (total time in seconds) x 60 = _____ words per minute

## Comprehension Check

**A.** Which of the statements are true about most *traditional* haiku? Write *T* (true) next to them.

_____ **1.** They are usually about nature.

_____ **2.** They are about everyday life.

_____ **3.** There is some reference to the time of year.

_____ **4.** They can be long or short.

_____ **5.** They have three lines and 17 sound segments.

_____ **6.** They include a shift or contrast of some kind.

_____ **7.** They have a feeling of peaceful sadness.

**B.** Read the statements in Exercise A again. Write a *C* next to the statements that are true about *contemporary* haiku.

**C.** Write a summary of the six steps involved in writing a haiku. Use your own words. Keep your summary short and simple.

First, _____.

Second, _____.

Third, _____.

Fourth, _____.

Fifth, _____.

Finally, _____.

**D.** Check your answers for the comprehension questions in the Answer Key on page 248. Then calculate your score and record it in the progress chart on page 246.

_____ (my number correct) ÷ 19 x 100 = _____ %

## > THINK BEFORE YOU READ

**A.** Work with a partner. Look at the picture. Ask and answer the questions. If you don't know a word in English, ask your partner or look in your dictionary. Then write your new words on page 233.

   **1.** Who are the people in the picture? What is their relationship?

   **2.** What are they doing?

   **3.** What kind of company or business is it?

**B.** Work with a partner. Ask and answer the questions.

   **1.** What are some of the ways that companies market their products or services?

   **2.** In your opinion, what kinds of marketing are most effective? Least effective?

   **3.** What are the challenges for a company that decides to market its products in a foreign country? For example, imagine that an American automobile company wants to enter the automobile market in your home country. What might some of the challenges be?

# Branding and Product Placement

## ▶ PREPARE TO READ

**A.** Look at the words and phrases in the list. Write the number(s) next to each word to show what you know. You may be able to write more than one number next to some of the words. You will study all of these words in this chapter.

1. I can use the word in a sentence.

2. I know <u>one meaning</u> of the word.

3. I know <u>more than one meaning</u> of the word.

4. I know how to pronounce the word.

**B.** Work with a partner. Look at the picture. Ask and answer the questions. If you don't know a word in English, ask your partner or look in your dictionary. Then write your new words on page 233.

1. Where does the picture come from? An advertisement? A television show? A movie? Do you recognize the actor in the red jacket?

2. What brand name do you see in the picture? What kind of business is this brand name associated with? Do you think that the association with this movie helped their business?

3. What are your favorite brands? Have you ever noticed one of your favorite brands in a television show or movie? Explain.

_____ awareness

_____ brand

_____ catch up 追いつく

_____ come to mind

_____ disregard ~を無視する
not pay attention

_____ likewise

_____ method

_____ setting

_____ standard

_____ strength

As you learned in Unit 1, *skimming* means to run your eyes very quickly over a text, without reading every word. Readers often skim to save themselves time or to get a general idea about the topic of a short reading before reading it. Here are some situations in which it might be appropriate to skim a text.

- You already know a lot about the topic of a reading. You skim it to see if there is anything new in it. Then you read that part carefully.

- You don't know much about a topic of a reading. You skim it first to get a general idea of what it is about. Then you read it carefully.

- You are in a hurry and don't have time to read something carefully for a class. You skim the text to get a general idea of what it is about.

**C.** Skim "Branding and Product Placement." Then read the questions and check (✓) the answers. Do not spend more than two minutes skimming.

1. Where does this reading probably come from?

_____ **a.** a business magazine

_____ **b.** a blog for people working in marketing

_____ **c.** a business textbook

2. Who is it written for?

_____ **a.** a graduate student getting an MBA in marketing

_____ **b.** an undergraduate student taking an introductory business course

_____ **c.** someone who is looking for a job in marketing

3. How much do you already know about the topic?

_____ **a.** a lot

_____ **b.** some

_____ **c.** a little

_____ **d.** nothing or almost nothing

4. How difficult do you think the article will be for you to understand?

_____ **a.** very difficult

_____ **b.** a little difficult

_____ **c.** not difficult

Read "Branding and Product Placement." Were your answers from Exercise C correct?

# Branding and Product Placement

1 Coca-Cola is the best-known **brand** in the world. It has often been said that if Coke needed money suddenly, it could borrow $100 billion on the **strength** of
5 its name alone. A brand name such as Coca-Cola serves many purposes. It sets Coca-Cola apart from the competition. It also establishes a **standard** quality that people can trust. You can buy Coca-Cola in
10 any country of the world and feel confident that it will always taste the same. This creates repeat customers. If consumers try Coke and like it, they will remember the brand name and buy it again.

15 **Building Brand Awareness**
When companies build their brands, their goal is to create brand **awareness**. They want to be the first company that **comes to mind** when consumers think of a type of
20 product. For example, imagine you need to ship a package. What is the first company you think of? For many people, the answer is FedEx. This means that FedEx's brand awareness is quite strong.

25 It is not easy to create brand awareness. It isn't cheap either. Internet brands are a good example. Google, eBay, and Amazon spend billions a year on advertising. But only one of them is among the fifty best-known
30 brands in the world: Google, at number thirty-six. Many Internet companies have failed because they were unable to build strong brand awareness.

Because brand awareness is so
35 important, marketers are always looking for new ways to create it. One **method** that has grown dramatically in recent years is *product placement*.

**Product Placement**
40 With product placement, companies pay to have their products appear in films, TV shows, and other forms of media. Media characters use real-life products in ways that make it easy for viewers to spot them.
45 In the films *I, Robot* and *Transporter 2*, for example, the main characters drive Audi cars. **Likewise**, BMW paid millions for its cars to appear in *James Bond* films. Another example of product placement is in the
50 movie *Cellular*. All of the characters in the movie use Nokia phones.

Product placement is even more common in television. In the popular show *The Office*, for example, the main character, Michael
55 Scott, once said, "I love my new Levis." The judges on the reality show *American Idol* all drink from cups with the Coca-Cola logo[1] on them. According to marketing research company TNS Media Intelligence,
60 there were 11 minutes and 46 seconds of brand appearances for every hour of prime time[2] network television programming in 2009. This was 31 percent more than in the previous year.

65 With product placement already so widespread in movies and television shows, companies are always looking for new places to market their products. Recently, product placement has begun to appear
70 in music and video games, too. Rapper

---

[1] **logo:** a small design that is the official sign of a company or brand
[2] **prime time:** the time in the evening when the largest number of people are watching television

Jay-Z mentions phone maker Motorola in one song. All of the car repair shops in the popular video game *Need for Speed* are Castrol Syntec shops. There is even product placement within more traditional advertising media, such as catalogs. For example, in the furniture maker IKEA's catalogs, Hewlett Packard computers are on every desk. But IKEA does not sell computers. Hewlett Packard pays IKEA to advertise its computers. This is an example of advertising within advertising.

### Costs and Benefits of Product Placement

Companies like product placement because it is effective. Consumers often **disregard** commercials, but they pay attention to movies and television shows. Films, songs, and video games are also attractive **settings** for products. The BMWs in *James Bond* movies appear next to beautiful people and places. Moreover, consumers associate products with the characters that use them. BMW owners may not be aware of it, but BMW's association with James Bond probably played a role in their decision to buy a BMW.

As product placement has increased, so has spending on it. Companies now spend over $5 billion a year on this form of advertising. Most of this is in television, but other forms of media are **catching up**. Some companies, such as Procter & Gamble, now spend more on product placement than on more traditional forms of advertising such as television commercials.

## Vocabulary Check

**A.** Work with a partner. Ask and answer the questions in full sentences. Use the boldfaced target words in your answers.

1. Which **brands** immediately **come to mind** when you hear the word *computer*?

2. What would be a good **setting** for an advertisement for an expensive perfume?

3. When you watch a movie, are you **aware** of which brands appear in the movie? Do you think your **awareness** will be raised after reading this article?

4. What are some of the personal and professional **strengths** that you need if you want to work in marketing?

**B.** Circle the letter of the correct answer to complete each sentence. The boldfaced words are the target words.

1. When you **disregard** something, you don't _____ it.

   **a.** pay attention to      **b.** enjoy            **c.** understand

2. It doesn't cost anything to set up an e-mail account with Google. **Likewise,** _____.

   **a.** many people have      **b.** Yahoo offers      **c.** you can pay extra for
       Gmail accounts             free e-mail               special services

3. When you have a **method**, you do something _____.

   **a.** in a specific way     **b.** in very little time    **c.** successfully

4. Fast food restaurants have a **standard** menu that is _____ in all locations.

   **a.** special               **b.** the same         **c.** unique

5. Pepsi is **catching up** to Coca-Cola. Pepsi's sales are _____.

   **a.** going up              **b.** slow             **c.** standard

## ▶ READ AGAIN

Read "Branding and Product Placement" again and complete the comprehension exercises. As you work, keep the reading goal in mind.

> 📖 **READING GOAL:** To pass a quiz on the most important ideas introduced in "Branding and Product Placement"

## Comprehension Check

**A.** Read the statements about the reading. Write *T* (true) or *F* (false). Then correct the false statements to make them true.

_____ **1.** Coca-Cola wants to borrow $100 billion dollars.

_____ **2.** Building brand awareness takes a lot of time and money.

_____ **3.** Google has been successful at building brand awareness.

_____ **4.** Product placement is an example of using brand awareness to increase sales.

_____ **5.** Product placement is a very successful marketing tool.

_____ **6.** Up to now, product placement has been used mostly in movies.

_____ **7.** You can buy a Hewlett Packard computer at any IKEA store.

_____F___ **8.** Most companies are now spending more on product placement than on other types of advertising.

_____T___ **9.** In the future, product placement will probably become more common than TV commercials.

**B.** What questions might be included on a quiz of the most important ideas in the reading? Write five questions.

1. _Who _____

2. _Why _____

3. _Why do media characters use real tv products?_

4. _How does product placement effective?_

5. _How much do company spend for their advertisement?_

**C.** Work with a partner. Take turns asking and answering the questions you wrote in Exercise B.

## ▶ DISCUSS

**A.** Work with a partner. Think of a product and a brand. It can be a brand that already exists, or you can invent your own. Develop a product placement strategy to build brand awareness of your product. Use the questions to help you develop your strategy.

1. What is your product? What is its brand name?

2. Who will want to buy your product? (children? teenagers? married couples? retired people?)

3. What is unique about your product? What are your product's strengths in comparison to similar products on the market?

4. What types of people and settings do you want your brand to be associated with?

5. In which media will you place your product? Movies? Television? Video games? Catalogs? Songs? Other? What specific kind of movie, television show, etc.? (Remember, product placement is very expensive, so you can't do everything!)

**B.** Present your product, brand, and product placement strategy to the class.

**C.** Listen to your classmates' presentations. Discuss who has the best strategy.

# CHAPTER 20

# Case Study: 3M's Entrance into the Russian Market

## PREPARE TO READ

**A.** Look at the words in the list. Write the number(s) next to each word to show what you know. You may be able to write more than one number next to some of the words. You will study all of these words in this chapter.

1. I can use the word in a sentence.

2. I know <u>one meaning</u> of the word.

3. I know <u>more than one meaning</u> of the word.

4. I know how to pronounce the word.

**B.** Work with a partner. Look at the picture. Ask and answer the questions. If you don't know a word in English, ask your partner or look in your dictionary. Then write your new words on page 233.

1. Which products do you see in the picture?

2. Do you buy these products?

3. Do you know the name of a company that makes all of these products?

_____ bribe　わいろ
_____ essential
_____ ethics
_____ expertise　専門知識
_____ found
　　　　　(a company)
_____ innovation
_____ mission
_____ operation
_____ potential
_____ refuse
_____ turnover　転倒・急転
_____ unstable　不安定な
_____ willingness　意欲・此力ず状態

turnover in personnel
= 人事異動

willingness
= 快
= 此力...
= 狀...

**C.** Read the abstract of "Case Study: 3M's Entrance into the Russian Market" on the next page. Then read the questions and circle the answers.

1. What do the words *this unstable period* (line 10) refer to?

    a. 3M's entrance into the Russian market

    b. the growth of 3M's business in Russia in the 1990s

    c. the time of dramatic political, economic, and social change in Russia

2. Which sentence expresses the main idea of the case study?

    a. The dramatic changes in the Russian business environment in the early 1990s were due to political, economic, and social change.

    b. The business opportunities in Russia in the 1990s were enormous, but the risks were even greater.

    c. 3M's success in the Russian market was due to the company's awareness of cultural differences and its ability to adapt to local conditions.

3. What is the <u>main</u> purpose of an *abstract* in a case study?

    a. to introduce the general topic of the case

    b. to give a brief summary of the issues and main points of the case

    c. to provide some background information about the case

# CASE STUDY: 3M's Entrance into the Russian Market

**Abstract:**

3M is an American-owned multinational corporation. This case study will discuss 3M's entrance into the Russian market in the early 1990s.

The 1990s were a time of dramatic political, economic, and social change in Russia. The business opportunities were enormous, but the risks were even greater. During this **unstable** period, 3M successfully entered the Russian market. Since that time, 3M's business in Russia has grown at an impressive rate.

Russian business expert Mikhail Gratchev has identified two main factors that contributed to 3M's success in Russia:

1. the company's awareness of the profound differences between American and Russian culture; and
2. the company's **willingness** to adapt its corporate structure to the local culture.

## Company background

3M was **founded** in 1902. **Innovation** has always been a part of 3M's corporate **mission**. One of the company's first big successes was the creation of the Scotch Tape brand in 1930. In the 1950s, 3M developed some of the earliest photocopying technology. In 1980, the company introduced another innovative product, the Post-It Note.

Scotch Tape and Post-It Notes are still among the company's most successful products, but other 3M products range from traffic lights to medical equipment. The company employs more than 76,000 people worldwide. Global sales are over $20 billion a year. $16.1 billion (64 percent) of sales come from outside the United States. 3M has **operations** in more than 60 countries and sells its products in nearly 200.

## Challenges

Entering the Russian market in the early 1990s was an enormous challenge. Gratchev has identified three main difficulties:

**1.** The political environment

The country was experiencing enormous political change. The Soviet Union had broken up. Almost overnight, Russia had become an independent country. There were new leaders and new laws. Along with excitement, there was a great deal of uncertainty and anxiety.

**2.** The economic environment

Under the Soviet Union, Russians had lived in a state-controlled economy. The shift to a market-based economy[1] was not easy for businesses, workers, or consumers.

**3.** The Russian mindset[2]

Gratchev identified three important differences between Russian and Western managers.

- Russian managers were more interested in short-term survival than long-term growth.
- Russian managers believed in strong leadership and fast decision-making. They were less likely than Western managers to listen to employees' opinions.
- Russian managers were used to change. In fact, one of their strengths was their ability to thrive in unstable business conditions. However, this also meant that they were not used to following rules. It was difficult to get them to follow standard business practices.

---

[1] **market-based economy**: a system of producing wealth based on the free operation of business and trade without government controls

[2] **mindset**: attitude

3M was not the only multinational corporation to enter the Russian market at that time. Others tried and failed. Some experienced very high **turnover** rates among their Russian 75 employees. Others were not prepared for the unstable environment. They found themselves paying protection money to criminal gangs[3] and **bribes** to politicians. In the early 1990s, many companies believed it was virtually impossible to 80 do business in Russia.

### The importance of cultural awareness

3M avoided many problems other multinationals experienced in Russia. Gratchev believes it was because the company understood Russian culture 85 and adapted to local conditions. This cultural awareness gave 3M an important edge in an unstable environment.

First of all, 3M designed policies to fit the local situation. They understood the powerful 90 appeal of freedom to Russians at the time. In the workplace, they stressed individual freedom and independent thinking. Employees were free to spend part of every work day on projects they had designed themselves.

95 3M directors knew that Russians were good at surviving and even thriving in unstable environments. Thus, they recognized that local **expertise** would be essential to their success. They decided not to bring in managers and 100 directors from outside the country. Instead, they designed a rigorous interview process to find Russians for top-level positions.

**Potential** employees had as many as eight separate interviews. They had to convince the 105 interviewers that they shared 3M's core values of innovation, creativity, and contribution from each employee. In the end, 3M was able to hire the best people locally.

3M also decided to continue a Russian 110 tradition of businesses contributing to local communities. 3M has given equipment to Russian schools and helped to fix damaged churches. These acts have helped 3M build strong, positive brand awareness in Russia.

### 115 Working in an unstable environment

At the time, it was easy to disregard Russian laws and make easy money. That is what other multinational companies were doing. But 3M did exactly the opposite. They trained both 120 employees and customers in business **ethics**. They insisted on openness and ethical behavior.

However, they also understood that their employees were part of a larger society. **Refusing** to participate in unethical or illegal activity could 125 be dangerous for individuals[4] and their families. When necessary, 3M provided employees with personal security protection.

3M protected its workers in other ways as well. At a time when many Russians were 130 losing government benefits,[5] 3M offered excellent health care. It also helped workers pay for housing. These are clear examples of the company's willingness to adapt to local conditions.

### 135 Conclusion

3M's cultural awareness has been **essential** to its success in Russia. Today, 3M is considered a model for other multinationals who wish to enter the Russian market.

---

[3] **criminal gangs:** groups of people who spend time together for criminal reasons

[4] **individuals:** people

[5] **benefits:** money, health insurance, or other advantages you get from your job

# Vocabulary Check

**A.** Read each question and circle the letter of the correct answer. The boldfaced words are the target words.

1. What does *business* **ethics** mean?
   a. how a business can become successful
   b. how a business can avoid paying taxes
   c. how to do business fairly and honestly

2. How do most people feel when they are in an **unstable** situation?
   a. absorbed
   b. disturbed
   c. enchanted

3. When you **refuse** to do something, what happens?
   a. You are successful.
   b. You don't do it.
   c. You have problems.

4. Who probably has the most business **expertise**?
   a. a twenty-five-year-old university student in an MBA (masters of business administration) program
   b. a fifty-year-old director of a successful multinational corporation
   c. a thirty-year-old professor of economics at an excellent university

5. Who is a **potential** employee?
   a. someone who has applied to work for a company but hasn't been hired yet
   b. someone who has just been hired by a company
   c. someone who has had an unsuccessful interview with a company

6. How can you show your **willingness** to do something?
   a. by refusing to do it
   b. by offering to do it
   c. by avoiding doing it

**B.** Read the definitions. Write the boldfaced word from the reading next to the correct definition.

1. _____ = necessary and important

2. _____ = money or gifts that you use to persuade someone to do something, usually something dishonest

3. _____ = the purpose or most important aim of an organization

4. _____ = a new idea, method, or invention, or the introduction and use of a new idea, method, etc.

5. _____ = to start an organization, town, or business that is intended to continue for a long time

6. _____ = a business or company, or the work of a business or company

7. _____ = the rate at which people leave a company or organization and are replaced by others

## > READ AGAIN

Read "Case Study: 3M's Entrance into the Russian Market" again and complete the comprehension exercises. As you work, keep the reading goal in mind.

> 📖 **READING GOAL:** To identify the problems and solutions in the case study

## Comprehension Check

**A.** Find the sentences in the reading. What do the underlined words refer to? Read each statement and circle the letter of the correct answer. The numbers in parentheses are the lines where you can find the sentences.

1. The business opportunities were enormous, but the risks were even greater. (9)

   **a.** the business risks

   **b.** the political, social, and economic risks

   **c.** the risks to Russians

2. 3M has operations in more than 60 countries and sells its products in nearly 200. (38–39)

   **a.** 200 3M products

   **b.** 200 countries

   **c.** 200 operations

*(continued on next page)*

**3.** However, <u>this</u> also meant that they were not used to following rules. (69)

   **a.** their strength

   **b.** their refusal to follow standard business practices

   **c.** their ability to thrive in unstable business conditions

**4.** It was difficult to get them to follow <u>standard business practices</u>. (70)

   **a.** illegal business activities

   **b.** rules of business that most corporations follow

   **c.** unethical ways of doing business

**5.** <u>They</u> found themselves paying protection money to criminal gangs and bribes to politicians. (76)

   **a.** all of the corporations that tried to enter the Russian market

   **b.** corporations that were not prepared for Russia's unstable conditions

   **c.** the Russians who stopped working for multinational corporations

**6.** Thus, they recognized that <u>local expertise</u> would be essential to their success. (97)

   **a.** 3M's knowledge of Russian culture

   **b.** Russian business people who understood Russian business culture

   **c.** top-level American directors who had studied Russian business culture

**7.** But 3M did exactly <u>the opposite</u>. (118)

   **a.** disregarded the laws

   **b.** followed the laws

   **c.** made easy money

**8.** 3M protected its workers <u>in other ways</u> as well. (128)

   **a.** by offering government benefits

   **b.** by offering health care and money for housing

   **c.** by paying protection money to gangs

**9.** <u>These</u> are clear examples of the company's willingness to adapt to local conditions. (132)

   **a.** protecting Russian workers

   **b.** offering Russian workers health care and housing

   **c.** paying for Russian employees' government benefits

**B.** What were the main challenges 3M faced when it entered the Russian market? How did it respond to those challenges? Complete the chart. Some of 3M's responses are not stated directly in the text. You will need to infer them.

| Challenge | 3M's Response |
|---|---|
| 1. | |
| 2. | |
| 3. | |

**C.** On a separate piece of paper write a paragraph explaining why 3M succeeded when other corporations failed. Make sure you explain what 3M did differently. Some of the reasons are not stated directly in the text. You will need to infer them.

## > DISCUSS

Prepare a role play. Half of the students are interviewers for 3M Russia (Group A). The other half are Russians looking for a job (Group B). Follow the steps.

### Preparation

**Step 1:** Meet with other people in your group to prepare for the interview.

*Group A:* You are interviewing someone for a job. You want to find out if he or she believes in 3M's core values: innovation, creativity, and contribution from each employee. How will you find out? What questions will you ask?

*Group B:* You are preparing for a job interview. You know that belief in 3M's core values is important for this job. How will you convince the interviewer that you believe in these core values?

**Step 2:** *Groups A and B:* Choose three representatives from your group (three from A and three from B) to role-play the interviews in front of the class.

### Role play

**Step 3:** *Group B representatives:* Wait outside the classroom until you are called in for your interview.

*Group A representatives:* Interview the job candidates one by one.

*The rest of the class:* Listen carefully to the interviews. You will help Group A make a decision about who to hire.

**Step 4:** *Group A representatives and the rest of the class:* Decide who is the best person for the job. Be ready to explain your decision to Group B.

*Group B representatives:* Wait outside the classroom while the interviewers make their decision.

**Step 5:** *Group A representatives:* Announce your decision to Group B. Give the reasons for your choice. Congratulate your new employee!

## > VOCABULARY SKILL BUILDING

### Vocabulary Skill: Collocations

In Unit 3 you learned about collocations—words that often appear together. Learning common collocations will help you use words the way native English speakers do. For example, native speakers say *do* business, not *make* business. If you say *make* business, people will probably understand you, but you will not sound natural.

Most fields, such as business, have their own collocations. *Brand name* is an example of a collocation frequently used in business. You can learn common collocations by reading a lot in a field and paying attention to which words often appear together. Dictionaries also contain common collocations.

**A.** Underline the collocations in the sentences. Some sentences have more than one collocation. All of the collocations are commonly used in business.

1. It is essential that all employees follow standard business practices.

2. It is illegal to take a bribe from a business associate.

3. Innovation is a part of our corporate mission.

4. In order to build a brand, it is necessary to spend a lot of time and money.

5. You can find Google's mission statement on its Web site.

6. We need to improve our brand awareness through better product placement.

**B.** Read the definitions. Write the collocation from Exercise A next to the correct definition.

1. _____take a bribe_____ = to accept money from someone to do something illegal or unethical

2. _____business associate_____ = a person who you work closely with in a business setting

3. _____corporate mission_____ = a written description of a company's values, basic beliefs, and goals

4. _____brand awareness_____ = the probability that consumers recognize the existence and availability of a company's product or service

5. _____build a brand_____ = to increase the recognition by consumers of a company's products or services

6. _____business practice_____ = to obey the rules and regulations and ways of doing business that are generally accepted in a business setting

7. _____corporate mission_____ = the most important goals of a company

8. _____product placement_____ = a form of "hidden" advertisement in which companies pay to have their products appear in movies, TV shows, and other types of media entertainment

# Learn the Vocabulary

### Using a Dictionary to Find Collocations

When you read a lot, you begin to recognize which words are commonly used together. You can also use a dictionary to find common collocation patterns.

Look at the dictionary entry for *bribe* from the *Longman Dictionary of American English*.

**EXAMPLE:**

> **bribe¹** /braɪb/ *n.* [C] money or gifts that you use to persuade someone to do something, usually something dishonest: *a judge accused of **taking bribes*** | *The officials said that they had been **offered bribes** before an important game.*

The **boldfaced** words in the definitions show you the verbs that collocate with the noun form of bribe: *take* and *offer*.

Sometimes collocations have their own specific meanings, so they have their own dictionary entries. These collocations are usually compound nouns. (See page 106 for more information on compound words.) Look at the example:

**EXAMPLE:**

> **'brand ,name** *n.* [C] ECONOMICS the name a company gives to the goods it has produced: *brand names such as Jell-O and Coca-Cola*

Different dictionaries have different ways of marking collocations. As you can see in the example entry, for *bribe*, collocations in the *Longman Advanced American Dictionary* are shown in ***boldfaced italics***. If the word is a part of a compound noun, it usually has its own dictionary entry.

**A.** Study the dictionary entries for *standard* and answer the questions.

> **stan·dard¹** /ˈstændərd/ *n.* **1** [C,U] a level of quality, skill, or ability that is considered to be acceptable: *teachers who have **high/low standards**. | Tricia's parents **set** very **high standards**. | Students have to **meet/reach** a certain **standard** or they won't pass. | national **academic/ health/environmental** standards* **2 by ... standards** compared to the normal or expected level of something else: ***By** American **standards**, Rafael's salary is pretty low.* **3 standards** [plural] moral principles about what kind of behavior or attitudes are acceptable: *She has very high **moral standards**.*
>
> **standard²** *adj.* normal or usual: *The shoes are available in all **standard** sizes. | Security checks are now **standard practice/procedure**.*

1. Which eight adjectives and nouns are commonly used with *standard*?

   _____

   _____

2. Which three verbs are commonly used with *standard*?

   _____

3. Which preposition is commonly used with *standard*? _____

**B.** Complete the sentences with the correct collocations from Exercise A. Be careful. You will not use all of the collocations.

1. That company has very _____ standards. Anyone can get a job there. Potential employees do not need to have any special skills or talent.

2. The managers at that corporation _____ very high standards for their employees. They only hire the best, and they expect everyone to work very hard.

3. _____ Russian standards, the health benefits that 3M offers are excellent.

4. My boss is the most ethical, honest person I know. He has very high _____ standards.

5. Employees must _____ certain standards in order to keep their jobs.

*(continued on next page)*

**6.** Strict _____ standards are essential. Without them, the future of our planet is in danger.

**7.** In our company, it is standard _____ to interview potential employees at least three times.

**C.** Make cards for any words that were new to you when you started the unit. Include target words and words that you wrote on page 233. Look in a dictionary to see if there are any collocations listed for the words. If there are, write them on the front of the card, under the word.

> BRIBE
>
> /braIb/
>
> <u>take</u> a bribe
>
> <u>offer</u> (someone) a bribe

**D.** Go back to the vocabulary list at the beginning of each chapter. What did you learn about the target words? Add numbers to the lists.

---

**Vocabulary Practice 10,** see page 243

# Biology: The Science of Life

## > THINK BEFORE YOU READ

**A.** Work with a partner. Look at the pictures. Ask and answer the questions. If you don't know a word in English, ask your partner or look in your dictionary. Then write your new words on page 233.

1. Describe the pictures. What are the words in English for the things you see?

2. Which of the things are plants? Which are animals?

3. Describe the picture in the middle. Which two animals does it look like?

4. What is the word in English for an animal that is a mix of two species?

**B.** Work with a partner. Ask and answer the questions.

1. Which of the living things in the list do you have direct experience with?

2. Which have you studied? Which would you like to learn more about? Explain your answers to your partner.

birds

insects

farm animals (such as chickens, goats, sheep, and cows)

land-based wild plants and animals

marine plants and animals

pets (such as dogs and cats)

# Symbiosis

捕 食者

## PREPARE TO READ

**A.** Look at the words in the list. Write the number(s) next to each word to show what you know. You may be able to write more than one number next to some of the words. You will study all of these words in this chapter.

1. I can use the word in a sentence.

2. I know <u>one meaning</u> of the word.

3. I know <u>more than one meaning</u> of the word.

4. I know how to pronounce the word.

**B.** Work with a partner. Look at the picture. Ask and answer the questions. If you don't know a word in English, ask your partner or look in your dictionary. Then write your new words on page 233.

1. Describe the picture. Which animals do you see? Are they touching?

2. The shrimp goby (the fish) and the shrimp have a unique relationship. What do you think it might be, based on the picture?

_____ astonishing

_____ classification

_____ concept

_____ dizzying

_____ interactive

_____ maintain

_____ organism

_____ predator

_____ reproduce

_____ shelter

_____ striped

_____ tail

## Reading Skill: Understanding Definitions

Textbooks teach students the important vocabulary in academic, technical, or scientific fields. That is why you will encounter a lot of unfamiliar terms when reading textbooks. At first glance, this can make the reading seem difficult. However, remember that one of the writer's goals is to teach you the meaning of the terms. Thus, the writer will usually give very clear definitions of the difficult terms.

The following are some common ways that writers show, or signal, definitions:

| PATTERN | EXAMPLE |
|---|---|
| X (Y)* . . . | Biology (the study of living things) . . . |
| X, Y, . . . | Biology, the study of living things, . . . |
| X is defined as Y. | Biology is defined as the study of living things. |
| X refer(s) to Y | Biology refers to the study of living things. |
| X is + general term + defining adjective clause. | A biologist is a scientist who studies living things. |

*X = term    Y = definition of X

**C.** Read the first paragraph of the chapter "Symbiosis." Then read the questions and check (✓) the answers.

1. Which of the following terms are defined? Check (✓) them.

_____ **a.** concept            _____ **c.** association

___✓___ **b.** symbiosis          _____ **d.** species

2. Which patterns does the writer use to define the terms in the first paragraph? Check (✓) them.

_____ **a.** X (Y) . . .         _____ **c.** X is defined as Y.

_____ **b.** X (Y) . . .         _____ **d.** X refer(s) to + general term + defining adjective clause

Read "Symbiosis." As you read, underline any definitions that you find.
Circle the term that is being defined.

# Symbiosis

1 ### Definition

Symbiosis is an important **concept** in biology.
Biologists define symbiosis as the close,
**interactive** association (living together) of
5 members of two or more species over a period of
time.

### Classification of symbiotic relationships

Symbiosis may have a good, bad, or neutral
effect on one or more of the species. One way
10 of understanding symbiosis is to consider the
benefit (positive effect) or harm (negative effect)
to each species in the relationship, as shown in
Figure 1. However, it is important to note that
many associations between species do not fit
15 neatly into one category. (See *One final note on
classification systems* below.)

**Figure 1**

| 0 no effect (neutral) | | |
|---|---|---|
| + beneficial effect | | |
| – harmful effect | | |

| Species A | Species B | Terminology used to describe symbiotic relationships |
|:---:|:---:|---|
| + | 0 | commensalism |
| + | + | mutualism |
| + | - | parasitism |

## Commensalism (+, 0)

Commensalism refers to an association in which
one or more species benefits. The other species is
20 not affected.

*Example*: the marine sponge and a variety of
small marine **organisms** including shrimp and
certain species of worms

The marine sponge serves as a "living
25 hotel" for certain marine organisms. There
are many benefits to the organisms living in
the sponge. These include **shelter**, protection
from **predators**, and easy access to food that
is washed into the sponge by the ocean. The
30 accommodating sponge does not appear to be
significantly affected by the association.

## Mutualism (+, +)

Mutualism refers to an association that is
beneficial to both species.

35 *Example*: the shrimp goby (a fish) and certain
varieties of shrimp

There are many varieties of shrimp gobies.
They come in many colors. Some are **striped**;
others are covered in spots. But they all have
40 one thing in common: They live in mutually
beneficial associations with certain shrimp.

The shrimp goby and the shrimp live together
in a small hole in the ocean floor. The shrimp
digs and **maintains** the hole. It also cleans the
45 goby by eating parasites that live on its body. In
exchange, the goby guards the entrance to the
hole. It warns the shrimp when a predator is near.
This is essential to the shrimp, which is nearly
blind.
50 When the shrimp is out of the hole, it always
keeps one of its antennae on the goby. If the
goby retreats into the hole, the shrimp feels the
movement and quickly follows. If the shrimp
is inside the hole and the goby is outside, the
55 shrimp reaches out with one of its antennae and
touches the fish's **tail**. If it is safe for the shrimp
to come out, the goby will move its tail from
side to side. Otherwise the shrimp will stay put,

60 protected from potential invaders by its constant companion.

**Parasitism (+, -)**

Parasitism refers to an association in which one species, the *parasite*, lives on or in a second species, the *host*, for a significant period of its
65 life. It uses the host for food, shelter, and/or protection. In the process, it harms the host in some way. A parasite does not usually kill its host. However, the harmful effects of the parasite's actions can lead to the death of the host.

70 *Example*: a tapeworm[1] and a dog

The tapeworm lives and **reproduces** inside the intestine[2] of the dog. It has no mouth, so it feeds by absorbing the contents of the dog's intestines through its skin. If the tapeworm is not
75 removed, there will be negative effects on the dog's health.

### One final note on classification systems

Clearly, man-made **classification** systems with distinct categories help us understand the natural
80 world. However, in nature such rigid categories do not exist. Rather, you might think of relationships among species as existing on a continuum.[3] For example, symbiotic relationships exist on a continuum from beneficial (+) to harmful (-). Very
85 few relationships fit neatly into just one category.

In addition, the system presented above is only one of many man-made classification systems. Biologists often disagree about which systems best describe the natural world. And
90 the **dizzying** number and **astonishing** variety of species, both plant and animal, mean that biologists are always making new discoveries. And with each new discovery, the existing classification systems must be adapted or new
95 ones created.

---

[1] **tapeworm:** a long, flat parasite that lives inside the intestines of people and animals and can make them sick

[2] **intestine:** the long tube that takes food from your stomach out of your body

[3] **continuum:** a scale of related things, on which each one is only slightly different from the one before

## Vocabulary Check

Cross out the one word in each group that does not belong with the other two words. The boldfaced words are target words.

1. cycles — lines — **stripes**
2. destroy — eliminate — **maintain**
3. **interact** — isolate — withdraw
4. creature — **organism** — **tail**
5. mate — **reproduce** — **shelter**
6. **classification** — facility — rank
7. eliminate — **shelter** — keep
8. **concept** — fate — idea
9. **dizzying** — dragging — thrilling
10. **astonishing** — **isolating** — interesting
11. communication — **interactive** — productive
12. killer — **predator** — **shelter**
13. **classification** — head — **tail**

Read "Symbiosis" again and complete the comprehension exercises. As you work, keep the reading goal in mind.

📖 **READING GOAL:** To understand definitions of technical terms and categorize information based on the definitions

## Comprehension Check

**A.** Write the letter of the correct definition next to the word. Do as many as you can without looking back at the reading. Then check your answers.

_____ **1.** symbiosis

_____ **2.** commensalism

_____ **3.** mutualism

_____ **4.** parasitism

_____ **5.** host

_____ **6.** parasite

_____ **7.** classification system

_____ **8.** predator

**a.** a man-made way of organizing complex information in order to understand it

**b.** an organism of one species that is harmed by another organism of a different species living on or inside it

**c.** a close, long-term association between two or more different species

**d.** a symbiotic association that benefits one species, while the other species is not affected

**e.** a symbiotic association that benefits both species

**f.** a symbiotic association that benefits one species and harms the other

**g.** a species that survives by killing and eating the members of another species

**h.** an organism (B) that lives on or in another organism (A) of a different species and causes harm to the other organism (A)

**B.** What is the effect of the association on each species? Write *B* (benefit), *H* (harm), or *Ø* (no effect).

1. _____ tapeworm

   _____ dog

2. _____ marine sponge

   _____ shrimp, worms, and other organisms living inside the sponge

3. _____ shrimp goby

   _____ shrimp

**C.** Read the examples and identify the type of symbiosis that exists between Species A and Species B. Write *C* for commensalism, *M* for mutualism, and *P* for parasitism. If you are not sure of the meaning of a word, ask a classmate or look in your dictionary.

| Species A | Species B | Type of Symbiosis |
|---|---|---|
| dogs | humans | |
| bacteria that live in the human intestine and feed on waste | humans | |
| bees | flowers to which bees are attracted | |
| barnacles | whales | |
| sharks | small pilot fish that swim into the sharks' mouths and eat food on the sharks' teeth | |

## ▷ DISCUSS

Work in small groups. Discuss your answers from Exercise C. Remember: In the natural world, symbiotic associations do not always fit neatly into one category, so there might be more than one answer for some of the associations.

# Mixing It Up

Hybrid = an animal or plant that is produced from parent animals or plants of two different species

## > PREPARE TO READ

**A.** Look at the words and phrases in the list. Write the number(s) next to each word to show what you know. You may be able to write more than one number next to some of the words. You will study all of these words in this chapter.

1. I can use the word in a sentence.

2. I know <u>one meaning</u> of the word.

3. I know <u>more than one meaning</u> of the word.

4. I know how to pronounce the word.

**B.** Work with a partner. Look at the picture. Ask and answer the questions. If you don't know a word in English, ask your partner or look in your dictionary. Then write your new words on page 233.

1. Look at the list of animal names on the next page. Then look at the names of animal hybrids. Which animals do the hybrids come from? Write the animal names next to the hybrid names. You will use one animal name twice.

_____ cub

_____ enchanted

_____ endangered

_____ exotic

_____ have a soft spot for

_____ hybrid

_____ itch

_____ offspring

_____ show off

_____ soul

_____ technique

| camel | horse | lion | whale |
| dolphin | grizzly bear | polar bear | zebra |
| donkey | lama | tiger | |

**Hybrid animals**

**a.** cama = _____*camel*_____ + _____*lama*_____

**b.** liger = _____ + _____

**c.** pizzly = _____ + _____

**d.** wholphin = _____ + _____

**e.** zonkey = _____ + _____

**f.** zorse = _____ + _____

2. Which of the hybrid animals in the list are shown in the picture on page 200 and in the pictures on page 193? List them.

_____

## Reading Skill: Skimming

You learned in Chapters 1 and 10 some of the reasons that you might want to skim a text rather than read it. Here are two more situations in which it might be appropriate to skim a text:

• You are reading for enjoyment. You are not sure if an article will be interesting to you. You skim it to see if you should read it.

• You are interested in a topic and already know a lot about it. You skim an article to see if there is anything new in it. People often skim newspaper articles for this purpose.

**C.** Skim the magazine article "Mixing It Up" on the next page. Do not spend more than two minutes skimming. Then answer the questions.

1. What is the article about? Do you already know a lot about this topic?

2. Do you think the article will be interesting to read? Why or why not?

Read "Mixing It Up." Is the article as interesting (or uninteresting) as you thought it would be after you skimmed it? Did you learn anything new?

# Mixing It Up

1 Zorses and wholphins. Ligers, zonkeys, and camas. These are some of the captive-bred[1] **hybrids** that exist. As a result of new scientific **techniques**, more hybrids are appearing every
5 year. We're learning that some of them—such as the pizzly, a cross between a polar bear and a grizzly—can occur naturally in the wild.

At The Institute of Greatly **Endangered** and Rare Species (TIGERS) in South Carolina (a
10 southeastern U.S. state), ligers (a hybrid that is a cross between a lion and a tiger) share 50 acres[2] with some 80 non-hybrid animals, including a white crocodile and an African elephant. Animal trainer Bhagavan Antle, 47,
15 runs TIGERS with a group of assistants who live there and learn how to work safely with the animals.

I first meet Antle on a cold, wet January day. He shows me recordings of his many media
20 and movie appearances. He's provided animals for such Hollywood films as *Ace Ventura: When Nature Calls, Forrest Gump,* and *Doctor Dolittle.*

Antle's **exotic** animal career just sort of happened after he started working at a health
25 clinic in Buckingham County, Virginia. In 1982, a visitor to the clinic gave Antle a tiger **cub**. By the mid-1980s, Antle had become a full-time exotic animal guy, breeding and training large species for exhibition and rental to the
30 entertainment industry. To his astonishment,

a few years later, his male lion Arthur successfully mated with one of his tigresses. A second liger litter[3] arrived in 2002.

After Antle finishes showing me around,
35 three of his assistants appear with Sinbad. The supersize animal has lighter stripes than a tiger and a lion-shaped head with no mane.[4] As we watch through a glass wall, a woman offers a piece of meat to make Sinbad stand
40 and **show off** his 12-foot frame. The assistants guide him around using chains and a baby bottle. Then Antle invites me out for a closer look. He walks up and snuggles[5] Sinbad's face. "Hi, bud," he says.

45 Sinbad could remove Antle's head with a single bite, but I'm more **enchanted** than scared. "In our core belief, people don't want to accept the idea that two distinctly different-looking wild animals can reproduce,"
50 Antle says. "Ligers make people understand that hybridization is real."

In Ramona, California, Nancy Nunke raises zorses and zonkeys at a 6-acre ranch called the Spots 'N Stripes Ranch. The ranch mainly exists
55 to breed zebras and miniature horses for show and for sale to private animal owners.

Nunke introduces me to her zorse, Zantazia. At seven months old, Zantazia is still a zoal.[6] This delicate[7] creature has a sorrel[8] coat, a
60 horse's long and thin face, and white stripes

---

[1] **captive-bred:** babies born to animals who do not live in the wild, but rather in zoos, as pets, etc.

[2] **acre:** a unit for measuring an area of land which is equal to 0.4046856 hectares

[3] **litter:** group of baby animals born at the same time, to one mother

[4] **mane:** the long hair on the back of a horse's neck or around the face of a male lion

[5] **snuggle:** to get into a warm and comfortable position

[6] **zoal:** (from *foal* and *zebra*) a baby animal with one horse parent and one zebra parent

[7] **delicate:** attractive, thin, and graceful

[8] **sorrel:** light or reddish brown (used to describe horses)

on her head, neck, torso[9], and legs. The **offspring** of a horse mother and a zebra father, she may grow to be taller than both.

Nunke **has a soft spot for** all "stripeys." She thinks they are more playful and loving than horses. "Horses will rub on you because they have an **itch**," she says. "A zebra will rub on you because he's your best friend." Zorses have the **souls** of zebras, she adds. "If they have one stripe, you train them exactly like you train a zebra. The Z is totally in them."

We walk over to meet the zonkey brothers, Zane and Zebediah, who have donkey faces and ears, caramel[10] coats, and a dizzying number of black lines. "They're the most striped zonkies in the world," Nunke says proudly.

---

[9] **torso:** the body, not including head, arms, or legs
[10] **caramel:** the color of caramel candy (brown)

## Vocabulary Check

Answer the questions in full sentences. Use the boldfaced target words in your answers.

1. Do you believe that animals have **souls**? Why or why not?

2. Do you **have a soft spot for** any animals? If so, which one(s)?

3. What are the young **offspring** of a tiger called? The young **offspring** of a house cat?

4. Which animals like to **show off**?

5. What is the most **exotic** animal you have ever seen?

6. Is it possible to **breed** a wolf and a dog?

7. What are some animals that are **endangered**?

8. In addition to tigers, what other animals have **cubs**?

9. What is a **hybrid** car? How is it similar to an animal **hybrid**?

*(continued on next page)*

**10.** Have you ever been **enchanted** by the beauty of an animal? Which one(s)?

_____

**11.** What do cats do when they have an **itch**?

_____

**12.** What **techniques** do trainers use to train circus animals?

_____

## > READ AGAIN

Read "Mixing It Up" again and complete the comprehension exercises. As you work, keep the reading goal in mind.

> 📖 **READING GOAL:** To identify the writer's point of view and explore your own point of view

## Comprehension Check

**A.** Complete the definitions of the words taken from the reading. If necessary, refer to page 195 to review some of the ways to write a definition in English.

**1.** A hybrid animal is defined as _____.

**2.** A pizzly refers to _____.

**3.** An exotic animal trainer is _____.

**4.** A baby horse is called a foal. A zoal refers to _____.

**5.** Sinbad is a liger, _____.

**6.** When Nancy Nunke refers to "stripeys," she is referring to _____.

**B.** Work with a partner. Answer the questions. The answers are not stated in the reading. You will need to infer them.

**1.** What is special about all of the names that Nancy Nunke gives to her hybrid animals?

_____

**2.** What does Nunke mean when she says "the Z is totally in them"?

_____

**3.** How do you think the writer feels about animal hybrids? Circle the letter of the correct answer.

**a.** worried
**c.** neutral
**b.** unsure
**d.** enchanted

**4.** What parts of the text support your answer to question 3? Underline them. Then explain your answer to a classmate by referring to the sentences you underlined.

_____

**5.** How do you feel about the breeding of animal hybrids? Circle the letter of your answer. Explain.

   **a.** worried         **d.** enchanted

   **b.** unsure          **e.** other? _____

   **c.** neutral

# DISCUSS

**Work in small groups. Follow the steps.**

**Step 1:** Invent an animal hybrid. (Do not choose one of the hybrids from the reading.) Give the new animal a name that reflects the parents of the hybrid. For example, the word for the hybrid zorse comes from the words _horse_ and _zebra_.

**Step 2:** Write a detailed description of your hybrid. What does it look like? How does it behave? For example, is it dangerous? Mild-mannered? Do not include the names of the parent animals in your description.

**Step 3:** Read your description out loud to the class. Can they guess which animals were bred to form your hybrid? Can they guess the name of your hybrid?

# VOCABULARY SKILL BUILDING

## Vocabulary Skill: The Adjective Suffix: _-ing, -ed_

You can add the suffixes _-ing_ and _-ed_ to some verbs to make them adjectives. The suffixes _-ing_ and _-ed_ have different meanings. Study the examples below.

VERB = _fascinate_

| **EXAMPLES:** | **MEANING:** |
| --- | --- |
| _You are fascinating._ | You are very interesting. Other people want to know more about you. You cause them to feel fascination. You fascinate them. |
| _You are fascinated._ | You are very interested in something. You want to know more about it. You experience fascination whenever you read about it. It fascinates you. |

Adjectives with _-ing_ tell about what something or someone causes others to feel or experience. Adjectives with _-ed_ tell about what someone feels or experiences about something or someone else.

**A.** Add the suffixes *-ing* and *-ed* to the verbs to make adjective forms.

| Verb | *-ing* adjective | *-ed* adjective |
|---|---|---|
| **1.** fascinate | fascinating | fascinated |
| **2.** enchant | _____ | _____ |
| **3.** thrill | _____ | _____ |
| **4.** astonish | _____ | _____ |
| **5.** threaten | _____ | _____ |
| **6.** absorb | _____ | _____ |

**B.** Complete the sentences with the words in parentheses. Use the correct form of the word.

1. Everyone was _____. We had discovered a completely new organism! It was an _____ discovery. (*astonish*)

2. I have a soft spot for cats. In fact, I am _____ by them. I think they are the most _____ creatures in the world. (*enchant*)

3. I know Sinbad is very big and looks _____, but there is no need to feel _____. He's really quite gentle. (*threaten*)

4. The movie was so _____ that I forgot all of my problems. I was completely _____ in it. (*absorb*)

5. You are a _____ speaker. Did you notice that everyone stayed put once you started your presentation? The audience was clearly _____. (*fascinate*)

6. What a _____ trip! We saw hundreds of exotic animals in the wild. Everyone was _____. We're already planning our next trip! (*thrill*)

# Learn the Vocabulary

## Strategy

### Choosing Words to Learn: Field-Specific Terminology

Every field has its own terminology. Field-specific vocabulary usually occurs infrequently in general English but very frequently in that field. For example, the reading "Symbiosis" contained field-specific vocabulary related to biology. If you are going to major in biology or a related field, it is important to learn terms such as *symbiosis* and *commensalism*. Otherwise, learning those terms may not be necessary.

The skills and strategies you have practiced in this book will help you learn any type of vocabulary, including field specific vocabulary. Here is a review of some of the skills and strategies, along with some additional tips for learning field-specific vocabulary.

- *Make word cards and review them regularly.*
  This is an effective strategy for all vocabulary learning. Make different types of cards depending on your level of knowledge of the word.

- *Use word parts to understand meaning.*
  This is especially useful when learning field-specific vocabulary because a large number of field-specific terms contain Latin and Greek prefixes and roots. For example, the word *symbiosis* is formed from two Greek roots, -sym-, meaning *together with,* and -bio-, meaning *life.*

- *Use a dictionary.*
  Purchase a high-quality, field-specific dictionary. Dictionaries written for general use do not include many field-specific terms. And sometimes a word has a nontechnical, general meaning that is distinct from its technical meaning. For example, compare the definition of *symbiosis* taken from a general use dictionary with the definition used by biologists:
  Definition from general use dictionary: a relationship of *mutual benefit*
  Definition used by biologists: the close, interactive association of members of two or more species over a period of time

- *Use the keyword technique.*
  This can be especially helpful for "big" words with very specific, technical meanings.

- *Learn how to pronounce the words.*
  This is especially important for words that are similar or even the same in your native language. Your natural tendency will be to pronounce them as you do in your native language. If you do, you will probably not be understood, and you also might not understand the words when you hear them.

- *Learn the signal words, sentence patterns, and punctuation that signal definitions.*
  Sometimes you will not need to look up field-specific terminology; it will be defined directly in the text.

**A.** Find something to read in a field that interests you or that you are planning to study. Highlight vocabulary that you believe is field-specific. Look for definitions of field-specific terms in the text and underline them.

**B.** Bring the reading to class. Exchange texts with a classmate. Discuss whether the terms you have chosen really are field-specific vocabulary.

**C.** Make cards for the field specific vocabulary that you have chosen. Follow the tips on page 207.

**D.** Go back to the vocabulary list at the beginning of each chapter. What did you learn about the target words? Add numbers to the lists.

**Vocabulary Practice 11,** see page 244

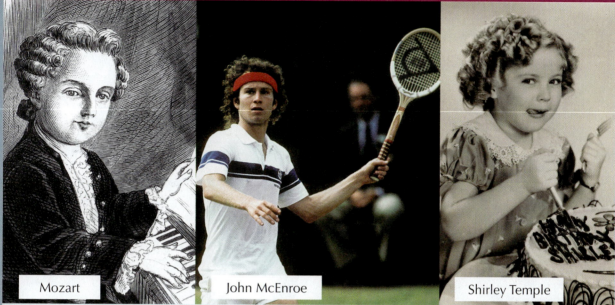

Mozart      John McEnroe      Shirley Temple

##  THINK BEFORE YOU READ

**A.** Work with a partner. Look at the pictures. Ask and answer the questions. If you don't know a word in English, ask your partner or look in your dictionary. Then write your new words on page 233.

   **1.** Who are the children in the pictures? What is special about them? What are the words in English for children who show unusual ability at a young age?

   **2.** Do you know any children like the children in the pictures? Describe them to your partner.

**B.** Work with a partner. Ask and answer the questions.

   **1.** What are some of the problems associated with being very talented at something at a very young age?

   **2.** Would you like to have a child with a remarkable ability? Why or why not?

# Being a Genius Is Hard Work

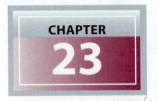
microsoft
bill

## > PREPARE TO READ

**A.** Look at the words in the list. Write the number(s) next to each word to show what you know. You may be able to write more than one number next to some of the words. You will study all of these words in this chapter.

1. I can use the word in a sentence.

2. I know <u>one meaning</u> of the word.

3. I know <u>more than one meaning</u> of the word.

4. I know how to pronounce the word.

**B.** Work with a partner. Look at the pictures. Ask and answer the questions. If you don't know a word in English, ask your partner or look in your dictionary. Then write your new words on page 233.

1. Who are the people in the pictures? What do they have in common?

2. In your opinion, are people like those in the pictures "born special" or do they become special through their own efforts? Or is their success a combination of both? Explain.

_____ acquire

_____ admiration

_____ adversity

_____ confirm

_____ exceptional

_____ exhibit

_____ hardly

_____ have access to

_____ individual

_____ minimize

_____ obsessively

_____ strive

_____ toddler

## Reading Skill: Paraphrasing

In academic classes, students are often asked to write a summary of something they have read. When you write a summary, never copy from the text. Instead, use your own words. This is called *paraphrasing*. When you paraphrase, you show that you understand the writer's main idea(s) and the main points that support his/her idea(s).

Here are some techniques to help you paraphrase. You should use a combination of these techniques whenever you paraphrase.
- Replace some of the words in the original sentence with synonyms (words with a similar meaning).
- Change the sentence structure. For example, change from active to passive voice or vice versa.
- Change the order of the clauses or ideas in the sentence.

Look at the example.

**EXAMPLE:**

Original sentence:

*Exceptional talent appears in a very small number of children at an early age.*

Paraphrase:

*The number of children who exhibit genius when they are very young is quite small.*

**C.** Review the Reading Skill: Understanding Basic Text Organization on page 21. Read the introduction to the magazine article "Being a Genius Is Hard Work" on the next page and preview the rest of it. Then answer the questions.

1. Is there a hook? If so, underline it.

2. What is the main idea? Underline it.

3. How many points does the writer make about the main idea?

4. How many paragraphs are there in the conclusion?

5. Is the main idea restated in the conclusion? If so, underline it.

Read "Being a Genius Is Hard Work." Check your answers from Exercise C.

# Being a Genius Is Hard Work

1   Lang Lang began playing the piano in his native China at the age of three, an age when most children are **hardly** able to hold a spoon. At age five, he won his first competition. At

5   thirteen, he was giving concerts in Beijing's main concert hall, earning the **admiration** of millions. Today, the adult Lang Lang is a superstar of classical piano. His popularity has motivated a new generation of Chinese

10  children. There is even an expression to describe the sudden increase in the number of young Chinese children taking piano lessons: the "Lang Lang effect." But will they succeed? What does it take to become the next Lang

15  Lang? Is it the luck of being born a genius or simple hard work?

Exceptional talent appears in a very small number of children at an early age. Frequently these prodigies **exhibit** talent in music and

20  math. They might also show special abilities in language and the sciences or art. Kim Ung-Yong of South Korea, for example, spoke four languages and could solve complex mathematical problems at age four. Akrit

25  Jaswal of India became interested in medicine while still a **toddler**. He performed his first operation at age seven and is now **striving** to find a cure for cancer.

Despite the early potential of these children,

30  it is difficult to know what will happen when they grow up. We still do not know exactly what genius really is, though many experts have tried to define it. The most famous predictor of intelligence is the Intelligence

35  Quotient (IQ) test. It was developed by the French psychologist Alfred Binet in the early twentieth century. However, many experts now **confirm** that this type of intelligence test only tells one side of the story. Most people

40  who score exceptionally high on intelligence tests as children never do anything particularly exceptional with their lives. This does not mean that intelligence testing is useless. It simply means that genius is still not very well

45  understood. Clearly, however, it involves much more than intelligence.

Tests that focus on creativity and problem solving skills have since been developed. On these kinds of tests, for example, children

50  might be asked to think of different ways to get from one side of the city to another. The children who score the highest can come up with forty or more possibilities in five minutes. Using helium balloons[1] to fly above the traffic

55  is just one example of the creative solutions children think of.

Experts are also looking at the importance of motivation and work in the development of genius. According to the writer Malcolm

60  Gladwell, many of the world's most successful people became great because they spent 10,000 hours or more **acquiring** and developing their skills. Microsoft founder Bill Gates, for example, spent many of his high

65  school years programming on one of the first commercially available computers. The Beatles spent their early years playing music anywhere they could. At one point they were playing seven nights a week for eight hours at a time

70  in nightclubs in Germany. By the time they

---

[1] **helium balloons:** balloons filled with helium, which is lighter than air

became successful, they had played together an astonishing 1,200 times.

Gladwell does not **minimize** the importance of natural talent to the success of the Beatles and Bill Gates of the world. However, he argues that the kids who will one day become superstars are almost always **individuals** with natural gifts who are *also* willing to work exceptionally, even **obsessively**, hard.

Environment may also play a role. Psychologist and researcher Mihaly Csikszentmihalyi says that many world-class[2] thinkers and artists grew up with either great **adversity** or great privilege. He suggests that in the first case, the children learn to focus their attention in order to escape their difficult lives. And in the second case, the children **have access to** information and resources that are not available to the average person. In both cases, the children start with talent. They then add the hard work necessary to become great economists, artists, or scientists.

The good news is that genius can appear at any time in life. Einstein is famous for failing algebra[3] long before he became a world-class scientist. The painter Grandma Moses completed her first painting when she was in her seventies. The lesson for parents is that the importance of hard work should never be minimized. For any child to reach his or her potential, hard work is at least as important as natural talent.

---

2 **world-class:** among the best in the world

3 **algebra:** a type of mathematics that uses letters and other signs to represent numbers

## Vocabulary Check

**A.** Complete the paragraphs with the boldfaced words from the reading. Use the correct form of the word.

Many children have the possibility, or potential to become exceptional at something. However, their parents do not always have the money to send their children to good schools or pay for special lessons. In fact, very few children (1) _____ the educational and cultural resources that could help them develop their unique abilities. As a result, many children who (2) _____, or show, natural talent at a young age—when they are (3) _____—don't have the chance to (4) _____ the skills they need to become successful adults.

Some experts do not think that natural ability is the most important thing for success. They (5) _____ its importance; that is, they believe that no one is born a genius. Instead, they believe that "geniuses" are simply people who work much harder than others. These hardworking

*(continued on next page)*

(6) _____ are not satisfied with being very good. They

(7) _____ to be the best at whatever they do. And to be the

best, they practice (8) _____, devoting tens of thousands of

hours to developing their skills. They are willing to work exceptionally hard

to become the best.

**B.** Cross out the one item in each group that does not belong with the other two items. The boldfaced words are the target words.

1. **admiration**     operation     appreciation

2. privilege     **adversity**     disability

3. barely     **hardly**     mostly

4. reject     agree     **confirm**

5. unique     **exceptional**     defective

## > READ AGAIN

Read "Being a Genius Is Hard Work" again and complete the comprehension exercises. As you work, keep the reading goal in mind.

> 📖 **READING GOAL:** To write a summary of the reading

## Comprehension Check

**A.** Complete the graphic organizer of "Being a Genius Is Hard Work." Do not write full sentences; write in note form only.

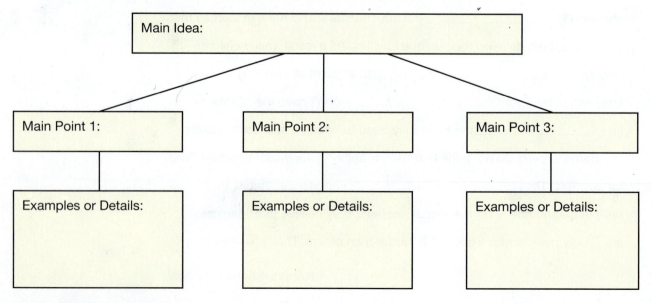

**B.** On a separate sheet of paper, use the information to write a one-paragraph summary of the reading. Do not look back at the text. Include only the main idea, the main points, and one or two details that support each main point.

**C.** Reread "Being a Genius is Hard Work." Make sure your summary accurately expresses the main idea and the main points. If any of your sentences are too close to the original sentences, use the paraphrasing techniques in the skill box on page 211 to rewrite them.

## ▷ DISCUSS

Read the statements and rate them according to your opinion. Then talk in small groups. Explain your opinions.

| strongly agree | agree | disagree | strongly disagree |
|:---:|:---:|:---:|:---:|
| 1 | 2 | 3 | 4 |

_____ **1.** Parents should help their children to identify their natural talents and abilities as early as possible so that they can develop those abilities at an early age.

_____ **2.** Parents should let their children discover their interests and abilities on their own.

_____ **3.** Parents have a responsibility to provide their children with access to as many different types of experiences as possible, such as music lessons, sports, art classes, etc.

_____ **4.** All children should have their intelligence tested at school.

_____ **5.** Children who exhibit signs of genius should be taught with other children who are similarly gifted.

# Through the Eyes of Love

## > PREPARE TO READ

**A.** Look at the words in the list. Write the number(s) next to each word to show what you know. You may be able to write more than one number next to some of the words. You will study all of these words in this chapter.

1. I can use the word in a sentence.

2. I know <u>one meaning</u> of the word.

3. I know <u>more than one meaning</u> of the word.

4. I know how to pronounce the word.

**B.** Work with a partner. Look at the pictures. Ask and answer the questions. If you don't know a word in English, ask your partner or look in your dictionary. Then write your new words on page 233.

1. Who do you think the boy is? How old is he? What special skill does he have?

2. Do you know what autism is? If so, explain it to your partner.

_____ accelerate

_____ adopt

_____ affection

_____ anticipate

_____ curriculum

_____ disorder

_____ extraordinary

_____ hyperactive

_____ livelihood

_____ pace

_____ repetitive

_____ scenery

_____ strain

**C.** Read the questions. Then scan the Web page excerpt "Through the Eyes of Love" and write the answers.

1. What is autism? _a brain development disorder which results in three distinctive behaviors._

2. How old was Ping Lian when he was diagnosed with autism? _When he was four years old._

3. What methods did Ping Lian's mother use to teach her son?
   _She uses the technique such as ABA_

4. When did Ping Lian's interest in art begin? _He is interested in art when he was eight_

5. Where has Ping Lian exhibited his artwork? _in the individuals people inside the_

6. Who is Dr. Treffert? _He is a world famous researcher on Autism._

## READ

Read "Through the Eyes of Love." Check your answers from Exercise C.

www.pinglian.com

# THROUGH THE EYES OF LOVE

1     Sixteen-year old Ping Lian looks ordinary. A handsome teenager with dark intense eyes, Ping Lian attends school during the day. When he is home, he draws, surfs the
5  Internet, watches television occasionally, and listens to music.

    But his mother, Sarah SH Lee, knew Ping Lian was different, even as a toddler. His verbal communication skills were limited. He
10  was also **hyperactive** and did not need much sleep. But what worried Sarah more was the fact that he showed no **affection** for people around him. "I would call him, but I would not be able to get his attention," Sarah said in an
15  e-mail interview.

    When he was four years old, doctors confirmed Sarah's suspicions—Ping Lian was found to be autistic. Autism is a brain development **disorder**, which results in three
20  distinctive behaviors. Autistic children have difficulties with social interaction, problems with verbal and nonverbal communication,

and **repetitive** behaviors or obsessive interests.
25     The early years were difficult for the family. Ping Lian's hyperactive behavior and sleeplessness put a **strain** on everyone. There were other problems, too. "I remember that I had to hold on tight to his hand
30  whenever we went to the mall. If he ran away from me, he would go into a fast food restaurant and help himself to someone else's drink," Sarah remembered.

    The only times when Ping Lian would
35  "lose" his hyperactivity was when he stopped to admire beautiful **scenery** or when he was looking through magazines such as *Home & Architectural Trends*, she added.

    But Sarah did not allow herself to think
40  about the negatives for too long. "I needed to face the reality of autism." Sarah motivated herself by setting goals and targets for both her and Ping Lian. She also **adopted** some of the techniques for teaching autistic children,

*(continued on next page)*

such as Applied Behavior Analysis (ABA).
The program helps to increase or decrease a
particular behavior, to improve the quality of
a behavior, to stop an old behavior, or teach
a new one by breaking down complex tasks
50 into smaller parts and teaching each one in a
repetitive manner.

Sarah remembers that Ping Lian could
hardly hold a pencil correctly to write, or
use a pair of scissors to cut when he first
55 started. In order to strengthen and develop
his fine motor skills,[1] his **curriculum** included
tracing[2] and coloring activities.

At the age of eight in mid-2002, Ping Lian
suddenly acquired an obsession for art.
60 Sarah remembers it well: "One day, after he
had finished eating an ice-cream cone, he
just started drawing the pictures printed on
the ice-cream wrapper," she said.

From that moment on Ping Lian's progress
65 in drawing and painting **accelerated** at
an amazing **pace**. Sarah sent him to art
classes in 2003 and started planning art as
a **livelihood** for him. "The art teachers were
nervous when I told them of my plan but I
70 assured them that I was willing to wait five,
ten, or even twenty years," she says. But
to her surprise, Ping Lian's art works were
quickly recognized. By September 2004, he
had already participated in six art exhibitions.
75 In November 2004, one of his watercolors[3]
sold for RM 100,000.[4]

Although Sarah's dream of Ping Lian
becoming an artist has become a reality, she
has not stopped striving to do better. Her
80 research on autism and art on the Internet led
her to learn about the savant syndrome[5] and
world-famous researcher on the subject, Dr.
Darold A. Treffert. She decided to get in touch
with Dr. Treffert, who is based in the United
85 States.

Dr. Treffert recognized Ping Lian as a
savant in September 2004. Dr. Treffert
said the artwork stands on its own and
demonstrates a remarkable ability. "Ping
90 Lian's work does show **extraordinary**
artistic talent in and of itself.[6] But when
seen in contrast to his limitations in other
areas, his artistic talent becomes even more
exceptional," Dr. Treffert said in an e-mail
95 interview.

Today, Ping Lian is recognized worldwide
as a gifted artist. He has had art exhibitions
in the United States, Australia and the United
Kingdom. And although Ping Lian still has
100 limited communication and social skills, Dr.
Treffert believes his savant ability will help
him in the future. Ping Lian's mother also
reports that his behavior and social skills are
much better. He is an affectionate person
105 who is no longer hyperactive, and he often
helps his mother around the house. She
**anticipates** that this trend wil continue.

---

[1] **fine motor skills:** the ability to use one's hands to do complicated and delicate things .

[2] **trace:** to copy a drawing by putting a piece of paper over it and drawing the lines you see through the paper

[3] **watercolor:** a picture painted with paint mixed with water

[4] **RM 100,000:** Malaysian Ringitt (RM 100,00 = about $30,000)

[5] **savant syndrome:** a rare condition in which people with developmental disorders (including autism spectrum disorders) have one or more areas of expertise, ability, or brilliance that are in contrast with their other limitations

[6] **in and of itself:** considered alone

## Vocabulary Check

Read the statements from the reading. Write *T* (true) or *F* (false). Then correct the false statements to make them true. The boldfaced words are the target words.

_____ 1. When a car **accelerates**, it slows down.

_____ 2. A **repetitive** action is one that is repeated many times.

_____ 3. If you have a physical **disorder**, you are healthy.

_____ 4. People show **affection** by hugging each other.

_____ 5. People under a lot of **strain** can relax easily.

_____ 6. **Hyperactive** toddlers are calm and easy to take care of.

_____ 7. When something is a part of the **curriculum**, it is taught.

_____ 8. If you want to enjoy the **scenery** when you travel, it is best to travel by plane.

_____ 9. A chef's **livelihood** is cooking.

_____ 10. If you **anticipate** something, you are not surprised when it happens.

_____ 11. Toddlers and adults naturally walk at the same **pace**.

_____ 12. When you **adopt** a new method, you reject it.

_____ 13. **Extraordinary** events are quite common.

## > READ AGAIN

Read "Through the Eyes of Love" again and complete the comprehension exercises on the next page. As you work, keep the reading goal in mind.

> **READING GOAL:** To write a summary of Ping Lian's life

## Comprehension Check

**A.** Check (✓) the statements that are true according to the reading.

_____ **1.** Ping Lian's mother spotted his artistic talent when he was a toddler.

_____ **2.** Dr. Treffert diagnosed Ping Lian with autism.

_____ **3.** Ping Lian's mother was surprised at her son's talent.

_____ **4.** It is rare for people with autism to be as talented as Ping Lian.

_____ **5.** Dr. Treffert believes that Ping Lian is talented because he is autistic.

_____ **6.** There is a good chance that Ping Lian's communicative and social skills will improve in the future.

**B.** Take notes about the most significant facts and events in Ping Lian's life on the timeline.

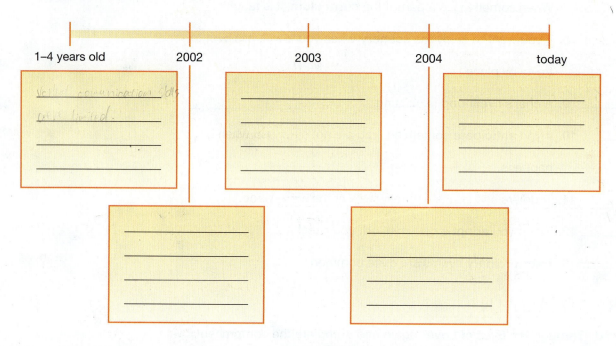

1–4 years old      2002      2003      2004      today

**C.** Using the information from the timeline, write a one-paragraph summary of Ping Lian's life on a separate sheet of paper. Do not look back at the text.

**D.** Work with a partner. Compare your summaries. Did you include similar information? Are any of your sentences too close to the sentences in the text? If so, change them.

Work in small groups. Ask and answer the questions.

1. In what ways might autism have contributed to the development of Ping Lian's talent as an artist? In what ways might it have interfered with the development of his talent?

2. What are some other extraordinary skills or talents that autistic savants have? In what ways might autism contribute to the development of these skills or talents?

3. If you could choose to be exceptionally talented in one area such as music, art, math, etc., which area would you choose? Why?

> **VOCABULARY SKILL BUILDING**

## Vocabulary Skill: Prefixes *extra-*, *hyper-*, *mini-*, *micro-*, *uni-*, *mono-*

Many prefixes in English come from Latin and Greek. It is common for there to be two prefixes with similar meanings, one derived from Latin, and the other from Greek.

| Prefix | Derivation and meaning | Example |
|---|---|---|
| *extra-* | Latin: outside of; beyond | *extraordinary* = **outside of** what is ordinary; **beyond** ordinary |
| *hyper-* | Greek: over; above; excessive | *hyperactive* = **excessively** active; **overly** active |
| *mini-* | Latin: small | *minimize* = to make something seem **smaller** or less important |
| *micro-* | Greek: small | *micromanage* = to manage even the **smallest** details of something |
| *uni-* | Latin: one | *unique* = being the only **one** of its kind |
| *mono-* | Greek: one | *monotone* = a series of sounds all repeated in **one** tone, without variation |

Complete the sentences. Add prefixes from the chart on page 221 to the words in the list to form new words. If you are not sure of a word, look in a dictionary.

| biologist | curricular | lingual | sex | skirt | tension |
|---|---|---|---|---|---|

1. My son is an excellent student. In addition to his schoolwork, he is involved in many ___extracurricular___ activities including tennis and music lessons.

2. In this building, all of the restrooms are ___unisex___. There are no restrooms specifically for men or women. Men and women use the same restrooms.

3. He needs to take medicine to control his high blood pressure. He suffers from ___hypertension___.

4. In the 1960s, the ___miniskirt___—a skirt that was high above the knee—was fashionable.

5. A ___microbiologist___ studies very small living things such as viruses and bacteria.

6. People who are ___monolingual___ speak only one language.

# Learn the Vocabulary

When you are learning new vocabulary, avoid studying two closely related words at the same time. This can make it more difficult for you to learn either word, as you will be more likely to confuse the two. There are four types of words you should avoid learning at the same time:

1. words that are very similar in spelling or sound, for example *adversity* and *advertise*

2. words that are similar in meaning, for example *extraordinary* and *exceptional*

3. words that are exact opposites, for example *accelerate* and *decelerate*

4. words that belong to one category, for example *infant* and *toddler* (category = small children)

**A.** Look at the words that were new to you in this unit. Make a list of any words that you should probably not try to learn at the same time.

    *exceptional*          *extraordinary*

_____     _____

_____     _____

_____     _____

**B.** Make cards for the words that were new to you when you started the unit. Include target words and words that you wrote on page 233. Separate any pairs of words that you wrote in Exercise A into different groups so that you do not review them at the same time.

**C.** Add your new cards to your old cards from previous units. Divide your cards into groups of thirty to forty cards each. Look through each group of cards carefully to make sure it doesn't contain words that you might confuse.

**D.** Review each group of cards separately for the next week.

**E.** Go back to the vocabulary list at the beginning of each chapter. What did you learn about the target words? Add numbers to the lists.

**Vocabulary Practice 12,** see page 245

# FLUENCY PRACTICE 4

## > READING 1

### Before You Read

**A.** Read the words and their definitions. You will see these words in the reading.

> **crystal:** high quality clear glass
>
> **botanist:** a person who studies the science of plants
>
> **bulb:** a root shaped like a ball, that grows into a plant
>
> **merchant:** someone who buys and sells large quantities of products

**B.** Preview "Tulip Fever." Check (✓) the main topic.

_____ **a.** an illness caused by tulips that killed many people

_____ **b.** an insect that killed almost all of the tulips in Holland

_____ **c.** a time when people sold everything they had in order to buy tulips

## Read

**A.** Read "Tulip Fever." Time yourself. Write your start and end times and your total reading time. Then calculate your reading speed (words per minute) and write it in the progress chart on page 246.

**Start:** _____ **End:** _____ **Total time:** _____ (in seconds)

**Reading speed:**
599 words ÷ _____ (total time in seconds) x 60 = _____ words per minute

# ✂ Tulip Fever ✂

1  It might come as a bit of a surprise, but tulips, the vividly colored yet rather ordinary flowers, have an extraordinary history. Today the country most commonly associated with tulips is Holland. However, that was not always the case. No one is sure where the first tulips came from, but we do know that
5  it was not Holland. The first wild tulips probably grew thousands of years ago somewhere in the region between Northern China and Southern Europe.

Turkish rulers, called sultans, were captivated by the tulip. From the late fifteenth to early eighteenth centuries, tulips were associated with wealth and high social position in Turkey. There were special festivals to celebrate the tulip.
10  On the night of the full moon, crystal vases filled with the most exceptional tulip varieties were placed around the Sultan's gardens. Crystal lanterns lit up the enchanting flowers. Songbirds in cages entertained the guests, who dressed in a dizzying range of colors to match the beautiful flowers. Access to the distinctive flowers was controlled by law. It was illegal for most ordinary Turks to grow, buy,
15  or sell them.

Europeans traveling in Turkey admired the beautiful flowers and brought back descriptions of the extraordinary Turkish tulips. As far as we know, the first tulip bulbs from Turkey were sent to the famous botanist Carolus Clusius (1526–1609) at the Royal Medicinal Gardens in Vienna in the late 1500s. The bulbs arrived in
20  Holland some years later when Clusius moved to Leiden, taking the Turkish bulbs with him. There he planted them in the Leiden Botanical Gardens.

At that time, merchants in Holland had become very rich from trading with other countries. These Dutch merchants built large, luxurious houses to show off their wealth. And like the Turkish sultans, they wanted the most dramatic
25  varieties of tulips for their gardens. But there was a problem. Clusius did not want to share his tulips. To get them, people had to sneak into the botanical garden and steal the bulbs.

Because tulips were so difficult to get and so many wealthy people wanted them, the flowers became very expensive. At first only wealthy merchants could
30  afford them. But in 1630 a new profession began: tulip trading. Traders bought tulip bulbs and then resold them at a much higher price. It seemed an easy way to make money fast.

Soon the obsession with tulips had become widespread. Everyone was borrowing money to buy tulip bulbs. Ordinary farmers and workers risked their
35  livelihoods to buy them. In 1633 one man traded his farmhouse for three bulbs.

*(continued on next page)*

In 1636 one bulb sold for an astonishing 5,200 guilders. That was as much money as a rich merchant made in a year! The whole country was wild for tulips. Soon, everyone had tulip fever.

40 Today, we can see that the Dutch were not thinking clearly. They believed that tulip prices would rise forever. But of course that was an illusion. The traders came to their senses first. From one day to the next, they stopped buying tulip bulbs. The demand for tulip bulbs evaporated, and the tulip markets crashed. Bulbs worth 5,000 guilders one day were worth nothing the next. The lives of ordinary people were destroyed. They lost everything: their homes, their land, their farms,
45 and their life savings.

Tulip fever was a disaster for ordinary people in Holland, but the financial markets survived. Today, the tulip is a flower for everyone, not just the rich. That is good news for the Dutch, who make hundreds of millions of dollars a year from tulip sales to ordinary people all over the world.

**B.** Read "Tulip Fever" again, a little faster this time. Time yourself. Write your start and end times and your total reading time. Then calculate your reading speed (words per minute) and write it in the progress chart on page 246.

**Start:** _____  **End:** _____  **Total time:** _____ (in seconds)

**Reading speed:**
599 words ÷ _____ (total time in seconds) x 60 = _____ words per minute

# Comprehension Check

**A.** Read the statements about the reading. Write *T* (true) or *F* (false).

_____ **1.** The first wild tulips grew in Holland.

_____ **2.** Tulips were popular in Turkey before they became popular in Holland.

_____ **3.** In both Turkey and Holland, tulips were an ordinary flower for ordinary people.

_____ **4.** When the tulip first arrived in Holland, it was mostly rich Dutch merchants who bought them.

_____ **5.** When tulip fever was at its worst, ordinary people were selling everything they owned to buy tulip bulbs.

_____ **6.** As a result of tulip fever, the Dutch economy was destroyed.

_____ **7.** Tulips are an important part of the Dutch economy today.

**B.** Complete the summary of "Tulip Fever" by circling the correct underlined word to complete the sentences.

(1) Everybody/<u>Nobody</u> knows exactly where tulips come from. We do know that tulips were popular in Turkey (2) after/<u>before</u> they became popular in Europe. Turkish (3) farmers/<u>sultans</u> grew tulips in their gardens. They also had tulip (4) festivals/<u>competitions</u>.

Clusius was a famous (5) <u>botanist</u>/farmer. He got tulip bulbs from (6) <u>Prague</u>/Turkey and planted them in a public garden. When he moved to Holland, he (7) <u>took</u>/left his tulip bulbs. He planted them in a botanical garden in Holland, but he didn't want to (8) <u>keep</u>/share them. If people wanted tulips, they had to (9) <u>steal</u>/buy them from Clusius.

Tulip bulbs became very expensive in Holland because it was so difficult to (10) <u>get</u>/sell them. For several years, tulip prices rose (11) a little bit/<u>dramatically</u>. People thought that the prices would keep going (12) <u>up</u>/down. Ordinary people (13) didn't buy/<u>bought</u> tulip bulbs for very high prices. Then one day, the tulip markets (14) <u>crashed</u>/opened. Ordinary people lost their (15) lives/<u>life savings</u>. However, the Dutch economy (16) <u>survived</u>/was destroyed.

**C.** Check your answers for the comprehension questions in the Answer Key on page 248. Then calculate your score and record it in the progress chart on page 246.

_____ (my number correct) ÷ 22 x 100 = _____ %

# ▶ READING 2

## Before You Read

**A.** Read the definition. You will see this word in the reading.

> **fraudulent:** intended to deceive people in order to steal money from them

**B.** Preview "Who Am I Today?" Check (✓) the questions that you think the reading will answer.

_____ **1.** Why is Frank Abagnale famous?

_____ **2.** How many children does Frank Abagnale have?

_____ **3.** What is a confidence man?

_____ **4.** How many confidence men are there in the world?

_____ **5.** How many careers has Frank Abagnale had?

_____ **6.** What are prisons in France like?

_____ **7.** What does Frank Abagnale do today?

## Read

**A.** Read "Who Am I Today?". Time yourself. Write your start and end times and your total reading time. Then calculate your reading speed (words per minute) and write it in the progress chart on page 246.

**Start:** _____   **End:** _____   **Total time:** _____ (in seconds)

**Reading speed:**
801 words ÷ _____ (total time in seconds) x 60 = _____ words per minute

# Who Am I Today?

1   Today Frank W. Abagnale, Jr. uses his expertise to help governments, banks, and other businesses to anticipate financial crime and protect themselves from becoming victims.
5   In fact, he is a worldwide expert on financial crime, and no one questions his professional ethics.

But this is not Abagnale's first career. Before his twenty-second birthday, he had tried being
10   a doctor, a college professor, an airline pilot, and a lawyer. And he did all of it without any professional training. How? Abagnale was a confidence man.

Confidence men, or con men for short,
15   get people to trust them. Then they steal their money. Abagnale was one of the most successful con men in United States history. Between the ages of 16 and 21, Abagnale cashed an astonishing $2.5 million in
20   fraudulent checks. He fooled people in every

state in the United States, and in 26 other countries too.

Abagnale's life as a con man began when he ran away from home at the age of 16. He arrived in New York City with only $100 in his pocket. He added ten years to his birthdate on his driver's license so that he could get a job. It was easy for Abagnale to fool people, because he looked much older than his age. At 16, he was six feet tall and his hair had already turned gray.

Over the next five years, Abagnale became a legendary con man. He pretended to be a pilot, and traveled all over the world for free. He pretended to be a doctor and worked at a hospital. He pretended to be a college professor, and taught courses at a university. He never went to law school, but he passed the exam to become a lawyer and worked in a law office.

Abagnale made some money from his jobs, but he got rich from his real livelihood: making and cashing bad checks. Bankers trusted him. Why? He pretended to be a professional, and they believed him. When someone started to suspect him, he moved to a new city or country. There he adopted a new identity, and began a new life.

The police finally caught up with Abagnale in France, and he went to prison. He was only 21 years old. Initially he was in a French prison, but later he was moved to the United States. After five years, the United States government agreed to release him, but with one condition. He had to work without pay for the FBI. His job? To help them fight financial crime.

For more than 30 years, that is exactly what Abagnale has strived to do. His mission is to help others avoid becoming the victims of financial crime. Years ago, he also paid back the $2.5 million that he stole. These days, he makes his livelihood legally through public speaking, writing books, and developing technologies to fight identity theft and other financial crimes. Abagnale has also maintained his close relationship with the FBI. Today, years after his legal obligation to the FBI ended, he still refuses to take any money for the work he does for them.

Over the years, Abagnale also maintained his close friendship with Joseph Shea, the FBI agent who was responsible for Abagnale's arrest. Abagnale has said about Shea, "He was a great help up until his death. He was obviously a big part of my life in getting me to work with the government. He was someone who saw that I had something to offer and he was very big on helping me do that. I think that when he started out, he thought I was some master criminal and he was going to catch me, but then he came to the realization that I was just a kid and I was a runaway."

Abagnale believes that it is even easier to commit financial crime today than it was when he was 16 years old. "Technology breeds crime—it always has and it always will." However, technology has changed the way people commit financial crime today, according to Abagnale. "There are really no con men anymore today like there were in my day, because you really don't have to associate with anyone. You don't have to be well-dressed and well-spoken. Everything's done on a computer. So even if you know who's doing it, you probably don't have the ability to go capture them. Chances are you have no idea what they look like; they can sit in their pajamas and commit all these crimes."

In 2002, a movie about Abagnale's extraordinary career as a con man, *Catch Me If You Can*, was released. It was based on a book Abagnale wrote about his life. In the highly successful movie, Leonardo DiCaprio played the role of Abagnale, and Tom Hanks played the role of FBI agent Joseph Shea.

**B.** Read "Who Am I Today?" again, a little faster this time. Time yourself. Write your start and end times and your total reading time. Then calculate your reading speed (words per minute) and write it in the progress chart on page 246.

**Start:** _____   **End:** _____   **Total time:** _____ (in seconds)

**Reading speed:**
801 words ÷ _____ (total time in seconds) x 60 = _____ words per minute

## Comprehension Check

**A.** Circle the letter of the correct answer to complete each sentence.

1. Abagnale got rich from _____.
   **a.** cashing bad checks
   **b.** his jobs as a pilot, a doctor, a lawyer, and a professor
   **c.** working with the FBI

2. From the ages of 16 to 21, Abagnale's real career was as _____.
   **a.** a banker
   **b.** a confidence man
   **c.** an FBI agent

3. Abagnale was able to fool bankers because they thought _____.
   **a.** he worked for the FBI
   **b.** he was a professional and trusted him
   **c.** he had a new identity

4. Abagnale learned a lot about financial crime _____.
   **a.** as a confidence man
   **b.** in college
   **c.** when he studied to be a lawyer

5. Today, Abagnale is _____.
   **a.** a confidence man
   **b.** an expert on financial crime
   **c.** the leader of the FBI

6. Abagnale still _____ the FBI.
   **a.** gives money to
   **b.** helps
   **c.** gets money for his work with

7. Abagnale thinks that committing financial crime is _____ today than in the past.

    **a.** easier

    **b.** more interesting

    **c.** more dangerous

8. Abagnale thinks that new technology _____ new kinds of financial crime.

    **a.** eliminates

    **b.** leads to

    **c.** minimizes

**B.** Complete the summary of "Who Am I Today?". Use the words in the list.

| adopted | caught | ethical | expertise | prison | suspect |
|---------|--------|---------|-----------|--------|---------|
| bad | criminal | exchange | mission | professional | teenager |

Today Frank Abagnale, Jr. is an expert on financial crime who uses his

(1) _____ to help the FBI. But when he was a (2) _____,

he was a (3) _____. He made and cashed 2.5 million dollars in

(4) _____ checks.

How did he do this? He got bankers to trust him by pretending to be a

(5) _____ such as a doctor, lawyer, professor, or airline pilot.

Whenever someone started to (6) _____ him, he moved to a new

place and (7) _____ a new identity.

After five years, the police finally (8) _____ Abagnale and

he went to (9) _____. Later, he made a deal with the FBI. They

released him in (10) _____ for his help fighting financial crime.

Abagnale has worked with the FBI for over 30 years. He thinks that it

is easier today than it was in the past for people to commit financial crime.

Today he is an (11) _____ man. His (12) _____ is to

minimize the damage done by financial criminals.

**C.** Check your answers for the comprehension questions in the Answer Key on page 248. Then calculate your score and record it in the progress chart on page 246.

_____ (my number correct) ÷ 20 x 100 = _____ %

# New Words

**UNIT 1**

**UNIT 2**

**UNIT 3**

**UNIT 4**

**UNIT 5**

**UNIT 6**

# New Words

---

**UNIT 7**

---

**UNIT 8**

---

**UNIT 9**

---

**UNIT 10**

---

**UNIT 11**

---

**UNIT 12**

## THINK ABOUT MEANING

Look at each group of words. Cross out the one word or phrase in each group that does not belong.

1. contemporary/current/explosion
2. marketing/movement/promotion
3. inspire/miss the boat/motivate
4. celebrity/legend/resource
5. influential/significant/slim
6. distraction/movement/trend
7. appeal/influence/role
8. sure/uncertain/undeniable
9. miss the boat/promote/sell out
10. legendary/ordinary/unique

## PRACTICE A SKILL: Parts of Speech

Read the sentences. Circle the correct form of the word to complete each sentence.

1. My daughter has a vivid/vividly imagination.
2. His popularity with teenagers is undeniable/undeniably.
3. I am interested in a career in market/marketing.
4. Please don't distract/distraction me when I am working.
5. To catch/Catching up with her, you will need to run fast.
6. He is unique/uniquely qualified to play that role.
7. What is the significant/significance of that event in history?
8. The tickets sell out/sold out just one hour after they went on sale.

## PRACTICE A STRATEGY: Making Word Cards

Make word cards for 10 more words that you learn this week. Add them to the cards that you made for this unit. Review your cards every day. Always change the order of your cards before you review them.

## THINK ABOUT MEANING

Circle the letter of the correct answer to complete each sentence. The boldfaced words are the target words.

1. People often show **appreciation** by _____ .
   a. apologizing
   b. giving a gift
   c. saying hello

2. When you study a **cross-section** of a population, you study people _____ .
   a. with different backgrounds
   b. from the same family
   c. with similar interests

3. **Reasoning** involves the _____ .
   a. brain
   b. feet
   c. lungs

4. A **load** is _____ .
   a. heavy
   b. slim
   c. unique

5. You **stride** with your _____ .
   a. arms
   b. legs
   c. shoulders

6. **Rewards** are given for _____ .
   a. good work
   b. luck
   c. rank

7. A **cycle** _____ .
   a. happens once
   b. is unique
   c. repeats

8. **Intense** exercise makes you _____ .
   a. elite
   b. a champion
   c. sweat

9. When a measurement is **accurate**, it is _____ .
   a. dramatic
   b. correct
   c. an exception

10. Food can be **stored** in a _____ .
    a. meal
    b. picnic
    c. refrigerator

## PRACTICE A SKILL: The Prefix *cross-*

Read the sentences. Are they true or false? Write *T* (true) or *F* (false). Correct the false sentences to make them true. Then check your answers by looking up the boldfaced words in a dictionary.

_____ 1. When a tennis player hits a ball **crosscourt**, the other player does not need to move to hit it back.

_____ 2. A **crosswise** pattern contains both horizontal and vertical lines.

_____ 3. If you and your partner are working at **cross purposes** on a project, you will probably complete the project quickly.

_____ 4. When a pilot does a **crosscheck**, he checks his instruments once very carefully.

_____ 5. To become a **crossover** success, a song needs to appeal to more than one type of audience.

_____ 6. A **crosswind** is a strong wind that is coming from one direction.

## PRACTICE A STRATEGY: Using different types of cards for different types of learning

Choose nine words that you want to learn (from another unit or book), three for each of the following categories: meaning, word form, pronunciation. Then add the cards to your other cards and review them frequently.

# VOCABULARY PRACTICE 3

## THINK ABOUT MEANING

Look at the words in the list. Think about their meanings, and decide if they have to do with money or technology. Write *M* or *T* next to each word. Some words will have both letters. Be ready to explain your decisions.

| _____ digital | _____ exchange | _____ expense | _____ income | _____ model |
|---|---|---|---|---|
| _____ operation | _____ property | _____ toy | _____ virtual | _____ vehicle |

## PRACTICE A SKILL: Collocations

**A.** Write the prepositions from the list next to the target words. Then check your answers in a dictionary.

| for | from | in | to | with |
|---|---|---|---|---|

**1.** merge _____          **3.** exchange X _____ Y

**2.** be absorbed _____          **4.** range _____ X _____ Y

**B.** Rewrite the underlined parts of the sentences with the collocations from Exercise A.

**1.** When she is <u>concentrating on</u> a project, she forgets everything else.

_____

**2.** The price of a personal computer can <u>be as low as $500 or as high as $3000</u>.

_____

## PRACTICE A STRATEGY: Finding the core meaning of words

Circle the core meaning of each word.

**1.** merge
  **a.** become unique                    **b.** form one from many

**2.** perform
  **a.** create something new              **b.** do something difficult

**3.** swallow
  **a.** take deeply inside one's body or mind    **b.** transfer from one place to another

**4.** operation
  **a.** something difficult involving many steps    **b.** something done by an expert

# VOCABULARY PRACTICE 4

## THINK ABOUT MEANING

Cross out the word or expression in each group that does not belong with the others.

1. fate/leisure/retirement
2. accumulate/pinch/sting
3. facility/leisure/university
4. isolate/participate/withdraw
5. forever/occasional/permanent

6. dance/keep time/ponder
7. gossip/promotion/slogan
8. catch up on/chat/reject
9. bother/disturb/inspire
10. claustrophobic/free/uneasy

## PRACTICE A SKILL: The Suffix –*free*

Complete the sentences with a hyphenated adjective ending in –*free*. Use the boldfaced words to form the adjectives.

1. Since my operation, I have not had any **pain** at all. I have been _____ for almost one year.

2. These eggs come from hens that were not raised in a **cage**. They are _____.

3. In Saudi Arabia, citizens do not pay any income **taxes**. Their income is _____.

4. There is no **risk** that you will lose your money. Our investments are _____.

5. It is now possible to buy a cell phone that you don't need your **hands** to use. These _____ models are becoming more and more popular.

6. Gum that has **sugar** in it is very bad for your teeth. You should chew _____ gum.

## PRACTICE A STRATEGY: Core meaning

Read the example sentences. Then write the core meaning of the boldfaced word(s).

1. **a.** Snow **accumulated** outside the door of their house.
   **b.** Over his lifetime, he **accumulated** a fortune worth over a billion dollars.

   core meaning: _____

2. **a.** He **withdrew** $300 from his checking account.
   **b.** The runner **withdrew** from the competition due to an injury.

   core meaning: _____

3. **a.** She felt **rejected** when she wasn't invited to the party.
   **b.** I'm sorry, but your credit card was **rejected**.

   core meaning: _____

# VOCABULARY PRACTICE 5

## THINK ABOUT MEANING

Read the questions and answers. Two of the answers are correct, but one is incorrect. Cross out the incorrect answer. The boldfaced words are the target words from this unit.

1. What can **wear off**?
   clothing/medicine/perfume

2. What happens when you **activate** something?
   You turn it on./It becomes active./It slows down.

3. What should you do with a **defective** product?
   exchange it/fix it/use it

4. What **flows**?
   furniture/music/water

5. When people **grin**, what do they show?
   feelings/ideas/teeth

## PRACTICE A SKILL: Adverb placement

Are the boldfaced adverbs in the correct place in the sentences? Write a check (✓) if the boldfaced adverb is placed correctly in the sentence or an X if it is placed incorrectly. If the adverb is placed incorrectly, move it to the correct position.

_____ 1. She answered his question **sympathetically**.

_____ 2. His thoughts **freely** flowed.

_____ 3. The two machines **simultaneously** were activated.

_____ 4. The effects of the drug wore off **slowly**.

_____ 5. She answered **hesitantly**.

_____ 6. Your endeavors **greatly** are appreciated.

## PRACTICE A STRATEGY: Guessing meaning from context

Read the sentences. Guess the meaning of the boldfaced words. Underline the words in the context that help you understand the meaning.

1. After the diagnosis, his condition **deteriorated** rapidly. He died soon after.

   _Deteriorate_ probably means _____

2. A feeling of sadness swept over him, and he began to **sob**.

   _Sob_ probably means _____.

3. She never seems to learn from her mistakes. I just heard that she is involved in yet another **foolhardy** endeavor.

   _Foolhardy_ probably means _____.

4. It won't be difficult to incorporate your suggestion into our proposal. We'll just need to **tweak** one of the sections.

   _Tweak_ probably means _____.

## THINK ABOUT MEANING

The sentences below do not make sense. Replace a word in each sentence with a word from the list so the sentences make sense. The boldfaced words are target words.

| | | | |
|---|---|---|---|
| dangerous | many | protect | school |
| impossible | party | outside | upset |

1. Jill is wearing a **costume** because she is going to a business meeting.
2. Tom becomes **anxious** in social situations, so it is easy for him to enjoy large parties.
3. You need to be **cautious**. This is a very nice area.
4. Parents have an **obligation** to forget their children.
5. We live in the **suburbs** in the city.
6. Maria is really excited. Her boss sent her another **threatening** e-mail.
7. That little boy is **barely** 10 years old. He should be at work.
8. The problem has become **widespread**. Few people are affected by it.

## PRACTICE A SKILL: Compound words

Form compound words by combining the target words in the list with the boldfaced nouns in the sentences.

| | | | | |
|---|---|---|---|---|
| costume | breed | instinct | partner | tap |

1. _____ **jewelry** is made out of inexpensive materials, for example plastic or glass instead of diamonds, or painted metal instead of gold or silver.

2. The **survival** _____ is the natural desire to live. All living creatures have it.

3. _____ **dance** is a theatrical dance involving special foot movements performed in special shoes with metal toes and heels so that the audience can hear the dance as well as see it.

4. A **dog** _____ is a group of closely related and physically similar domestic dogs.

5. A **silent** _____ is someone who privately invests in a business but does not make his/her involvement in the business public.

## PRACTICE A STRATEGY: The Keyword Technique

For the next three weeks, make a few cards every week using the keyword technique (see page 107). Try to use it every time a word in English sounds like a word in your native language.

## THINK ABOUT MEANING

Match the words to the definitions. Be careful. There is one extra definition.

_____ **1.** destination

_____ **2.** violent

_____ **3.** foresight

_____ **4.** fee

_____ **5.** wade

_____ **6.** submerge

_____ **7.** retreat

**a.** the ability to imagine what might happen in the future, and to consider this in your plans

**b.** an amount of money that you pay for professional services or that you pay to do something

**c.** the complete circle that an electrical current travels through

**d.** strong and very difficult to control

**e.** to walk through water that is not deep

**f.** to put something under the surface of the water

**g.** the place that someone or something is going to

**h.** to move away from a place or person

## PRACTICE A SKILL: Understanding Core Meaning

Read the definition of the boldfaced target word. Then read the sentence and write a definition for the underlined expression.

**1. dawn**: the time of day when light first appears

It finally <u>dawned on me</u> that he was lying.

*to dawn on someone*: _____

**2. subscribe**: to pay money regularly to have a newspaper or magazine sent to you, or for a particular service

I don't <u>subscribe to that theory</u>, but I understand it.

*to subscribe to a theory*: _____

**3. flood**: a very large amount of water that covers an area that is usually dry

She hadn't seen her sister in 50 years. <u>A flood of emotions</u> swept over her when they finally met.

*a flood of emotions*: _____

## PRACTICE A STRATEGY: Using a dictionary to find the core meaning of related words

**1.** Which words are repeated or related in meaning in the entries of both the target word from Unit 1, *promote*, and the entries nearby? Write them here.

_____

**2.** Based on your answer to question 1, which of the words on the page share a core meaning with *promote*? Write them here.

_____

## THINK ABOUT MEANING

**A.** Look at the words in the list. Circle the words that are associated with food or cooking. If you haven't made word cards for them, do so now.

| | | | | |
|---|---|---|---|---|
| (agriculture) | distinct | jaw | profound | stem |
| approach | enable | lead to | scent | stroke |
| coat | enhance | mate | shift | terrace |
| devote oneself to | flame | nutritional | slide | thrill |
| digest | gather | pityingly | stay put | |

**B.** Now look through your other word cards and find words that are associated with food or cooking. Add them to your word cards from Exercise A.

**C.** Over the next week, review your cards for the food/cooking words as a group. Make sure you change the order of the cards <u>every time</u> you review them.

## PRACTICE A SKILL: Cause and Effect

Read the sentences. The boldfaced words are the target words. The underlined words will help you identify the causes and effects. Rewrite the sentences with *enable* or *lead to*. Make sure you keep the same meaning.

1. Because of a **shift** in wind direction, the firemen <u>were able to</u> put out the **flames**.

   enable: _____

2. The development of **agriculture** <u>made it possible for</u> many humans to **gather** in one place and **stay put** for long periods of time.

   enable: _____

3. **Agriculture** <u>was responsible for</u> the construction of the first cities.

   lead to: _____

4. News of the **approaching** hurricane <u>caused</u> widespread panic.

   lead to: _____

## PRACTICE A STRATEGY: Changing order and grouping of word cards

Regroup your word cards by meaning. Make nine groups of cards, one each for the following topics, plus an additional group for words that don't fit into any of these topic areas. Over the next week, review your cards in these groupings. Make sure you change the order of the cards in each group every time you review them.

| | | | |
|---|---|---|---|
| Animals | Arts and culture | Business | Food/cooking (from Exercise C above) |
| Medicine | Sports/exercise | Technology | Travel |

# VOCABULARY PRACTICE 9

## THINK ABOUT MEANING

Read the statements and pay attention to the boldfaced target words. Write *T* (true), or *F* (false). Correct the false statements to make them true.

_____ **1.** It is difficult to **chip** a **fragile** plate.

_____ **2.** The loser of a race **trails behind** the winner.

_____ **3.** If you put too much water in a glass, it will **overflow**.

_____ **4.** In a flood, water from a river or ocean **overflows** and covers the land.

_____ **5.** When you accommodate someone, you **insult** that person.

_____ **6.** When you **get used to** something, it feels strange to you.

## PRACTICE A SKILL: Understanding idioms

**A.** Look up the meanings of the idioms online and write the definitions. The boldfaced words are the target words.

**1. drag** one's feet: _____

**2.** have a **chip** on one's shoulder: _____

**3.** What a **drag**!: _____

**4.** to add **insult** to injury: _____

**B.** Complete the sentences with the idioms from Exercise A. You may need to change the form of some of the words in the idiom.

**1.** "I can't go to the party because I have to work."

   "_____ Can't you ask for a day off?"

**2.** He _____ because he didn't get invited to the party.

**3.** Stop _____ and get to work!

**4.** He lost his job. Then, _____, his wife left him.

## PRACTICE A STRATEGY: Adding visual images to word cards

**A.** Make word cards for the four new idioms in Exercises A and B of *Practice a Skill* (above). Add visual images to those cards.

**B.** Show your cards to a classmate. See if your classmate can guess the idiom.

## THINK ABOUT MEANING

Are the meanings of the words in each set similar or different? Write *S* or *D*.

_____ 1. standard/unusual

_____ 2. likewise/in contrast

_____ 3. come to mind/think of

_____ 4. strength/weakness

_____ 5. disregard/ignore

_____ 6. expertise/knowledge

_____ 7. found a company/start a business

_____ 8. willingness/refusal

_____ 9. essential/necessary

_____ 10. innovation/ancient practice

## PRACTICE A SKILL: Collocations

Read the two example sentences, and underline the word(s) that collocate with the boldfaced target word. Write the collocation and its meaning. Then write your own sentence with the collocation.

1. **a.** We are trying to raise **awareness** of the need for more cancer research.

   **b.** In recent years, public **awareness** of environmental issues has risen significantly.

   Collocation: _____

   Meaning: _____

   Your sentence: _____

2. **a.** What is the **essential** difference in their positions on healthcare?

   **b.** The **essential** difference between the two products is price.

   Collocation: _____

   Meaning: _____

   Your sentence: _____

3. **a.** This is the perfect **setting** for a horror movie!

   **b.** We've found the perfect **setting** for the wedding.

   Collocation: _____

   Meaning: _____

   Your sentence: _____

## PRACTICE A STRATEGY: Using a dictionary to find collocations

Look up the words in the list in a dictionary. Write any collocations you find, along with the meaning of the collocation. Make your own sentences for each collocation, and add them to the word card for that word.

| | | |
|---|---|---|
| foundation | operation | strength |
| mission | refuse | willing |

# VOCABULARY PRACTICE 11

## THINK ABOUT MEANING

Read the statements and pay attention to the boldfaced target words. Write *T* (true), or *F* (false). Correct the false statements to make them true.

_____ 1. The **offspring** of two animals often look like their parents.

_____ 2. A **cub** is the **offspring** of a dog.

_____ 3. **Endangered** species are dangerous and should be killed.

_____ 4. A car that uses only gasoline is an example of a **hybrid** vehicle.

_____ 5. Animals seek **shelter** to stay warm and dry.

_____ 6. Humans have **tails**.

_____ 7. Adventurous people like to go to **exotic** destinations.

_____ 8. **Predators** hunt and kill other animals.

## PRACTICE A SKILL: The adjective suffix: -*ing*, -*ed*

Complete the sentences with the correct adjectives. There are two extra words.

| | | |
|---|---|---|
| absorbed | enchanting | threatened |
| astonishing | fascinating | thrilled |

1. She has traveled all over the world visiting many exotic destinations. She's _____ to talk to.

2. I was _____ when I found out that I was going to be a grandmother. I've been waiting for this moment for a long time!

3. Their discovery was _____. Nobody expected it.

4. He was so _____ in his book that he missed his stop on the train.

## PRACTICE A STRATEGY: Choosing words to learn

Read the sentences. Circle the words that would NOT be useful to learn unless you were interested in that particular field. In some sentences, you will need to circle more than one word. In others, you will not need to circle any words.

1. Nuclear fission produces energy for nuclear power and to drive the explosion of nuclear weapons.

2. The scientific name for the domestic dog is Canis lupis familiaris.

3. The construction of emergency shelters was the government's first priority after an unprecedented series of natural disasters.

## THINK ABOUT MEANING

Are the meanings of the words in each set similar or different? Write *S* or *D*.

_____ **1.** accelerate/speed up

_____ **2.** exhibit/show

_____ **3.** exceptional/extraordinary

_____ **4.** have access to/make allowances for

_____ **5.** adversity/good fortune

_____ **6.** toddler/predator

_____ **7.** confirm/deny

_____ **8.** hardly/barely

_____ **9.** disorder/illness

_____ **10.** strive/try

## PRACTICE A SKILL: Latin and Greek prefixes

Look in your dictionary for words that begin with the boldfaced prefixes. Write the words that you find next to the prefix.

**1. mono-** _____

**2. uni-** _____

**3. hyper-** _____

**4. extra-** _____

**5. mini-** _____

**6. micro-** _____

## PRACTICE A STRATEGY: Deciding which words to learn

Choose the words from *Practice a Skill* that you think would be most useful to learn, and make word cards for them. If you choose two words with the same prefix, you can avoid learning interference if you learn one of the words very well before trying to learn the other one.

# Fluency Progress Charts

## FLUENCY PRACTICE 1

| | Words per Minute | |
|---|---|---|
| | **First Try** | **Second Try** |
| Reading 1 | | |
| Reading 2 | | |
| Comprehension Check Score _____% | | |

## FLUENCY PRACTICE 2

| | Words per Minute | |
|---|---|---|
| | **First Try** | **Second Try** |
| Reading 1 | | |
| Reading 2 | | |
| Comprehension Check Score _____% | | |

## FLUENCY PRACTICE 3

| | Words per Minute | |
|---|---|---|
| | **First Try** | **Second Try** |
| Reading 1 | | |
| Reading 2 | | |
| Comprehension Check Score _____% | | |

## FLUENCY PRACTICE 4

| | Words per Minute | |
|---|---|---|
| | **First Try** | **Second Try** |
| Reading 1 | | |
| Reading 2 | | |
| Comprehension Check Score _____% | | |

# Fluency Practice Answer Key

## Fluency Practice 1

### Reading 1

#### Comprehension Check, p. 54

**A.** *(Answers do not count toward score)*

**1.** c   **2.** b

**B.**

**1.** T   **2.** F   **3.** F   **4.** T   **5.** F   **6.** T   **7.** T   **8.** T   **9.** T   **10.** F

**C.**

**1.** inexpensive   **2.** surprised   **3.** college students   **4.** video
**5.** Internet   **6.** creatively   **7.** marketing   **8.** likely
**9.** good   **10.** successful

### Reading 2

#### Comprehension Check, p. 58

**B.** *Answers may vary slightly.*

**1.** He dreamed of becoming a doctor.
**2.** He was 13.
**3.** He was very tall.
**4.** He didn't like it. He fell and cut his face.
**5.** He got an academic scholarship.
**6.** He went to Georgetown.
**7.** He became an NBA player in 1991.
**8.** His mother had died because she couldn't get to a hospital in time to save her life.

**C.**

Dikembe Mutombo was born in Africa. When he was young,
he dreamed of becoming a ~~basketball player~~ *doctor*. His parents pushed
him to play basketball because he was so ~~smart~~ *tall*. He played
on the Zaire national team for two years. In 1985, he won
~~a basketball~~ *an academic* scholarship to study at Georgetown University in
the United States.

At Georgetown, Dikembe became a great basketball player.
~~Before~~ *After* he graduated, he started playing for the NBA. He
stopped dreaming of becoming a doctor.

Dikembe became rich and famous as a professional
basketball player. Then one day his ~~father~~ *mother* died because ~~he~~ *she* could
not get to a hospital in Kinshasa. Dikembe made a promise. He
would build a hospital in his hometown. In ~~1997~~ *2007*, Dikembe's
dream came true when the Biamba Marie Mutombo Hospital
and Research Center opened in ~~Washington, D.C.~~ *Kinshasa*

Dikembe didn't become a doctor. However, he is helping
more people in his country than he could help if he were a
doctor. He believes that it is important for successful people to
help others to become successful, too.

## Fluency Practice 2

### Reading 1

#### Comprehension Check, p. 111

**A.**

**1.** b   **2.** b   **3.** c   **4.** a   **5.** c   **6.** b   **7.** b

**B.** *Answers may vary slightly.*

**1.** recognize or reproduce musical notes   **2.** identify with the
condition   **3.** noise   **4.** avoid places where there is music
**5.** they can become isolated   **6.** be a relief

### Reading 2

#### Comprehension Check, p. 114

**A.**

**1.** F   **2.** T   **3.** F   **4.** T   **5.** T   **6.** T   **7.** T   **8.** T   **9.** F

**B.**

| Insects | Function of pheromones |
|---|---|
| moths | to attract members of the opposite sex |
| ants | to tell others where to find food |
| ants | to warn others of danger |
| fire ants | to confuse their enemies |
| Large Blue caterpillar | to protect itself from being eaten |
| Large Blue caterpillar | to get another species to take care of it |
| bolas spider, ants | to get food |

## Fluency Practice 3

### Reading 1

#### Comprehension Check, p. 168

**A.**

**1.** over 1,000  **2.** in Ueno  **3.** in 1656  **4.** His master died.  **5.** Edo
**6.** banana tree  **7.** He loved bananas so much that his friends
started calling him "Basho."  **8.** 3 times  **9.** 12  **10.** Osaka

**B.**

The great Japanese poet, Matsuo Kinsaku, better known
as "Basho," was born in 1644 in the ~~large~~ *small* city of Ueno, Japan.

When Basho was 12 years old, his father died, so he left home
to ~~study~~ *work*. He worked for a ~~poor~~ *wealthy* young man named Todo for ten
years. Basho and Todo both loved to write poetry, ~~but~~ *and* they were
~~not~~ close friends. When Todo died after a ~~long~~ *short* illness, Basho
lost his job and his home.

Basho then went to the capital city of Edo to ~~work~~ *start a new life*. His
poems attracted attention, and he started to ~~attend~~ *teach* school. Basho
was ^ *not* happy in Edo, but his friends were ~~not~~, so he moved to
the countryside. There he lived in a ~~large~~ *small* house and planted a
banana tree. He wrote many haiku about the tree, so his friends
started to call him *Basho*, which means ~~blossom~~ *banana tree*.

One day, the house burned down, and for the ~~second~~ *third* time in
his life, Basho had nowhere to live. He then decided to travel to
all 12 of the Japanese ~~cities~~ *provinces* between Edo and Kyoto. For years,
he traveled around Japan and wrote ~~novels~~ *haiku*. He died when he
was ~~40~~ *49* years old in the city of Osaka.

## Reading 2

#### Comprehension Check, p. 172

**A.**

Traditional haiku:

1, 3, 5, 6, 7

**B.**

Contemporary haiku

1, 2, 5, 6

**C.** *Answers may vary slightly.*

First, decide what you want to write about. Second, decide on
the form of your haiku. Third, include some sort of shift or
contrast. Fourth, include a season word if you want to. Fifth,
practice. Finally, have fun.

## Fluency Practice 4

### Reading 1

#### Comprehension Check, p. 226

**A.**

**1.** F  **2.** T  **3.** F  **4.** T  **5.** T  **6.** F  **7.** T

**B.**

**1.** Nobody  **2.** before  **3.** sultans  **4.** festivals  **5.** botanist
**6.** Prague  **7.** took  **8.** share  **9.** steal  **10.** get
**11.** dramatically  **12.** up  **13.** bought  **14.** crashed
**15.** life savings  **16.** survived

### Reading 2

#### Comprehension Check, p. 230

**A.**

**1.** a  **2.** b  **3.** b  **4.** a  **5.** b  **6.** b  **7.** a  **8.** b

**B.**

**1.** expertise  **2.** teenager  **3.** criminal  **4.** bad  **5.** professional
**6.** suspect  **7.** adopted  **8.** caught  **9.** prison  **10.** exchange
**11.** ethical  **12.** mission

# Pronunciation Table

## Vowels

| Symbol | Key Word |
|---|---|
| i | beat, feed |
| ɪ | bit, did |
| eɪ | date, paid |
| ɛ | bet, bed |
| æ | bat, bad |
| ɑ | box, odd, father |
| ɔ | bought, dog |
| oʊ | boat, road |
| ʊ | book, good |
| u | boot, food, student |
| ʌ | but, mud, mother |
| ə | banana, among |
| ɚ | shirt, murder |
| aɪ | bite, cry, buy, eye |
| aʊ | about, how |
| ɔɪ | voice, boy |
| ɪr | beer |
| ɛr | bare |
| ɑr | bar |
| ɔr | door |
| ʊr | tour |

/t/ means that /t/ may be dropped.
/d/ means that /d/ may be dropped.
/ˈ/ shows main stress.
/ˌ/ shows secondary stress.

## Consonants

| Symbol | Key Word |
|---|---|
| p | pack, happy |
| b | back, rubber |
| t | tie |
| d | die |
| k | came, key, quick |
| g | game, guest |
| tʃ | church, nature, watch |
| dʒ | judge, general, major |
| f | fan, photograph |
| v | van |
| θ | thing, breath |
| ð | then, breathe |
| s | sip, city, psychology |
| z | zip, please, goes |
| ʃ | ship, machine, station, special, discussion |
| ʒ | measure, vision |
| h | hot, who |
| m | men, some |
| n | sun, know, pneumonia |
| ŋ | sung, ringing |
| w | wet, white |
| l | light, long |
| r | right, wrong |
| y | yes, use, music |
| t̬ | butter, bottle |
| t̚ | button |

# Vocabulary Index

The numbers following each entry are the pages where the word appears. All words followed by asterisks* are on the Academic Word List.

## A

absorbed /əbˈsɔrbd/ 43, 45
accelerate /əkˈsɛləˌreɪt/ 216, 218
accommodate /əˈkɑməˌdeɪt/ 94, 96, 103
accumulate /əˈkyumyəˌleɪt/ 61, 63, 159
accurate* /ˈækyərɪt/ 27, 29, 45, 113
acquire* /əˈkwaɪə/ 210, 212, 218
activate /ˈæktəˌveɪt/ 77, 79
admiration /ˌædməˈreɪʃən/ 210, 212
adopt /əˈdɑpt/ 216, 217, 229
adversity /ədˈvɜsəti/ 210, 213
affection /əˈfɛkʃən/ 216, 217
agriculture /ˈægrɪˌkʌltʃə/ 141, 144
ancient /ˈeɪnʃənt/ 43, 46, 143, 160
anticipate* /ænˈtɪsəˌpeɪt/ 216, 218, 228
antique /ænˈtik/ 124, 126
anxiety /æŋˈzaɪəti/ 100, 102, 182
appeal /əˈpil/ 2, 5, 12, 53, 56, 183
appreciation /əˌpriʃiˈeɪʃən/ 20, 23, 57, 168
approach* /əˈproʊtʃ/ 134, 136, 160, 171
as far as we know /əz far əz wi ˈnoʊ/ 37, 38, 225
at first glance /ət fɜst glæns/ 27, 29
astonishing /əˈstɑnɪʃɪŋ/ 194, 197, 213, 226, 228
attractive /əˈtræktɪv/ 43, 46, 70, 160, 177
awareness /əˈwɛrnɪs/ 174, 176, 182, 183

## B

barely /ˈbɛrli/ 100, 101,
be associated with /bi əˈsoʊʃiˌeɪt wɪθ/ 117, 119, 120, 167, 225
be at it /bi ˈæ dɪt/ 152, 155
bend /bɛnd/ 94, 95, 136
beneficial* /ˌbɛnəˈfɪʃəl/ 27, 28, 196
brand /brænd/ 174, 176, 182, 183
breed /brid/ 100, 102, 113, 202, 229
bribe /braɪb/ 180, 183

## C

capacity* /kəˈpæsəti/ 20, 22, 95, 110
captivating /ˈkæptəˌveɪtɪŋ/ 124, 126, 168
carefree /ˈkɛrfri/ 61, 63, 70
catch up /kætʃ ˈʌp/ 174, 177
catch up on /kætʃ ʌp ɑn/ 68, 70
catch up with /kætʃ ʌp wɪθ/ 2, 5
cautious /ˈkɔʃəs/ 94, 95, 102
celebrity /ˈkɔʃəs/ 2, 4
championship /ˈtʃæmpiənˌʃɪp/ 27
chip /tʃɪp/ 158, 159
circuit /ˈsɜkɪt/ 124, 126
classification /ˌklæsəfəˈkeɪʃən/ 194, 196, 197
claustrophobic /ˌklɔstrəˈfoʊbɪk/ 61, 63, 70
coat /koʊt/ 134, 136
colleague* /ˈkɑlig/ 94, 96, 126
come to mind /kʌm tə ˈmaɪnd/ 174, 176
companionship /kəmˈpænyənˌʃɪp/ 152, 154
concept* /ˈkɑnsɛpt/ 194, 196

confirm* /kənˈfɜm/ 210, 212
conflict* /ˈkɑnˌflɪkt/ 86, 87
conservative /kənˈsɜvətɪv/ 86, 87
contemporary* /kənˈtɛmpəˌrɛri/ 9, 11
costume /ˈkɑstum/ 100, 101
course /kɔrs/ 86, 88
crate /kreɪt/ 124, 126
creature /ˈkritʃə/ 37, 38, 46
cross-section /krɔs ˈsɛkʃən/ 27, 29
cub /kʌb/ 200, 202
currently /ˈkɜəntli/ 9, 11, 39
curriculum /kəˈrɪkyələm/ 216, 218
cycle* /ˈsaɪkəl/ 20, 23

## D

dawn /dɔn/ 124, 126
decipher /dɪˈsaɪfə/ 158, 160
default /dɪˈfɔlt/ 77, 80
defective /dɪˈfɛktɪv/ 77, 79, 110, 160
depth /dɛpθ/ 124, 126
destination /ˌdɛstəˈneɪʃən/ 117, 119, 120
destroy /dɪˈstrɔɪ/ 43, 45, 70
devote oneself to /dɪˈvoʊt wʌnsɛlf tə/ 141, 144
diagnosis /ˌdaɪəgˈnoʊsɪs/ 86, 88
digest /daɪˈdʒɛst/ 141, 143, 146
digital /ˈdɪdʒɪtl/ 37, 39
disability /ˌdɪsəˈbɪləti/ 100, 103
disorder /dɪsˈɔrdə/ 216, 217
disregard /ˌdɪsrɪˈgard/ 174, 177, 183
distinct* /dɪˈstɪŋkt/ 141, 143, 197, 202, 217, 225
distraction /dɪˈstrækʃən/ 2, 5
disturb /dɪˈstɜb/ 61, 64, 119, 136
dizzying /ˈdɪziɪŋ/ 194, 197, 203, 225
dragging /ˈdræg ɪŋ/ 152, 154
dramatic* /drəˈmætɪk/ 20, 23, 57, 160, 176, 182, 225

## E

eliminate* /ɪˈlɪməˌneɪt/ 158, 160, 171
elite /eɪˈlit/ 20, 22, 29
enable* /ɪˈneɪbəl/ 141, 143
enchanted /ɪnˈtʃæntɪd/ 200, 202
endangered /ɪnˈdeɪndʒəd/ 200, 202
endeavor /ɪnˈdɛvə/ 77, 80
engulf /ɪnˈgʌlf/ 117, 119, 126, 170
enhance* /ɪnˈhæns/ 134, 135, 144, 168
enormous* /ɪˈnɔrməs/ 20, 22, 29, 38, 53, 119, 182
essential /ɪˈsɛnʃəl/ 180, 183, 196
ethics* /ˈɛθɪks/ 180, 183, 228
evaporate /ɪˈvæpəˌreɪt/ 152, 155, 226
exception /ɪkˈsɛpʃən/ 27, 29
exceptional /ɪkˈsɛpʃənəl/ 210, 212, 218, 225
excerpt /ˈɛksɜpt/ 68, 69, 79, 159
exchange /ɪksˈtʃeɪndʒ/ 37, 39, 57, 64, 120, 196

exhibit* /ɪgˈzɪbɪt/ 210, 212
exotic /ɪgˈzɑtɪk/ 200, 202
expense /ɪkˈspɛns/ 37, 39, 46, 53
expertise* /ˌɛkspəˈtiz/ 180, 183, 228
extraordinary /ɪkˈstrɔrdnˌɛri/ 216, 218, 225, 229
explosion /ɪkˈsploʊʒən/ 9, 11

## F

facility* /fəˈsɪləti/ 68, 70
fate /feɪt/ 61, 54, 70
fee* /fi/ 117, 119
ferry /ˈfɛri/ 124, 126
firsthand /ˌfɜstˈhænd/ 117, 119, 171
flame /fleɪm/ 134, 136
flood /flʌd/ 117, 119, 126
flow /floʊ/ 86, 87, 88
foresight /ˈfɔrsaɪt/ 117, 119, 126
found (a company) /faʊnd/ 180, 182, 212
fragile /ˈfrædʒəl/ 158, 160
freak out /frik ˈaʊt/ 158, 160

## G

gather /ˈgæðə/ 134, 136, 144
genius /ˈdʒinyəs/ 94, 95, 210, 212, 213
get used to /gɛt ˈyust tu/ 152, 154, 168
give someone an edge /gɪv sʌmwʌn ən ˈɛdʒ/ 20, 22, 29, 46, 183
gossip /ˈgɑsəp/ 68, 70
grasp /græsp/ 86, 88, 110
grin /grɪn/ 86, 88, 159

## H

hardly /ˈhardli/ 210, 212, 218
have a soft spot for /hæv ə ˈsɔft spɑt fə/ 200, 203
have access to /hæv ˈæksɛs tu/ 210, 213, 225
hesitate /ˈhɛzəˌteɪt/ 77, 80, 119
hook /hʊk/ 77, 79, 88
horizontal /ˌhɔrəˈzɑntəl/ 27, 29
hybrid /ˈhaɪbrɪd/ 200, 202
hyperactive /ˌhaɪpəˈæktɪv/ 216, 217

## I

identify with /aɪˈdɛntəˌfaɪ wɪθ/ 86, 87, 110
illusion /ɪˈluʒən/ 86, 88, 226
implication /ˌɪmplɪˈkeɪʃən/ 2, 4, 95
income* /ˈɪnkʌm/ 37, 39, 53, 57
incorporate* /ɪnˈkɔrpəˌreɪt/ 77, 79
individual* /ˌɪndəˈvɪdʒuəl/ 210, 213
influence /ˈɪnfluəns/ 2, 4, 5, 11, 12
initially* /ɪˈnɪʃəli/ 27, 29, 53, 56, 229
innovation* /ˌɪnəˈveɪʃən/ 180, 182, 183
inspire /ɪnˈspaɪə/ 2, 4, 12, 168
instinctively /ɪnˈstɪŋktɪv li/ 94, 95, 102
insult /ɪnˈsʌlt/ 152, 154
intense* /ɪnˈtɛns/ 20, 22, 23, 29, 56, 88, 217